The Man-of-Words
in the West Indies

JOHNS HOPKINS STUDIES IN ATLANTIC HISTORY AND CULTURE
RICHARD PRICE AND FRANKLIN W. KNIGHT, GENERAL EDITORS

The Man-of-Words in the West Indies

Performance and the Emergence of Creole Culture

Roger D. Abrahams

The Johns Hopkins University Press
Baltimore and London

See p. 203 for permission notices.

Copyright © 1983 by The Johns Hopkins University Press
All rights reserved
Printed in the United States of America

The Johns Hopkins University Press, Baltimore, Maryland 21218
The Johns Hopkins Press Ltd., London

Library of Congress Cataloging in Publication Data

Abrahams, Roger D.
   The man-of-words in the West Indies.
   (Johns Hopkins studies in Atlantic history and culture)
   Bibliography: p. 187
   Includes index.
   1. Storytellers—West Indies—Addresses, essays,
lectures. 2. Story-telling—West Indies—Addresses,
essays, lectures. 3. Communication in folklore—West
Indies—Addresses, essays, lectures. 4. Blacks—West
Indies—Folklore—Addresses, essays, lectures.
5. Sociolinguistics—West Indies—Addresses, essays,
lectures. I. Title. II. Series.
GR120.A27   1983   398′.092′2   82-16235
ISBN 0-8018-2838-4
ISBN 0-8018-2839-2 (pbk.)

To John Szwed

Contents

Preface

This collection of essays on the place of performance and performances within Afro-American communities records a continuing preoccupation with creativity within cultural and historical settings. It registers, in immediate terms, a sense of wonder at the ability of human beings—especially Afro-Americans—to endure with spirit in the face of continuing adversity.

I have kept the essays as they were originally published, for the most part. But I like to think that I have become a better writer, so when, on rereading, I encountered especially infelicitous passages, I changed them—even to the point of eliminating whole pages. But I have not attempted to bring them up-to-date in the scholarly references in any full sense. On the one hand, the bibliography in the areas covered here is extensive; on the other, nothing has emerged in the last five to ten years in West Indian studies that has made me want to change my mind substantially. I have changed my intellectual concerns considerably, but that is what these essays demonstrate, a point detailed in my introduction.

I do not mean to say that no work of substance has been carried out on West Indian folklore during this period. On the contrary, important monographs have emerged; for instance, Errol Hill's (Hill, 1972) monograph on Trinidad Carnival and Donald Hill's (Hill, 1977) on Carriacou folk culture; and a number of important articles by Karl Riesman on Antigua talk and world order, and a fine book by Jane C. Beck on an *obeahman* (Beck, 1979). But when one compares such work to the major studies carried out in Afro American history, especially those drawing on black folk culture in the United States, the record for the West Indies looks slim indeed, especially with regard to developing useful new ways of treating materials from this area. The only exception I would note to this generalization is the continuing work of Sidney Mintz, Richard Price, Michael Craton, Barry Higman, and Edward Brathwaite, all of whom have done marvelous work in filling in the record of the social and cultural history of the region.

I like to think that these essays have some interest in themselves as records of the planting, germination, the reaping and refining of ideas. I hope that it will interest the reader to be able to see, for instance, the way in which the distinction between the two types of the man-of-words came to be attached to the sociolinguistic notion of diglossia, to the historical process of creolization, and, finally, to the social structural dichotomy between notions of respect- and reputation-seeking. Such developments also record my desire to use these materials as a means of commenting on the received ideas about language and culture, about black language "problems," and about anthropological (especially social anthropological) notions concerning gossip, ritual, and festival, and the notion of performance itself.

Chapter one was written primarily while I was in the field in the West Indies and rewritten in only minor ways while I was engaged in library work at the Institute of Jamaica, the British Museum, and the Barker Collection at the University of Texas.

Most of the rest of the essays were written on request from one quarter or another and then were published in divers places. Yet I hope the reader finds them informed with a common purpose and reflecting related preoccupations and cognate materials. Indeed, it is as much because of the dispersion of these arguments as for any other reason that it seems useful to bring them together.

Inevitably, there are areas of overlap between these essays, for each was written as a self-sufficient argument. I have made extensive cuts in most of them where a point made in passing is covered at some depth elsewhere.

Acknowledgments

Field research for most of these essays was carried out while I held a John Simon Guggenheim Foundation Fellowship in 1965-66, and a National Institute of Mental Health grant in 1968. Most of the essays were written while I was on research leave sponsored by the Center for Urban Ethnography, directed by John Szwed. I would like to thank the kind folks at these institutions, especially Gordon Ray, of the Guggenheim Foundation, who has exhibited interest in my work all these years.

As always, a great number of people assisted me in various ways, some of whom I mention in the introduction or in one or another of the chapters. My thanks then—and in abundance—to my coworkers in the charnel house: Tom Kochman, Mervyn Alleyne, Bill Stewart, Sid Mintz, Karl Reisman, Richard Wright, Geneva Gay, Joel Sherzer, Rich Price, Michael Holquist, Don Brenneis, John Baugh, Dell Hymes, Bill Labov, Ken Goldstein, Dan Ben-Amos, Roger Renwick, and Archie Green; so many of the fine graduate students at the University of Texas who kept asking embarrassing questions; and Rudy Troike, Mary Galvan, Riley Smith, and all the other wonderful folks in the East Texas Dialect Project. And my undying blessing on those who helped out so much in the field. I wish to thank my parents, who were so enthusiastic about Nevis life—my father remains so and tries to get our family to return as often as possible. The greatest native philosopher I have encountered, Samuel Hunkins, has provided a moral vision and a center of gravity throughout the years. Hyacinth Liburd of Morningstar, Nevis, has always looked after our needs so calmly. I would like to also thank Melly, Rosalee Jeffers, Pops, and the many Daniels, and, especially, Spencer Howell, who taught me how to relate to Nevisians and how to get around the island. On Tobago, Charley and Pusher and Isaac were my special, special friends. And on St. Vincent, Douglas and Mabel Brisbane made the collecting possible, and Freddie, Mommy Mack, and Caloo kept me going through some very rough times. Just to name them is to bring on an avalanche of grateful memories. I am especially indebted to my collaborators Dick Bauman and John Szwed, as well as to Bob Thompson, my near-collaborator. And again, my special thanks to Rich Price for his continuing interest in, and support of, my work, and to Henry Tom and Jane Warth, editors at the Johns Hopkins University Press. And Janet, who held my hand, encouraged, edited. To all, my thanks.

Orthographic Note

I have italicized important "native" terms the first time I use them in each chapter. Thus I distinguish West Indian terms of description and analysis from my academic terms of art, which I put in quotation marks. The West Indian words I draw on are spelled as they are spoken, as often as possible. I have eliminated as many footnotes as possible and done the references in anthropological style, referring to the author in parentheses, and giving the full reference in the bibliography.

Introduction

As *The Man-of-Words in the West Indies* suggests, this book focuses on the role of the verbal performer in the English-speaking Caribbean. Based on my field studies in village settings on Nevis, St. Kitts, Tobago, and St. Vincent carried out in the 1960s and early 1970s, it attempts to establish the presence and importance of a performance complex, a set of traits that articulate expressive relationships.

I first formulated the concept of the man-of-words in my study of black folklore in Philadelphia, *Deep Down in the Jungle,* and in that setting it referred to great street performers. I then went to the West Indies, partly in order to see if words and word control played an analogous role in nonurban Afro-American communities and if such verbal dexterity conveyed the same kind of status. My findings surpassed all expectations, for they led me to recognize that by observing street life and lore I had only dealt with one of the many possible settings in which such men (and women) held forth with mighty voices. Thus, in my report from the field, "The Shaping of Folklore Traditions in the British West Indies" (Abrahams, 1967), I already saw the distinction emerging between different types of men-of-words.

There are two kinds of men-of-words: good talkers and good arguers. The distinction is important because the two types function at different kinds of traditional performances—one characterized by the use of long speeches suffused with "fancy talk," the other by strongly colloquial diction and the rapid thrust of invective. One may may be proficient at both uses of words, but the two abilities are only rarely called for on the same occasion. The decorated and decorous verbiage of the good talker arises at serious community events: wedding receptions, christening parties, funerals, church meetings, arrivals and departures, political gatherings, *thanksgivings* (parties given after a sickness or some other such trial), and many other sentimental occasions. The good talker usually expresses himself in toasts, speeches, or recitations. The colloquial invective of the good arguer, however, usually occurs at the least solemn times, and it is this man-of-words who is capable of turning any conversation into a show.

Both types of man-of-words use set pieces as part of their verbal arsenal. Some performances call for a greater amount of improvisation than others, but even then the patterns for improvising are traditional. For instance, while many toasts are set pieces, others are made up of traditional clichés in combinations appropriate to the occasion. Similarly, a speech or a recitation is usually memorized, whereas the various verbal contests generally consist of an impromptu arrangement of curses, riddles, rhymes, or insults, most of them learned in the past, but some made up on the spot on the pattern of the older ones. (There is a higher incidence of improvisation in Trinidad and Tobago than on other islands I have investigated.)

On certain occasions, the man-of-words must combine the talents of the good talker and the good arguer. This is the burden of the *chairman* at wakes and *tea meetings* (the latter a combination of variety show and church social, with a little bit of fertility worship thrown in; the name derives from a Methodist attempt to substitute a tea-drinking occasion in the place of the slave's *ball* or *play* in which alcoholic refreshments predominated). The chairmen (there are generally two) decide who is going to perform what and when. But they also provide a major part of the entertainment by their competitive speechmaking and occasional arguments. They begin each phase of the meeting with an elaborate macaronic introduction and give a speech of thanks and congratulations after every performance. When the performance has been a speech, it is usually answered by another by the chairman, who uses its subject as a basis for his own oration. This often leads to a rebuttal speech from the cochairman, and with each speech the rhetoric becomes more decorated with Latin and Latinate phrases. The object of each competitor is to be recognized by the audience as "the cock with the brightest comb," the one who can best control and arouse them.

Such chairmen show that the man-of-words not only provides the tone and subjects for traditional performances but also serves as the principal organizer of the activity. The performing troupes that roam abound at Christmas and Carnival are similarly organized around a *captain*. In such Carnival troupes as *Calypso Mas'* or Tobago *Speech Mas'*, the captain is generally the best performer, the wittiest of the witty. In the Christmas serenading groups, he is the speechmaker who begins and ends the performance; in the Christmas mumming plays (on Nevis and St. Kitts, as well as in the celebrated *Jonkanoo* on Jamaica) he is the one who knows the entire play and who teaches the other players their parts. In those troupes that involve dancing, acrobatics, or fighting, he has his equivalent, one we might call the man-of-action, the physically adept one who brings focus to the proceedings by his leadership and performance abilities.

The man-of-words or the man-of-action exhibits his talents best in contest with other performers. Many West Indian entertainments are simply traditional occasions for these battles. Here, for instance, is a description of one such activity, the Trinidad Carnival *Devil Band*:

> There was a reigning beast, a man so dexterous and inventive in his dancing and portrayal of the beast as to be proclaimed best. Each year aspirants for his crown would "challenge him to combat." The challenge to combat occurred automatically when the two bands met for the first time. The combat took the form of the execution of the reigning beast of various dance steps which the challenger had to imitate. If he succeeded in imitating them he then executed steps of his own for the reigning beast to imitate. The beast who first failed to imitate the other's steps lost the contest. (Procope, 1956, p. 279)

This pattern of confrontation is found in most other Carnival groups, even the historical mas'es. The whole proceedings have been formalized recently by the addition of official judging and the awarding of prizes. The contest element was more basic to the old Carnival performances such as Calypso Mas', *Midnight Robber,* and Speech Mas'. These were groups that openly sought a battle with rival organizations in which boastings and invectives were the major weapons of the battle, and each performer or group had a time to compete.

This pattern of competitive interaction is observable in many other traditional activities, such as the tea meetings described previously. More frequently held are riddling sessions (held at wakes or on moonlit nights), and *rhyming,* a trading of curses directed against the mother of another contestant, a practice commonly known as *playing the dozens* in the United States. These contests are so central to the sense of entertainment in the West Indies that they are observable whenever people congregate, whether for a special event or in the marketplace or rum shop. In all of these activities, little effort is made to declare a winner or a loser; it is the entertainment value of the battle that matters most (Abrahams, 1967).

This perception of difference between those who control words primarily to demonstrate eloquence and rhetorical invention and those who seek to enter into verbal contests led me to recognize that there were different varieties of speaking to be found in these pursuits and that the differences were spatial, temporal, and social. This book illustrates the development of the idea of different kinds of performances into contrarieties and oppositions that operate in virtually every facet of village life—and perhaps elsewhere in Afro-America. These studies also document my recognition that these data commented upon more than folkloric traditions and might be employed usefully in the larger public debate about the existence, nature, and character of Afro-American culture.

The 1960s was a period of dramatic juxtapositions of different social and political perspectives as they affected us "where we live." Ideas and actions came together in special ways simply because suddenly social change seemed possible, change engineered on the basis of percieved (and studied) inequities. Inadvertently, I found myself in the midst of some of these controversial "scenes" because I had set out in the late fifties on a personal quest to understand black culture (we did not call it that then, of course) and, because I had written of my experiences and observations, I found myself with a vested interest in the black question. I had lived in a black neighborhood in South Philadelphia for a couple of years and, as a folklorist, had recorded a tremendous amount of lore as actively performed on the streets. In discovering these materials and the process by which they were learned, rehearsed, transmitted, understood, and used, I became aware that many of the received notions concerning blacks and their language abilities were wrong-headed and misleading.

Because of the more public interest in such questions, I found myself discussing black lore (and "the Afro-American expressive system," as I came to call it) with people who were not folklorists: educators, sociologists, ethnographers, sociolinguists, and formulators of public policy. Those were heady days, for folklorists were not used to such attention unless it was of a negative, blacklisting sort. But naturally there were questions raised with regard to my data—and the underlying system I perceived there—that I could not begin to answer. The most troubling of the questions were those concerned with the social and cultural history of blacks—especially how I might attempt to account for how such a different cultural system of expressivity could possibly exist among a people who had been actively deculturated under slavery. I came to realize that answers did not exist in the literature on the black experience, though I did see a glimmer of hope in the writings of Melville J. Herskovits. My training in literature did not prepare me to even recognize that the Herskovitsian argument was a generally discredited one within the social scientific community. I had taken no courses in sociology or anthropology and even had to be told by a colleague at the University of Texas that my work in South Philadelphia betrayed a naive approach to ethnography. Taking this as a challenge, I began reading more than just the ethnographies and sociological studies that had been carried out on black communities. But it soon became evident that I needed to carry out further fieldwork and that the dimension of the problem I was most concerned with investigating—the distribution of performance styles and traits—could best be carried out in remote agrarian communities.

As I was teaching at Texas by this time, I thought I might work someplace in the New South. In the meanwhile my parents had bought a place in the West Indies and begun to fix it up. Because Herskovits had carried out some powerfully attractive work in that part of the world, I decided to go in that direction. So in the summer of 1962 I began the West Indian fieldwork out of which these studies grew. I went to Nevis, then, with set goals: to discover how much of the performance pattern I had observed in my Philadelphia work was characteristic of the black world in general, and how much was American, urban, and contemporary. I was self-consciously looking for the most archaic material in the most removed and backwater areas of Afro-America. My most pressing goal as a folklorist was to discover the cultural conditions of creativity as well as to document the dissemination patterns of style in performance.

"The cultural conditions of creativity"—how ponderous the project now seems. Mostly, as it turned out, I pursued performers to their front gate, asked them embarrassing questions about how they cobbled together their performances and received from them overly kind, commonsensical responses. Fortunately I was living within their community and observing not only their performances but their rehearsals, interacting with their friends and audiences, and getting involved in gossip and other kinds of simple talk, and by this declension was forced to recognize that talk is never cheap and that every group I dealt with had a profound notion of their own speech economy. Creativity came to mean only how the performers saw fit to deal in expressive currency with care and abandon, and with charity. That is to say, I became more interesting in expressive exchange than the process by which performers husbanded their energics so that they might appear unique. The old virtues of wit and cleverness being reestablished, I sought only to record performances and less dramatic but still significant behaviors, the ways in which the everyday and the extraordinary were chained to each other, and how they were discussed. Somehow creativity seemed less important than how a group managed to achieve meaning while celebrating community. And out of this came a recognition that expressive resources are remarkably limited in range and tenaciously tied to recurrent occasions in peasant communities. But within such a restricted vocabulary, an amazing potency of meaning and subtlety of expression can be achieved.

This realization came upon me in my initial Nevis research, though it took me many years to work it through. It occurred primarily because the performance occasions for Nevisians were not the same as those I had found in Philadelphia; rather, they were tied to certain times of the year and to community occasions of fun-making. That first summer, I attended my first Nevis tea meeting and heard from so many of the high-spirited folk involved about the big times taking place during the Christmas season. I mainly applied myself to working with children, which is always the easiest way to ease into the lore of a community; but here too I found myself chained to the concept of seasons, for many of the sports and games I asked the Nevisians to perform for me were not regarded as appropriate to that time of year, and I was regarded as more than a little bit strange for even asking about them.

By wonderful fortune, I discovered that there was an anthropologist on the island that summer, the late Richard Frucht, who was carrying out a study on the cultural ecology of the island for his dissertation. Rich introduced me to a great number of things that summer, including some of the anthropological classics. Of course, I received stern lectures on field methodology and ethics—but then *he* was alerted to the tremendous fund of extremely archaic expressive resources I was discovering.

Perhaps the lesson of greatest importance that I learned during those first couple of sojourns was that on Nevis and St. Kitts there were a number of traditional practices that textually were European in origin (a number of very old ballads, for instance, and the St. George and the Turk mumming) but performed in Afro-American style. Thus, the distinction between repertoire and performance patterning began to become clear to me. The relationship of the performer to his material and to his audience was quite similar to that which I had perceived in Philadelphia.

Taking the cue from my informants, I returned in the fall of 1965 to study the preparations for the Christmas sports and to work with the various kinds of performing groups: the *Serenaders,* the *Cowboys and Indians,* the *Saguas,* the *Buzzards,* and the *Masqueraders.* My project was specifically to collect the Christmas plays. Fortunately I was able to spend the entire fifteen months from June 1965 to September 1966 in the West Indies, and rather than staying the entire time on Nevis, where I felt constrained due to my family's living situation, which created a certain social distance from those with whom I was working, I went scouting for other promising village settings. Fortunately at that time, the *Federal Palm* and the *Maple* still went from one island to the next between Jamaica and Trinidad and back, so that I was able to survey the entire range of the Anglophonic Lesser Antilles. These ships, which were presented to the islands when a West Indian federation was envisaged, were supposed to provide a link between the various islands. I had already established that I would spend some time working on Tobago, having been led there by the folklorist Jacob Elder, himself a Tobagonian. We took the *Palm* from St. Kitts to Trinidad and stopped in Montserrat, Antigua, Dominica, St. Lucia, St. Vincent, and Grenada. And, again, after a short time we went back up the chain, establishing that St. Vincent would be our third island to look into. Thus it was that we made our way to Plymouth, Tobago, for a couple of extended stays, and later to Richland Park, St. Vincent, again and again throughout the late sixties and early seventies, whenever it could be wangled.

During the year 1965-66, while in the field I wrote a general overview of what I was beginning to observe about the area. This paper was written to be delivered at a meeting of the Congress of Americanists in Mar Del Plata, Argentina, in the fall of 1966, at a session organized by Richard M. Dorson on the factors in the creation of folklore traditions in various parts of the New World. Written without benefit of library or time to transcribe tapes and field notes, it was a folklorist's overview of the common and uncommon features of the traditions I had observed. It recorded my bewilderment at the number of variable factors one had to take into consideration to study with effect any one of the island communities in which I had been working—the differences arising from who settled the island, what was cultivated there and for how long and intensively, where its slaves originated from, what markets the plantations served, when manumission occurred, whether nonblack workers were brought in, and so on and on. The article, "The Shaping of Folklore Traditions in the British West Indies," went on, nonetheless, to notice the similarities in theme, in structure of performances, and in the place of the performer in the various islands, including my new and broadened concept of the man-of-words, which I had first developed with regard to the Philadelphia material.

The article was noticed by Sidney Mintz, who promptly not only contacted me but put me in touch with the other major Caribbeanists at work at the time. Moreover, through his good offices, I was asked to join the Social Science Research Council Committee on Afro-American Societies and Cultures. Thus, I suddenly found myself working in an area-studies format, which forced me to recognize that whatever I wrote might be of interest and relevance beyond my immediate community of folklorists. It also made me aware of the political potential in scholarship, for I found myself engaged in commenting on the "soul movement" from my strange comparatist perspective, with my point of view skewed because my concerns (and thus my data) commented upon the cultural deprivation argument. All my findings dictated that I put forth the argument for the systematic character of Afro-American expressive culture as strongly as possible, for everywhere I looked in the black world I found analogous and complementary materials and attitudes, and the data themselves argued for a trans-Atlantic retention at a deep cultural level. However, the questions to which I found myself responding went far beyond the maintenance of expressive traditions; they had to do with how the very idea of culture, as it was being employed by social scientists, did not really encourage appropriate ways of looking at the various Afro-American situations. For there was—and is—little doubt that the complex tribal traditions seldom made it to the New World in a whole piece—and especially not to the areas I was engaged in studying. Yet there were cultural features that were shared and could not be explained in any fulsome way as simply a shared response to enslavement and emancipation.

Two other factors arose at the end of the sixties that affected the direction and intensity of this work. The first was a convocation of Afro-Americanists and anthropologists to survey the state of the art, called by Norman Whitten and John Szwed and held at the annual meetings of the American Anthropological Association in 1967. This provided my first opportunity to try out ideas on this audience, most of whom were unknown to me. Fortunately, there was a good sense of coming together in spite of the participants' growing anxiety that we were dealing with politically sensitive matters. The result was the groundbreaking book *Afro-American Anthropology: Contemporary Perspectives,* which was edited by the organizers. The first chapter in this book is a revision of the paper I developed for that conference and represents an attempt to begin to clarify the concept of the man-of-words as it is found in its various settings, and to demonstrate how it might be used as an introduction to a performance complex that could be employed to demonstrate both cultural continuities and local differences in Afro-American culture.

The second and perhaps most important influence on my work was that I began teaching courses for desegregating school districts, mostly in East Texas, on language and cultural differences as they might affect schooling. Rudolf Troike and Mary Galvan and I, along with a number of other investigators, developed a quick course on the systematics of language and culture, with a special focus on culture conflict in the school setting, and techniques for taking the evidence of such conflict and using it as an educational resource in teaching the lesson of linguistic and cultural relativity. Engaged in such practical projects, I was forced to think through the social and cultural implications of what my field data had begun to suggest.

The most immediate outgrowth of this development in my thinking and writing was a pair of "practical" works, *Positively Black* and *Language and Cultural Diversity in American Education,* in which I attempted to use materials of expressive culture to cast light on immediate social problems. Neither work drew in any substantial degree on my West Indian experience except as it commented on mainland analogues. But because I found myself on the firing line constantly defending a developing position that insisted that the question of African cultural retentions must remain an open one, my writings became more defensive, and the materials I chose more susceptible to being used in the black cultural integrity and dispersion argument. Moreover, I had been forced to look at whatever historical records I could find of how and where these patterns originated and developed. Naturally, I found myself attempting to make common cause with others who were undergoing similar experiences. Chapter three is one of the products of this essentially group effort. There was so much shooting in the dark going on at the turn of the sixties that a number of investigators decided to discover how much was really known about the black cultural experience. In league with John Szwed and others, we began to compile bibliographies and to attempt to bring historical notices to bear on as the contemporary ethnographic record. Szwed and I pooled our resources so that we could work toward the annotated bibliography that we felt the field really needed—the first two volumes of which were issued in 1978. We discovered such a gold mine of materials in travel accounts and plantation journals that, when the Herskovitseans organized their counterattack to the deculturation argument, we were ready to enter into the discussion. Published originally in a symposium edited by Daniel Crowley in Research in African Literatures, this argument forms the basis of our continuing argument, most recently surveyed in our "After Africa" (forthcoming). It carries the core of the debate that I argue with other materials and on other dimensions of Afro-American expressive culture in chapter two and in a paper on the history and diffusion of the tea meetings (Abrahams, 1977), which is not included here because of space limitations and its overspecialized character.

Most of the other chapters represent my joy at discovering that, because of developments in a number of related fields, investigators other than folklorists were interested in the performances I had discovered and observed. Mirroring this enlarged audience, I published these in a range of journals and anthologies: five in area studies publications; four focusing on the Americas (especially Latin America) and Africa; one in a sociolinguistics journal; another in a book on Afro-American styles of expression; yet another in a book exploring the interface of folklore, communication, and sociolinguistics; three in anthropological publications; and only one in a traditional folklore journal.

Richard Bauman, my colleague at the University of Texas, introduced me to the wonders of "the new ethnography" and more specifically of the ethnography of communication. This led to our collaboration on a number of essays, one of which appears here in somewhat revised form as chapter six. Although we only formally coauthored one article, he assisted me in thinking through and writing *Talking Black,* which was written during this same period, as well as a number of the essays in this volume addressed to sociolinguistic problems.

If the data reported in this volume came more from the St. Vincent fieldwork than elsewhere, it is because that is where I was able to do the greatest amount of fieldwork after I came to know which sister disciplines were interested in cultural performances. Indeed the chapters in the last part of the volume reveal my excitement in seeing the convergence of folklore, sociolinguistics, ethnography of communication, symbolic interactionism, and symbolic anthropology. Folkloristics had taken a decisive turn in the postwar years, one that brought together fieldwork and theory in the desire to understand the activities of tradition-bearing as well as the products of tradition. This meant, among other things, that folklorists became more interested in performers and performances, and somewhat less interested in texts to be collected. Moreover, folklorists began to look at the related notions of context and genre in order to understand actual performances more fully—for it is in these notions that we begin to discover what one has to know ahead of time in order to understand what is going on in a performance. That this brought folklorists closer to the traditional concerns of social and cultural anthropologists is obvious. But the interaction between the disciplines was facilitated all the more as both were influenced by European formalism and structuralism. Perhaps most important was that a great many more theoretical works bearing on these matters were translated and read. Strongly influenced by the cultural by-products of the international exchanges that took place during and after World War II, European and American thought began to merge. This process was intensified because of the tremendous number of international conferences held from the late fifties on, which brought people together from both sides of the Atlantic.

This exchange has had so many repercussions just in the way in which man's expressive capacities are studied that I cannot recapitulate them. But most important as far as my work represented here is the alterations that occurred in some the basic notions of what the important dimensions of the human condition are, and how we ought to go about studying them in their various manifestations. Indeed, what has happened in these fifteen or twenty years is a change in the way in which culture itself is being defined, a change that places folkloric phenomena and other expressive and stylized materials more solidly at the center of anthropological concerns. Indeed, our revised notions of what culture is and how it operates through symbolic behaviors begin to come together nicely with the assumed task of the social anthropologist: to reveal the social orders and common understandings of human collectivities. In this, we suddenly find ourselves in a vastly enlarged dialogue, one that spans the Atlantic. Arising from this dialogue is the growing accord on the character of the cultural dynamic, including the presumption that order is not a *given* in the human condition, but rather an achievement, one that must constantly be revalidated even on a second-by-second, minute-by-minute basis. (This essentially phenomenological approach to ethnography is widely practiced; see especially Geertz, 1973; Peacock, 1968; Turner, 1974; and Sahlins, 1976.) *Society* and *culture,* in this way of conceiving of problems, are terms for the highest level of abstraction of these achieved orders and, therefore, between them constitute and contain native notions of both how life is lived and how it should be lived.

Moreover, discussing culture as achievement and as discovery process not only underscores the importance of the emergent elements of experience but also places performers and performances, festive and ritual celebrants and their intense interactions much more at the center of the ethnographic enterprise. Rather than viewing such display events as epiphenomenal we can now listen to our informants, who have long been telling us that it is in such events that a people depict themselves most fully and regard themselves most seriously (even when the event is carried out in fun).

In placing intensive and stylized events at the center of ethnographic descriptions, we can observe extraordinary, if ideal, order being negotiated and achieved plainly and openly. Moreover, describing such expressive phenomena allows us to approach the areas of meaning and value as well as order. This descriptive and analytic project thus brings together ethnographers of various disciplinary backgrounds: sociolinguists, symbolic interactions, and folklorists, as well as social and cultural anthropologists. Ultimately we begin to conceive of questions in the structural-functional mold of Malinowski and Radcliffe-Brown; but we all attempt to break away from the limitations of such a method by introducing one or another kind of confounding notion. The effort is in behalf of an ever subtler exposition of the dialectics by which culture is achieved, and in search of ways in which the alternative and often self-canceling character of this achievement can be depicted and celebrated.

This enables us to register the variety and even the agony of the life-as-lived rather than revealing human beings as simply order-seeking working and playing animals.

It is the special task of ethnographic fieldworkers of various persuasions to discover how groups derive order, meaning, and value out of the random flow of experience. Of all the sorts of ethnographers, folklorists apparently have an easier time in carrying out such a project. The materials of greatest interest to us are repeatable, memorable, preformulated in a sense, and embodied in performances, ceremonies, and celebrations that are stylized and therefore self-consciously ordered and predictable. Moreover, as opposed to most every-day exchanges, folklore carries its own meanings and values on the surface of its enactments: members of the culture learn early and often what meanings are to be achieved through the play and replay of traditional expressive events. Indeed, such meanings are often explicitly spelled out in the course of the ceremony's storytelling, singing, and dancing. But because we deal with emergent performances that are conventionally jocular, even ridiculous and nonsensical (therefore attacking the usual concepts of ordering), and because we work closely with those to whom the community has given the gift of un-predictability and the status of outsider, we constantly discover ourselves to be working in the margins of meaning and value. Yet, like our colleagues in anthropology, we revel in the deep orders we discover, rendering our texts without the tumult in which we encountered them. This is especially so when the texts arise within festive events, for these are by definition the most intense and the most dizzying cultural engagements. In presenting these texts in orderly form, we convey a strange impression of life, for now festivity begins to be equated with norms and quotidian concerns, even as these norms are being abrogated at a high pitch. Moreover, I am increasingly un-comfortable the more I find that my analyses of life and lore can be presented in the parsiminious fashion developed out of the ethnoscientific developments of these classic social anthropological concerns.

The point of all of this, I suppose, is that scholarship is as responsive to social situations and political and economic impulses as anything else in culture. The enterprise seems, especially as I look back, as if it were only in part under my control; I feel more like a pilot, in other words, than a shipwright. When I look closely at the data I bothered to collect in depth, so often the depth itself seems to occur not necessarily because this reflected an area of importance to those among whom I lived and worked, but rather was my personal response to a particular upset that I was involved in and felt the need to "work through." Let me dwell on one example, for it not only illustrates this but it is also as good a point as any to enter into a discussion of West Indian village culture as I interpret it today.

Unforeseen occurrences and the shock to our systems that accompanies them so often deeply affect the directions in which we proceed and the kinds of questions we ask, especially when we are confused or embarrassed by the experience. The subject comes up often in the natural course of conversation with other ethnographers, especially because such discussions so easily become sessions of "field stories." Yet how few of these formative upsetting experiences are included in our write-ups, even when they have forced us to reexamine and refocus our ways of looking and seeing. To get such information into the record, the experience is told in short-story form and published separately—as with Laura Bohannon's classic "Shakespeare in the Bush" (Bohannon, 1966; but see Geertz, 1973, as well). Even in this article, personal embarrassment is submerged in favor of the lesson to be learned, or the "amusing things" that can occur.

In my pursuit of men-of-words and their performances on St. Vincent, I asked about the events of oratorical display and contest I had observed on other West Indian island communites, events called *concert, service of song,* or, most commonly, tea meeting. On arriving at my Vincentian base of operations, Richland Park, I inquired whether this form of *old talk* was still practiced, only to find that a tea meeting was being planned in the neighboring community of Biabou.

Indeed, I discovered that in preparation for this speechmaking contest to be held in six weeks, the great men-of-words who would *chair* the occasion were holding *colleges* in which the young *scholars* from their home areas were being taught their *lessons*; that is, not only specific speeches but also the techniques for performing them fluently and in competition with other fledgling orators. In this practice the island was unique. I was invited by one of these chairmen to observe how they trained their charges. By attending these classes, I was able to get a glimpse of how the chairmen and orators function and how speeches were put together and then learned. Because I exhibited this interest, I was asked to be a judge for the occasion itself (teachers are traditionally the judges anyhow). I agreed with great reluctance.

Even though I was prepared to be surprised and even embarrassed, I had *no* idea in what ways and how deeply. Although I had seen a number of tea meetings elsewhere, I knew enough about them to know they were played in a quite different fashion from island to island. Further, no place I had worked had such an elaborate and careful process of preparation, especially in involving the young.

The evening arrived and I found myself positioned on the stage with the two chairmen and the choir. The orators sat in the front rows, and the rest of the lodge hall was filled—to the point that many people were hanging out of the windows. I was neither prepared for the mob nor for the incredible amount of noise it generated, especially the rhymed curses and challenges that were screamed out as the young scholars went to the stage solemnly to present their orations. But I had heard the shrill market women do similar comic routines on other islands during tea meeting. What really took me back was that as the evening progressed, the meeting became dominated by the *pit boys* in the rear, who, by beating sticks against the backs of the benches in front of them, were apparently able to bring the proceedings to a total halt again and again. My fellow judges assured me through their laughter that this was not only permitted but an important feature of the event—even if it did prevent the speeches from being finished. Sentimentalist that I am, I felt miserable for the now stony-faced youngsters who had put so much time and energy into the preparation and were being prevented from speaking their piece.

Then, much to the embarrassment of the other judges, the hosts, and the chairmen, as the evening progressed the *bad johns* got more and more unruly, drowning out everything else in their call for the refreshments, the *beer and buns*. When the beer arrived, those carrying the bottles in were tackled and pummeled, and the rest of the audience cleared out quickly, singers and orators, chairmen and judges, including, of course, myself, with my tapes and tape recorder.

I was troubled by the experience, of course, as were those who had gone to such pains to involve me. This upset, however, gave me an opportunity to enter openly into discussion about what had happened. I learned a great deal about Vincentian ways of judging, explaining, and making social repairs from these heated conversations. Indeed, because this opened up the talk about talk, I was able to gather sociolinguistic information, for I was in a speaking network in which I could freely gossip (or *make commess*) about this ruptured social event. My field notes were soon filled with Vincentian comments on right and wrong ways to talk and to act. This traditional performance gave me an opportunity to tie tea meetings to the larger expressive system: now I saw the continuities in both form and criteria of judgment between successful and unsuccessful encounters, good and bad performances.

This material had come my way because of a chance occurrence. But my development as a folklorist had been progressively away from a comparatist perspective and more toward models that related traditional materials to the occasions on which they were performed and the preparation and learning and composition process one went through to be regarded as a performer. The performance-centered "school" of folkloristics that I was practicing focuses primarily on the expressive system within which creative interactions are generated, how the performer and audience relate to one another in performance, and how traditional genres of performance enter into the intense and prepared-for events of a culture (Bauman, 1978).

Ideally, performance-centered folklorists place specific occasions in the context of the expressive repertoire of the culture. By entering into the project of giving at least a profile of the ways in which occasions of per-formance and celebration enter into the regular flow of group life, the folk-lorist-ethnographer attempts to situate creative interactions and their tech-niques of composition. This branch of folkloristics, then, illustrates the range of ways in which expressive individuals, and especially performers, inherit devices of value, power, and meaning in the traditional repertoire. In line with other ethnographic enterprises, the profile is carried out to discover whatever systems (the poetics of the community) underlie the interactions of the group. Thus it carries with it the usual warnings: that the relationship between the system as it is conceived and as it is actually practiced is problematic and to be discovered; and that the performances themselves emerge out of the fruitful union of a performer, a repertoire of available past "texts," and an appropriate situation and occasion for performance. Moreover, it overlooks, for the moment of description at least, that any such repertoire is subject to being used differentially by individuals and is therefore susceptible to analysis in rhetorical terms (who expresses what to whom, in order to move them in what direction) and thus may be looked at with regard to the ways in which individual employment of the system enters into the expressive process.

I had begun drifting in this direction because my informants in Philadelphia kept pushing me that way by insisting on the importance of the performer and his or her text only as it emerged on specific performances. As opposed to the Appalachian singers I had heard sing a song in essentially the same way each time, the street-corner bards change their performance in response to external forces, such as who was listening and responding and under what conditions. Perhaps even more important is the different relation white Appalachian and black Philadelphia performers have to their materials; the white singers regard themselves as vehicles of tradition, whereas the black street performers employ their skills to enhance their personal reputations.

Quite appropriately critics have objected to the apparent emphasis upon the street culture of these studies, for they seem to skew our understanding of Afro-American culture by neglecting the more private, orderly, and "respect-seeking" dimension of black life. These West Indian studies suggest that the vitality of the street world is predicated partly on an opposition of values and behaviors between this locus as a world of action and "reputation-seeking" and the "respect-seeking" segment living primarily in the more private and orderly spaces of the home and the church. This was especially clear in the performance economy of Vincentians, especially in their display events, for they were judged to be either *sensible* ("respect-seeking") or *nonsense* times by where and when they were held, who entered into them, and so on. What had gone on in the Biabou tea meeting could best be understood, then, by recognizing the event's similarities with the respectable household events in which speeches were made of the same general sort, and the nonsense times like carnival, played on the streets and encouraging rude behavior for the fun of it.

In the circumscribed symbolic environment of the lodge hall, the front stage operates in competitive balance with the back area of the pit boys. In this face-off is an explicit confrontation between the values of the house and yard and those of the crossroads. And, needless to mention, on at least one occasion, the force of the crossroads won, bringing down the house.

This occurrence reverberated around the island. Everywhere I went for the next week or two, there were those who wanted to discuss what had happened. Among other things, all of the conventional bromide routines about judging youth with being "rude, rude, rude" were once more called upon by the crossroads philosophers. But interspersed with these formulaic exchanges were those in which the politicians and the government in general were scored for permitting uncontrolled change to occur on the island by improving the roads, by introducing truck-buses that traversed the island, by providing wage-paying jobs—all of which took the young away from the governing power of the family. An important feature of this argument was that young people—especially boys—have always been rude. Their untrustworthiness and nonsense-making potential is simply built into the system as it is recognized and discussed by Vincentians. The unexplored element of this way of looking at life is that any alternative to working on the land for wages is regarded as the preferable way to direct one's children. They are, as many have noted of similar Afro-American communities, educated to emigrate—and to send home regular remittances.

It is just at points such as this that the concerns of the anthropologist and the student of expressive culture come together. Much of the literature on black creativity, as previously noted, has stressed the forms that arise at places of public congregation, contest (or *cutting*) forms like *jazz, calypso, capoiera,* and playing the dozens. But without placing these forms, on the one hand, within the expressive resources of the community, and, on the other, within the situated processes by which social structure is put into practice, their force, passion, and craft cannot be comprehended.

The tea meeting that brought down the house in St. Vincent is, from such a perspective, a special case of an Afro-American performance technique that went awry, and then only slightly so. By recognizing the value systems operating in constant opposition, especially in display events, we can begin to come to grips with what went on with the dissolution of the Biabou tea meeting. Even more important for my folkloristic purposes is the opportunity the event provided to open up for discussion the interesting larger question of the relationship between social upset and cultural creativity. The alternative worlds of order and behavior and of rudeness and nonsense are clearly perceived by Vincentians as the most important dimension of the social organization in their home communities. Moreover, it is customary to bring the two segments into intense confrontation as part of this event and others. A meeting is not regarded as a success unless a good deal of tumult occurs, tumult in which the interest of everyone involved may then be sustained all night. Vincentian tea meeting, then, involves a game of brinksmanship, "deep play" if you wish, a contest in which the highest ideals of the community are put to a test as they are displayed. For this one meeting the men-of-words did not triumph. I was repeatedly told that one of the main reasons why the upset occured was that the chairmen were not strong enough, or did not have sufficient guile, to win over the audience.

Such considerations take us to the heart of the Vincentian—indeed, the more general Afro-American—aesthetic. Performances of all sorts, to be well-received, must be judged on their ability to contend with opposing and competing forces and to keep the contest going indefinitely. A man-of-words is worth nothing unless he can, on the one hand, stitch together a startling piece of oratorical rhetoric, and, on the other, capture the attention, the allegiance, and the admiration of the audience through his fluency, his strength of voice, and his social maneuverability and psychological resilience. What I interpreted at the time as chaos and mob rule always was regarded as one possible outcome to the event, albeit one that seldom occurs. Vincentian creativity, West Indian creativity, and, indeed, Afro-American creativity are built upon this competitive and highly contrastive superimposition of voices, ones that speak in different codes and cadences. All Vincentian occasions demand such participation, through contest or at least through a willingness to practice performance skills as part of a larger chorus of sounds. Most occasions call for each performer to "play apart," to "do his own thing," not in order to quiet everyone else but to gain control through an active leading of these others. But for one such as myself, who did his first fieldwork listening to high lonesome singers around the fire in the Appalachians, the shock of encounter was great—and I anticipate many other such traumas before my days of observation and collecting are finished.

These chapters were not written as a unit. Rather, as the call for a particularistic ethnography of experience has come together with a thorough tryout of the dramatistic metaphor used to describe observed life, it has seemed important for folklorist-ethnographers to become involved in the project. After all, folklorists have been involved with collecting and analyzing performances since the founding of the discipline. My most recent writing has been in response to these analytical programs more than to the sociopolitical concerns of the earlier studies.

With these attempts to enter into that dialogue, however, it has become clearer to me that the dramatistic metaphor is ever in jeopardy of being overemployed, and that, indeed, in describing all interactions with regard to "scenes," "scripts," "scenarios," "actors," and the vocabulary of mimesis, in general, we lose the particular virtues of such terms to describe actual performance occasions. My response to this, registered in some part in this volume's final chapters, as well as the introduction to my forthcoming book "Folktales of the Black World," is an attempt to cling to "native" terms to describe what is going on in a tale-telling or any other traditional performance. It becomes increasingly clearer to me that a ritual or a festival, a game or a debate, is not a performance, and to describe them in performance terms is to break down certain ontological distinctions that we find useful to cling to. Thus, though it was tempting to describe the range of Vincentian traditional occasions and genres in terms of dramatic performance so that I might more fully become a voice in that rich discussion, I inclined away from doing so, hoping thereby to maintain the sense of unique vibrancy to be discovered in Afro-American speechmaking and storytelling. They are performances, to be sure, and they do approach theater—even great theater—at certain points. But the personae taken by the men-of-words in each case differ from those of stage characters, and the qualities of these enactments differ precisely because they are not theatrical but engage the audience in an entirely different manner.

The Man-of-Words
in the West Indies

Patterns of
Performance
in the West Indies

In his survey of Afro-American folklore studies in 1943, Melville Herskovits made a call for a reexamination of the materials of traditional performance, and practice in terms of similarities and differences on a regional basis. Only in the area of religious practices has this been carried out, but not with the materials central to the study of expressive culture: tales, riddles, proverbs, singing and music-making, oratory, and sermons, as well as the more everyday ways of talking and interacting. There is an attitude concerning speaking and speech, to words and word usage in conversation, discussion, debate, and performance throughout Afro-America. This approach to talk emerges most clearly in a common pattern of performance. Because speaking and other display activities are so important in the carrying out of everyday life, this pattern may be used both in defining a culture area and in pointing to important local and regional differences within that area. That this pattern is not merely a configuration of cultural traits, most of which can be observed in any oral culture, will become self-evident.

MEN-OF-WORDS

Communities have devised only so many ways to organize themselves. Once a program or arrangement develops in one sector of life, it tends to repeat itself in other areas. Principles of family organization in certain regards may be echoed in other structures of government, or of economics, and the same principles of order may also be seen in the structure of traditional performances. Folklore seems especially susceptible to this kind of analysis. As the expressive and aesthetic dimension of the culture of tradition-oriented groups, folklore is made up of items and performances that are self-consciously and artistically constructed. And because the performances are of a totally public nature, and therefore are conceived in terms in which under-

1

standing may be achieved by all, outlines of aesthetic organization are clearly stated. Folklore is constructed of conventional materials, and these conventions organize performance in the areas of form, content, imagined roles and role relationships, and in relationships between participants in the aesthetic transaction. Because the performance is public and unrecorded, the audience must have a constant sense of orientation; that is, its members must be aware at all times at what point they are in the performance.

Conventions of performance therefore provide the kinds of markers the performer and the audience need to establish this constant sense of orientation. For instance, virtually every scene of a folk play or a folktale must imply the totality of the composition, where it has been and where it is going. This is why convention must dominate folk performance. Because folk arts are so conventional, it is not difficult to describe their organization. However, though folk art is, by necessity, conventional, the typical forms and styles of performance differ from group to group. One may learn a great deal about a group from discerning what these stylistic abstractions are and therefore what its expectations are toward the performance situation.

In 1958 and 1959, while living in a predominantly black neighborhood in South Philadelphia, I observed a number of traditional performances and began to perceive a pattern of traits in the roles played by the performer, his relation to his material and his audience, and in the audience's attitude toward the performer and his enactment. This pattern centered upon the acclaim given those individuals who were good at using words—individuals I came to call "men-of-words." Significant in their performances was the way in which these artful narrators became closely identified with the style and action of the heroes they described. The audience seemed almost as fully involved, physically and verbally, in the enactment as the speaker. My examination of how this situation was structured centered upon the relative lack of psychic distance between the performer and his performance and between the audience and the described actions. A further trait inducing this strong sense of sympathetic involvement and vicarious identification was the repeated and insistent use of the first-person singular pronouns by the man-of-words. This I termed the "intrusive 'I.'" Finally, it became clear that these performances almost always arose in contests with other men-of-words, and that such contests were a community-accepted manner of establishing and maintaining a public (or *street*) reputation. Although other performance traits were discussed in my report on my Philadelphia findings (Abrahams, 1970), these were the ones that carried a kind of cultural signature.

My assumptions while writing the volume were that this pattern was probably unique to urban black performers in the United States, and so I described the pattern in terms of "oikotypicality" (local configuration of traits). Since then, field experience in the southern United States and in the West Indies has convinced me that this pattern is considerably more widespread and may be characteristic of performances in most New World Afro-American communities. This becomes clear, for instance, in a casual comparison of blues and calypso singers, for both build their art on personal identification, singing of what purports to be their own experiences or observations; and calypsonians perform most characteristically in the context of situation. Furthermore, both types of performer are capable of achieving high status in their respective communities through practice of their art.

The widespread nature of this performance pattern is even more forcefully demonstrated by one type of verbal contest observed in many Afro-American communities in the New World. This practice is often called *playing the dozens* or *sounding* in the United States and is commonly called *rhyming* in the West Indies (Abrahams 1962b, 1964). This adolescent verbal activity involves invective contests in which one youth insults a member of another's family—usually his mother—knowing that he will be answered in kind. The ensuing battle is recognized simply as boasting, and though the contestants become deeply involved in the proceedings they seldom regard it as anything but entertainment. In the West Indies the rules are occasionally spelled out by the boys before they begin to rhyme.

Most of the performance characteristics outlined above can be observed in this obscene oral exchange: the constant insertion of the first-person pronouns, the close identification of the speaker with an imaginary situation, the achievement of sexual identity and (peer-group) status through good word usage, and the word-contest structure of performance. Of course, the verbal effects are not as witty, subtle, or complex as those of adult entertainments.

Rhyming is practiced, unlike more complex verbal traditions, by most young men in West Indian villages, though some are regarded as better talkers than others. In combination with the teasing and taunting also found as a well-developed verbal art among black children in many communities, this rhyming type of verbal interplay develops into two kinds of folklore activities and two kinds of men-of-words: *good talking* or *talking sweet*; *broad talking* or *talking bad.* Badinage remains an integral part of the expressive and communicative dimensions of everyday life there. Almost any extended conversation can develop into an entertainment, especially a contest of wits. I have witnessed these impromptu performances at casual gatherings on the steps or at the pool hall in the big-city atmosphere of South Philadelphia, as well as in markets, rum shops, and especially on buses and boats in the West Indies. This kind of activity gives rise to the person adept at repartee, the broad-talker. Women are often as quick to enter such an on-the-spot contest of wits as men.

The good talker, however, needs a more highly structured situation and more time to exhibit his talents. He commonly purveys a highly decorated and self-consciously artificial rhetoric; for these effects he must have a situation in which he can gain the complete attention of his audience. In the United

States, the good talker tends to hold forth at private parties or religious meetings, though there are street situations in which he may be invited to indulge in his fancy talk. In the West Indies, he may channel his talents exclusively into preaching, but more commonly he holds forth at special performances traditional in festivals such as Carnival or Christmas, or at occasions such as wakes or wedding feasts. On both the islands and the mainland, some men-of-words have in the past specialized in writing friendship or love letters for other members of the community.

Although the ubiquity of the man-of-words has been emphasized here, the more interesting aspect of his presence is the way in which he develops his powers in different ways in the various Afro-American communities responding to different historical, geographical, and cultural conditions. Of equal importance is the way in which the good talker fits into the total picture of a community's traditions and institutions and how great the part he plays in the total range of its expressive culture. Communities on two West Indian islands, Tobago and Nevis, will be described to illustrate the varieties of this man-of-words tradition, how traditional expression harmonizes with the ethos in these communities, and what recent forces have effected changes in folklore, specifically in modifying the performance pattern.

TOBAGO

In Tobago there have been numerous traditional occasions for the man-of-words to exhibit this power: at a *bongo* (wake) as a storyteller or sermonizer; at a *thanksgiving* as a speechmaker, and, most notably, as a central performer in a Carnival *mas'*, as the touring groups of masqueraders are called. In these Carnival mas'es the stylistic traits of the man-of-words performance pattern are harmonized with certain Carnival characteristics. Most of the groups found on Trinidad and Tobago during Carnival represent a self-banded group of a community or neighborhood. They have traditional roles as part of the performance roles designated by traditional naming practices, costumes and masks, and by a certain type of performance consonant with the role. The roles are usually power figures, either characters from the underworld (criminals, devils) or impersonations of heroic types (military figures, warriors). Performers usually take on stage names that are appropriate to the character being played. They usually accumulate groups of followers who dress in a similar style. Although the performer may perform simply by interacting with the audience, he nevertheless finds opportunity for the fullest statement of his abilities in competition with another performer playing the same type of role.

This kind of *old mas'*, which still is the rule in village Carnival, if not in the cities, is organized around a virtuoso performer: a singer, a dancer, a stick fighter, or a speechmaker. He often performs alone, and especially in those roles in which money-making is the primary motivation. More often, he performs alone on the first day of Carnival and with a group the next. When he performs with his group, it is generally recognized that they represent the reputation of their community, and they may use this factor in building up the dramatic interest in contests with other groups.

Most of these contests call for the performance of certain set pieces prepared by each virtuoso ahead of time, and then an improvised battle. This is true, for instance, in the *Caiso Mas'*, the ancestor of the modern calypso competitions, found on both Trinidad and Tobago. The various *chantwells* or master singers composed a song for the season and each tried to have it widely sung. Then when a chantwell met another calypsonian, he and his group traded songs and the two chantwells generally engaged in a "war," or contest of invective. As with most of these conflicts, they were for the amusement of the crowd; seldom was a winner declared.

Although Trinidad and Tobago share many of the same mas'es, Tobago has developed at least one, Speech Band, which seems unique to that island. This troupe for the most part follows the same kind of organization as the Trinidadian groups. It has one additional characteristic usually found at Carnival, but more often in relation to the fancy costume mas'es: a fascination with exotic hierarchies. The members of the group organize themselves in a rigid status order, modeled after British courtly hierarchy, rank depending primarily on speechmaking ability and experience. Characteristically, each performer takes on an appropriate name, the leader being King George. When they march, the hierarchical arrangement is fully revealed. First comes the Showboy, a clown figure who clears the way for the group. Then comes the apprentices, all called Robins. Then come, in a cluster, the members of the King's Court, the knights such as Hero, the Conqueror, Duke of York, Warrior Sealey, and many others. The King is immediately preceded by his "sons," the Prince of Wales and the Duke of York. The King's organizer, called Commander, determines who speaks and in what order. As the names of the characters suggest, the speechers are properly heroic in tone and diction. They have a wide range of subjects and themes, but they always rhyme, use inflated rhetoric, and are strongly hyperbolic.

There are significant differences between Speech Mas' and most of the groups in Trinidad. Most notably, in Speech Mas', though the King is the acknowledged master at speechmaking, everyone in the group is given an opportunity to perform.

When two bands sight each other, one draws a line in chalk over which no member of the other band may step. This announces the challenge. "You are barring them there. They cannot pass the road without they don't answer those questions." Those questions are ones of a prescribed nature and constitute a preliminary sparring. They are posed by one Commander and directed to the other. The following is an example:

> Stop the Bow! [The command at the beginning of each speech, directed toward
> the accompanying musicians, especially the fiddler.]
> Great champion, great champion, great champion am I. What champion are you?
> Champion of war.
> War of what?
> War of Old England.
> Old England of what?
> St. 'Bastopol.
> Of what?
> Gold.
> Of what?
> Mold.
> And the next one?
> What [if] your sister are not able to control [herself sexually]?

At this point the Commanders of both groups will get together and make arrangements to battle in speeches. Usually each contestant will make two or three speeches. If one group has five members and the other ten, then each member of the first group will make more speeches than those in the second. The members of one band will make all of their speeches and then give way to the other group. The Commander indicates who will make the speeches in what order. The Robins always go first but after that the order may vary. The first "champion" will give his speeches and then engage in a short dialogue or, more likely, a short exchange of insulting or boasting verses, such as:

> I must come from across the sea.
> King, oh King, remember me.
> Duke of York must come to me,
> I mus' go and make kisses to his mommee.

To which the Duke will reply:

> I just arise from Italy
> Where Tarawaro cried for me.
> Is you they sent to speak to me?
> Man of full quality,
> Deat', oh deat', remember me.
> You best not to carry none of you blame for me
> Because I made your mother breathe through my pee-pee.

Or the performer will take a few lines from the final speech of the man before him and improvise one in which he shows himself to be an even greater champion. For instance, if one has given a speech that ends:

> I call my King and Commander not to keep that in the memorandum.
> Let us bring them under perpendicular rules and regulation.
> When they call for food let us give them bread and saffron.
> When they call for water, let us give them Candice Lotion.
> When they rebel for mercy from their poor generation,
> We'll badger them for a cheap sale to the American.

The next will give one that goes:

> We'll badger them cheap sale to the American.
> I'll stretch forth my left hand to them but not my right hand.
> I want to meet them that day, man to man,
> And I show them I'm water, stone, cement, and sand.

In this way, aggressions are playfully directed against members of one's own band, dissipating the possibility of more active conflict with the other band. However, the possibility of conflict remains and sometimes has to be taken care of by other means. "When everyone is finished [their speeches], they shake hands and go and part. If a man want to fight, you say, 'Man, go on and pass, and go if you come to fight!'" (Abrahams, 1968, pp. 134-136).

The team character of Speech Mas' performance, in the past, has enabled communities to feel more fully involved in the contest of wits that occurs on Carnival Tuesday when one Speech Band encounters another on the road. Further, the pageantry of the costumes and the system of performance etiquette involving the careful enunciation of the rules of battle provide as much dramatic interest as the boasting and cursing contest itself. These performances of local men-of-words are, then, considerably more egalitarian in organization and less severely focused on the virtuoso abilities of the individual performer.

This style of expressive organization in which dramatic focus is passed from performer to performer is characteristic of most entertainments on Tobago. Furthermore, recently this egalitarian approach to performance has become even more pronounced in certain Tobago communities, including Plymouth.

Perhaps the most important force affecting this change has been the identification of the virtuoso performance with Trinidadian self-centered and mercantilistic motives. Since Trinidad and Tobago achieved independence in 1962, Tobagonians have sensed that its second-class satellite status, already present before nationhood, has become more pronounced. Although the islands are geographically close and have shared a great deal historically and culturally, they are different in many important respects. Trinidad is dominated by urban population centers and therefore has a predominantly mercantilistic way of looking at life. Its economy is based, to a great extent, upon a surplus production of goods and a high degree of division of labor. Trinidadians suffer from a complex cultural situation in which people from many different islands have been brought together in shanty housing, and strong resentments have arisen between resident Afro-Americans and East Indians. All of these factors have created tensions, which are further exacerbated by the lack of employment and by overpopulation.

Problems of this sort are not so profound on Tobago, even in Scarborough, the seat of government and the center of population. In towns like Plymouth, because there has been such a steady migration from the town to Trinidad and elsewhere, there is little problem in providing enough food and employment for anyone who wishes to stay. Although half of the men in Plymouth work in the fields, life really centers on the beach, where the men fish with seines. *Fishening,* as they call it, not only provides Plymouthians with their main source of protein but also with income when the catches are large enough to yield a surplus. In fact, life on the beach projects a model pattern for all social and economic activities of the Plymouthian.

The most important value in beach life is cooperation. There are usually thirteen to fifteen seines in use, but only two can be cast at a given time because of the size of the beach. Therefore they must run by a system of *chances;* that is, the fishermen wait their turn. The two seines that are on their chance are thrown until a reasonable catch is made (sometimes a week goes by without one). The three to six men who throw the seine are the principals in the catch, but everyone else on the beach at the time of the catch shares it. Furthermore, when repairs must be made on a boat or seine, those who are best at such things automatically help, and when a new seine is being *tied* nearly all of the men do some knitting.

Existence of this sort calls for long periods in which no fishing is done, when the men *lime* (relax); they drink, do repairs, sleep, and talk. Those with more sense of initiative and individual enterprise can fish for themselves from a small one-, two-, or three-man boat. The men on the beach do not resent this because there is a ready, lucrative market for all the fish caught.

Although there are conflicts that recur in Plymouth life, even among the men on the beach, the spirit of cooperation dominates. Such conflicts are commonly ascribed to outside influences, an ascription that has some basis in reality. When cooperation is threatened, the beach group and their families cohere and continue their way of life with self-conscious recalcitrances.

This ethos pervades all aspects of Plymouth life, especially in regard to the holding of property and in social and governmental status arrangements. There are provisions for achieving status in Plymouth, and even on the beach. One man can become a net *owner* (who gets 40-75 percent of the take in good catches), or the *captain* of a net team (who gets two *shares*); nevertheless, these bestow no special social distinction. The men on the beach are consciously defensive about such subjects, insisting that anyone, even the Prime Minister, is just another "nigger" when he comes to Plymouth. This is not a pious platitude; in a number of cases, men have left Plymouth and achieved some measure of status elsewhere, and then returned to find their outside position of little account within the community.

For example, one retired policeman who had status elsewhere vocalized his frustrations, to the point of attempting to "organize" the men on the beach under his leadership. The men acquiesced in his activities, because they promised merely to add an element of formal organization to an already orderly existence. However, the government attempted to get the men to organize a cooperative to provide more surplus fish for the rest of the island at lower prices. Because the ex-policeman was not elected to the presidency of the cooperative, he stirred things up sufficiently, drawing on the Plymouthian distrust of outsiders, and caused most of them to refuse to join. Consequently, this cooperative fishing enterprise, encouraged and underwritten by the government, was primarily made up of agricultural workers, shopkeepers, and retired civil servants. An atmosphere of conflict by this outside intervention has arisen, which is resented by members of both factions.

The problem involves much more than just factions. Essentially, the government, and the cooperative as its agency, asked the fishermen to break up their beach life and to reject beach values in favor of a fully capitalist and competitive world view. The fishermen felt that this would not only destroy their way of life but in its place would introduce the attitudes and values of the Trinidadians, whom they regard as thieves and, in personal relationships, dangerous and unpredictable. They feared the incursion of big-city ways and values.

This cooperative pattern is reiterated in nearly all aspects of the lives of Plymouthians. It is reflected in their attitude toward making the family as extended as possible (each person has two godfathers and godmothers and the entire family tends to refer to those individuals by this relationship); it is seen in the large number of savings groups, *susus* (sharing groups), sports clubs, and steel drum bands; but it is most fully seen in the traditional expressions that are still widely observed in the town. Most dramatically, the cooperative motive arises in times of crisis, such as when a member of the community dies. Immediately, nearly all work in town stops, and friends and family gather around the ones most affected. As many as forty or fifty men collect wood, cut it up, and put together the coffin. The same is true of the digging of the grave; each male friend takes his turn with the shovel, while the others stand around watching. After the burial, a *bongo* (wake) is usually held; the first night is devoted to hymn-singing, but subsequent nights are given over to games, dances, and riddling. Storytelling, once favored, is no longer the most common entertainment. The games are usually played in a circle; their accompanying song is performed in the chanter-response pattern usually associated with African practices, with the position of song leader changing often. The dances are the same; they are performed in a circular arrangement, each dancer coordinating his movements with those of dancers on each side of him.

Other festival occasions reflect the same communal preoccupation. Any new boat or seine calls for a *fête*, a *christening,* the appointment of godfathers and godmothers, and so on. Similarly, when someone has returned from a trip or recovered from an illness or had a similar experience a *thanksgiving* is given. Finally, the most important holiday of the year is St. Peter's Day, *Fisherman's Fête,* in which not only Plymouthians but fishing folk from all over the island gather for games and the blessing of the boats. All of these occasions call for the same kind of performances as those outlined in regard to the bongo, except that on St. Peter's Day all the local fishermen and many of their friends from other locales are called upon to improvise a speech or a song for the occasion. These single-person performances have diminished because they are difficult to perform for an audience that has been greatly enlarged by the improved roads and transportation system, which make it easier for people in one community to go to the celebrations in others. But in this development the singular focus on cooperative activity has encouraged the maintenance of a great many other traditional forms—specifically those in which the role of the central performer is passed around.

The practices that have replaced them harmonize with the traditional extended-family ideals of the residents. Essentially, there is no sense of rejecting the ways of the past, as one finds in a number of other West Indian communities, but rather a selective emphasis on an alternative pattern of traditional performance: the group game or song or dance.

NEVIS

The island culture of Nevis contrasts dramatically with that of Tobago. Nevis, which endured for over three hundred years under British domination, has a style of performance and an accompanying ethos that emphasizes solo performance and an image of life as isolated and full of anxiety and conflict. The folklore of Nevis is—like that of Tobago—the result of a coming together of African and European traditions. In the actual texts performed, Nevis folklore is predominantly British. But in terms of the context, the way in which a performance is organized, traditional expression in Nevis is a development of the man-of-words pattern with its many African antecedents and analogues.

On Tobago there was always a balance between the two patterns of performance, the integrated and the virtuoso types, and recent developments away from the latter simply illustrate that a choice is being made. On Nevis, for very different reasons, there has also been a drifting away from the man-of-words pattern. Whereas on Tobago the situation develops because of a defensive shoring-up of the sense of community enterprise, on Nevis the only shoring-up and defense done is that of individuals retreating into themselves. On Nevis there is very little community activity or feeling.

Nevis occupies a satellite status to St. Kitts not unlike that between Tobago and Trinidad. It is one of the smaller of the Leeward Islands, which were formerly British. With St. Kitts, Antigua, and Barbados, it was one of the "Mother Colonies" in the British Caribbean. Tobago was never regarded as one of the great outposts of European power, was never a highly successful plantation enterprise, and therefore has never been fully cultivated and populated. However, Nevis, which was settled in 1628, was one of the places in which West Indian sugar fortunes were made (Pares, 1950; Merrill, 1958) and that attracted a large slave population.

A hot springs system there was developed into a luxurious spa, which became a favorite vacation spot for British visitors and for planter residents of other West Indian islands. Consequently, Nevis has been dominated politically and economically by Great Britain for over three hundred years. Add this to the fact that the first field workers on the island were English-speaking Irish peasants transported for "political" crimes and the strongly British flavor of their traditional expressions begins to be accounted for.

The Irish brought their countryside amusements with them, and many have been perpetuated by the Africans who followed them. But these would not have become established were there not elements in the situation of blacks on Nevis that made the British entertainments understandable and appropriate. One of the appropriate features was that the British amusements permitted a number of aesthetic features to be maintained and elaborated, such as the use of topical satire for aggressive purposes and social control and, most important for the concerns of this study, the good-talker type of man-of-words performance. But the British folk ethos emphasizing the futility of love and any interpersonal involvements was also seized upon by the Nevisians and integrated with the kinds of distrusts and divisions that are endemic to the Afro-American family system as it comes under the pressures of economic marginality and the need to migrate to places in which wage labor is viable. This tension and distrust becomes especially evident in sexual involvements. Not only are there many proverbs that argue that man and woman cannot live together effectively (unless man uses force), but songs and dialogues emphasize the same point of view. Perhaps the most dramatic example of this is the widely sung Nevisian adaptation of the English folk song "Johnny's So Long at the Fair." In English versions the maiden sings of Johnny, who is late in returning from the fair, and of the presents he has promised her. On Nevis the song has become a recitation of all the things Johnny has already given the maiden.

> The ring on my finger is Johnny give me,
> The ring on my finger is Johnny give me,
> The ring on my finger is Johnny give me,
> Johnny alone until morning.

Johnny also gives her shoes, a hat, and a number of other personal items. After all of these things are listed, she finally sings:

> Johnny says that he love me, but I do not believe,
> Johnny says that he love me, but I do not believe,
> Johnny says that he love me, but I do not believe,
> Johnny alone until morning.

This divisive and affectless vision of life, in combination with a high degree of competition in economic, social, and aesthetic areas of life, is a reflection of the sense of personal alienation so often discussed by Nevisians. Because the land has been misused, it is still owned primarily by the plantocracy or the government, which often will not let it be planted, and, because of the lack of any other means of livelihood, the island has been in an economically depressed state for over a century. But these conditions are not only a result of economic factors, for in those instances in which a cooperative enterprise has been suggested, which might lead Nevisians out of the spiral of economic stagnation, there has been no widespread move to act on the plan. On the most populous side of the island, the peasants plant vegetable crops that are not highly suited to the land and that have a limited market. They are, however, crops that can be vended by individuals in market competition and thus affect their way of viewing life in terms of competitiveness.

This bankrupt and alienated condition has led many residents of Nevis to envision themselves as living in a prison, quite different from the image of the "tropical paradise" held by most of the visitors and part-time residents from Canada and the United States. Consequently, there has been a series of mass emigrations from Nevis to areas in which employment possibilities are better. Many Nevisians went to New York and New Haven around World War I, others to the Dominican Republic in the 1930s, to Great Britain from 1945-63, and to the U.S. Virgin Islands recently. Naturally the ones who leave are the more adventurous and often the more intelligent. Although those who have remained are often severely tradition-oriented, they have not always been the best performers, and on Nevis only a charismatic speaker is capable of winning an audience.

As on Tobago, on Nevis festivals provide the most important occasions for traditional performances. The two most notable Nevisian occasions are Christmas and tea meeting. Both provide opportunities for the dramatic exercise of verbal dexterity in the framework of a contest situation. But whereas Tobagonians have had an alternative of virtuoso or group performances, on Nevis the only type acceptable in this conflict-oriented community is the virtuoso contest. Group-style performances on Nevis are primarily performed by children in their *ring play,* and by small groups of chantey men moving houses or boats. Not only is the man-of-words given the opportunity to display his powers in these festival performances, but almost the only kind of performance to which an audience listens is one in which an individual arises and seizes attention by virtue of his entertainment abilities. Inevitably, such attempts are rewarded with oral retorts and heckling, for the entertainment value of virtuoso performance relies strongly on the introduction of the contest element.

There are a number of occasions in which such contests are an integral part of the festivities. Wedding feasts, for instance, usually include a session in which toasts of an obscene, boastful, and comical nature are proposed by a succession of orators. The following is part of such a toast:

> Here's to the girls that dress in black;
> When they dress they never look slack.
> When they kiss, they kiss so sweet,
> Makes Tommy stand without feet.

Almost any other formal occasion calls forth speeches in contest of one sort or another.

On Nevis, where the land and the money are still in the hands of the few, the songs and speeches of compliment and respect play an important part, even in the most raucous groups of Christmas revelers:

A merry Christmas to the Master
A merry Christmas to the Master
A merry Christmas to the Master
And a merry Christmas to you all.

A merry Christmas to the Mistress
A merry Christmas to the Mistress
A merry Christmas to the Mistress
And a merry Christmas to you all.

A merry Christmas to the children
A merry Christmas to the children
A merry Christmas to the children
And a merry Christmas to you all.

Master, Mistress and children
A merry Christmas, a merry Christmas,
Master, mistress and children
A merry Christmas to you all.

Perhaps because Nevis (and St. Kitts) had a longer history under British rule than other islands in the area, the English manner of celebrating the Yule season was even more profound and long-lasting there. Not only has the night-time caroling persisted, but also the *mummings*—short entertainments performed for the benefits of households throughout the countryside. The attribution of this custom to English manner of observance is as definite as possible, for two of the more ubiquitous mumming plays from Great Britain, *St. George and the Dragon* and *The Christmas Bull Play* (Abrahams, 1968, 1971), are still performed on these islands, as well as a version of the English Morris here called *Masquerade*. Not only has the mumming persisted, it has also proliferated to the point that a number of other plays are performed during this season in the same way, including one called *Cowboys,* taken directly from Street and Smith publications of the 1930s and from Western movies (Abrahams, 1964).

While newly conceived, the cowboy play is built on the older pattern of the hero-combat dramas in which each character introduces himself with a boast, leading to a scene of argument and finally to armed battle. In the *Cowboys,* however, the battle is between whole groups, while in the more archaic St. George *Mummies* the fights are serially carried out between pairs.

Of the older plays, there are two types of play, each performed by different kinds of troupes. The first are "wooing plays," domestic farces that call for a good deal of sexual play—ribald seduction and courtship scenes that are primarily enacted in terms of an argument or contest of wits between the man and the woman or between the husband and his rival; the second are ritual-combat plays in which the dialogue between the combatants is rendered in elaborate language. In a sense, the farces elevate the broad talker to thespian status, whereas the combat-dramas bring good talkers onto the stage.

The plays divide themselves by their kinds of troupes. The farces are carried on in broad creole by cross-dressed players. The combat dramas, which are played only by men in beautiful costumes and acted out in stentorian tones and stately movements, are in the most elevated sort of oratorical English. Shakespeare texts are used, which is not uncharacteristic of the Eastern Caribbean. While *Richard III* is the most common, *Julius Caesar* is also found on Nevis:

Cinner.   I dreampt last night that I did feast with Caesar, and things un-luckily change my fancy. I have no will to wander forth of doors, yet some-thing lead me forth.

Lucius.   What is your name?

Antony.   Are you a married man?

Cassius.   Are you a bachelor?

Marcus.   Answer every man directly.

Octavius.   Where do you dwelt?

Cinner.   What is my name? Am I a married man? Am I a bachelor? Answer every man directly. Where do I dwelt? Directly I am going to seize a funeral.

Marcus.   As a friend, or an enemy?

Cinner.   A friend.

Marcus.   That answer is directly.

Cinner.   To answer every man thus briefly, truly, and wisely, I said I am a dandy bachelor and my name is Cinner the poet.

Marcus.   Tear him to pieces, tear him to pieces.

Cassius.   Tear him for his bad verses, tear him for his bad verses.

Marcus.   Tear him to pieces, tear him to pieces no matter, his name is Cinner the conspirator.

Cinner.   I am not Cinner the conspirator, I am Cinner the poet.

Lucius.   Come brand, fire brand. Some to Brutus, some to Cassius, some to Lagarirus, and away go with him.

Caesar.   The evil that men live after death let it be so with Brutus, as Caesar was ambitious I slap him, blows for his ambition, and death for his honour, and pride for his valor.

Antony.   For fifteen hundred years ago the power of Rome city was destroy by the Nineveh again I will take my seat as a Roman citizen for they are

famous in waters, blood, sword, halters, and poison, for I remember it
was a summer when I put on this mantle and I will die for my country
Rome and citizen.

Caesar.   Roman, Country men, and lover lend me your ears, lend me your
ears. As the noble Brutus to told you Caesar was ambitious and it not so
it was a grief and a grievous fault against Caesar.

[*They kill him.*]

Lucius and Choius.   We are in deep distress for our brother who was so
valiant and brave for our country Rome. Oh, let us weep for him and over
his silent tomb.

Antony.   Is there no voice to be heard of my repealing banish brother.

Sardius.   I come to bury the body of Caesar that all the world may see that
he was the famous captivity of Rome.

This *lesson* is not characteristic of those of such performance groups,
however. Most are considerably longer and make much more verbal and
dramatic sense. But even Shakespeare was judged with regard to his entertainment potential, and this scene is not only laughed at but commented upon
by the audience, and accompanied by music and dancing. This blending of
music, dance, and drama is characteristic of all performances still observable
on Nevis.

Every playing group is accompanied by some kind of musical aggregation,
and the divisions of the scenes are punctuated by music from them and by the
dancing of the players. This tends to isolate scenes and break up any sense of
dramatic development in the pieces, causing the players to forget about this
implied construction and to skip backward and forward from one scene to
another, as they go from house to house. This is possible only because the
audience knows the story that the piece enacts. In some cases, this fragmenta-
tion has dictated the construction of the piece, as in *Giant Despair,* in which
the passages taken from *The Pilgrim's Progress* are chosen without thought of
portraying the story of Christian's journey to the Holy City, but rather to give
interesting confrontations that occurred to Christian and Great Heart along
the way.

Such plays are never presented in toto in any yard. Indeed, one scene from
The Pilgrim's Progress might be given in one yard, and another from a different story completely might be performed in the next. Troupes, which
perform two or three plays during any given season, are organized by one
older man-of-words, the *captain,* who knows the plays by memory. The parts
are written out and taught to the others. The members change from year to
year, but organized as the troupes are around the captain, there is no threat of
a break in the tradition. The captain usually has a *number-two man,* who
helps him put together the production every year. New troupes usually are
formed when a number-two man goes off on his own. This is an apprentice
system similar to that of the Speech Band on Tobago, but there are inherent

weaknesses in this arrangement as developed on Nevis, which have recently led to a breakdown in the performance of these Christmas *sports*.

A certain amount of community cooperation is called for in organizing the troupe. In the past this was put into effect through the respect accorded the man-of-words; he usually was a highly regarded member of the community because of his verbal abilities. Emigration has carried away many of the best virtuosos. It has become more difficult for those remaining to attract personnel to their troupes, a situation aggravated by the increasing egotistical involvement of the captains.

These factors have created a situation in which the position of captain is no longer one of such high status. The remaining captains react to this change by insisting that they be given their proper respect, especially by the younger members of the community, who are, as always in such mumming situations, the potential additions to the troupe. Although the young may earn their Christmas money in this way, they find that they not only have to learn their parts from the captain but also have to demonstrate their respect for him over and over again. They react by refusing to join him in spite of the economic motivation.

The Cowboy groups have less of a problem in this regard because of the number of status roles within the play itself, and because the role of the captain has devolved upon a number of players. The young players are anxious to graduate to important roles, and the *Cowboys and Indians* allows them to do so because any number of combats can be added without altering its shape. One captain of an older play, *The Christmas Bull,* found that the only way he could hold his troupe together was to rewrite the play. In the original there was a role for one bull who had a comic fight with an inept local plantation owner, but in the revision eight bulls were added. Most of the captains are not willing to make such changes. If changes are made they are generally to enhance the captain's part, already the largest and most heroic one.

The language of most of these plays, especially the hero-conflict dramas, is extremely ornate and hyperbolic. A champion must, after all, excel both in words and deeds. The boasting speeches are not, however, quite so broad in style and outlandish in diction as the speeches made during tea meetings.

The Nevis tea meeting is a remarkable combination of pageant, mock fertility ritual, variety show, and organized mayhem. The proceedings, which probably developed most immediately out of fund-raising church events introduced in the nineteenth century, are still found on a number of other islands in the West Indies, but in many different forms (DeCamp, 1968). Until recently, tea meetings were often held on Nevis on summer evenings during the full moon. A hall was engaged, and a *King* and *Queen* and their *court* chosen. Costumes were carefully prepared for the royalty and for the other performers. On the night of the performance, the King and Queen were called for by a fife and drum (*Big Drum*) band. They went to the place of the meeting, where the rest of the community had gathered. They sat on the stage while members of the audience came up and performed some prepared routine—a song, poem, dialogue, speech, or dance, done by one or two performers, or a team song and dance such as Japanese Fan Drill or Baby Drill. The participants wore costumes appropriate to whatever role they played. In the middle of the evening tea (cocoa or some other hot drink) was served, and some ceremonial cakes, fruit hanging from a *harbor* (*sic*), and kisses from the King and Queen were ceremoniously auctioned. Then the King, the Queen, and members of the court made elaborate and ironic speeches. The speeches were followed by other acts from the audience, which continued until dawn if the meeting was a good one. In the back sat the scoffers, who made loud and often obscene comments about the performers and their routines.

Organizing, or attempting to organize, the proceedings were two *chairmen*. They were supposed to give a sense of continuity and order to the show and to determine who should perform at what time and when the tea should be served. One of them usually called the meeting to order by making a plea for decorum; this speech announced the tone for the night.

> Ladies and gentlemen, this afternoon we stand here to accompany this company here, ladies and gentlemen, and I want to here, this afternoon, have decorum. Decorum. Remember the alphabet, ladies and gentlemen: A is for attention, B is for behavior, C is for conduct, and D is for DECORUM. And ladies and gentlemen, as we march on further, we go to J is for justice and P is for peace that is Heaven for the flocks. I ask you to remember those few letters in the alphabet: A, B, C, D, P, and J. Ladies and gentlemen, I won't procrastinate much more of the valuable time while I ask ____ to provide me with a piece.

As the chairmen continued to make their introductions and to comment on each act, it became clear that they are the premier performers. They not only had to make these interpolated speeches but also had to attempt to outshine the other performers, and, most important, each chairman had to prove himself the best speaker there. As they put it, each wanted to be regarded as "the cock with the brightest comb." They preened their feathers by making long, inflated, macaronic speeches.

> That song reminded me of Moses standing on the banks of the Red Sea. It fills my heart with phil-long-losophy, entrong-losophy, joken and conomaltus. Impro, imperium, pompry, comilatus, allus comigotus, which is to say I come here today without any study. Dia Gratia, by the grace of God, I have tried my best. Time is tempus fugit. The same. I will say a few words about Moses. His life he went into different parts; he spent forty years in Egypt, forty years in Medea, and forty years in the wilderness. I shall now, sum bonum, malcum cum shalltum propendum peerum, desideratum, wobiteratum attitaratin. I shall now say veedie, veedie, amrie, which is to say, I came, I saw, and I conquered. And shall now leave my stand backon-awalum, aloquent, precipitie, matic-matic, savong-savong. For I'm

well-known for this, a wild cannonball speaker. Who thinks they can come over harder than I? Why if anyone here come from the school, I come from the college. If they're from the college, I'm from the Temple Bar. If they are from the Temple Bar, I am from the House of Parliament. If they are from the House of Parliament, I am from the city of Cairo that is in Egypt.

Speeches of this sort simply proclaimed the challenge that the other chairman or some other performer felt called upon to accept. Meanwhile, each flourish of language caused the emotions of the audience to rise, including those of the hecklers in the back. As the noise mounted, the chairmen felt more of a need to assert their control, not only by becoming more eloquent but louder and, quite often, insulting. In one tea meeting reported to me, the only way one of the chairmen could reassert control was to grab his wife and to begin to do a highly obscene dance; obscenity was not out of bounds on an occasion like this.

Most Nevisians will tell you they still love tea meetings. However, recently there have been very few of them. The reasons are primarily the same as those that are causing the demise of some of the Christmas sports. The chairmen become egotistical all too often, and this is sensed by the audience, especially the hecklers. There is little attraction in placing oneself in such an assailable and potentially embarrassing position, and few young men are willing to learn the speechmaking craft. All of the chairmen, consequently, are middle-aged or older, and therefore of the age that is becoming less respected and obeyed by the young. The brightest of the young, moreover, continue to leave the island.

The breakdown of the traditional practices is part of the larger degeneration of communication channels. People on Nevis in many cases have retreated into themselves, lashing out at anyone who happens to come too close. In certain cases, this has resulted in a family banding together in the face of the threat from others in the community, but in other situations it is only the individual who becomes defensive.

THE SOCIAL USES OF THE PATTERN

In presenting Nevisian and Tobagonian man-of-words traditions in terms of their constituent elements and their recent changes, an attempt has been made to show that a variety of nonaesthetic forces may have important repercussions on aesthetic performances. But it has also been pointed out that these performances, as aesthetic entities, represent a model of interpersonal relations in the surrounding community. When forces inside or outside the community bring about changes in these relations, they will be reflected within the structure of the traditional performance. The performance is, after all, a stylization.

The Nevisian Christmas plays are, as pointed out, very similar to the Tobagonian Carnival Speech Mas'es especially in regard to the boasting rhetoric and the combative scene presented. But there is a wide divergence between the two islands in regard to the model of interpersonal relationships provided by these activities. These differences reflect a real divergence of world view. In the Speech Mas', the band is organized on a double principle of status. The King is regarded as the finest speechmaker, but the Commander handles the business affairs—collecting the money, holding it, arranging with Commanders of competing groups who should speak first and for how long. It is these two who must keep order throughout the contest. This dual responsibility, in addition to the provision for apprenticeship, diffuses attention away from a single performer. A sense of hierarchical order and decorum is built into such performances, bringing about a sense of control at all times in the proceedings. However, this very sense of order allows for greater flexibility in regard to the poetic orations. There are two kinds of speech made by members of the Speech Band: prepared and improvised speeches, the latter of which reply to one or another piece of the other team (usually the one just before the improvisation). The strength of the group therefore resides in part in its members' ability in composition and memorization, and in part in their ability to improvise in proper style. The emphasis always is on coordination, even in the contest atmosphere. Conflict becomes a positive mode of socialization.

On Nevis, the freedom to improvise is totally absent in the Christmas plays. The captain knows the plays, teaches all the parts, and takes the most important and heroic part himself; it is his show from beginning to end. Such plays call for a high degree of coordination, and this coordination can only occur through community acquiescence to the leadership of the captain and, to some extent, his number-two man. It is up to these leaders to see that the players speak their lines as taught them.

The Nevis tea meeting does, however, call for ability to improvise on the part of the chairmen. But once again, there are significant differences between this technique and that of the members of Speech Mas', for while the Nevisian man-of-words calls attention to himself through his improvisation, the Tobagonian speaks both for himself and his team. Not only is there more occasion for improvisation on Tobago, but a greater range of freedom of topics the speaker may explore in his speech. The tea meeting chairman, to be sure, must *answer* the challenges hurled at him, and in the same terms as the challenge, but usually he merely uses the other speaker's theme to introduce his speech; and once the introduction is over he falls back on set pieces he has used in the past. He may thus say, in answer to the speaker before him, "That magnificent, fantastico-fantastical rendition of that song of sorrowful parting brings to mind Ruth and Naomi standing 'midst the alien corn," and then he is free to give a speech learned in Sunday School about Ruth and Naomi, embellishing it with choice phrases from Greek and Latin. On Nevis, in other words, the man-of-words is just as restricted in his expressions as the community is in other aspects of life. The interpersonal contests that feature the performances are fraught with anxieties and tensions and are focused upon the individual performer; in throwing so much of himself into the performance, he reflects, in a heightened fashion, the day-to-day interpersonal relations of most members of peasant groups on the island. Traditional contests, once a viable model of socialization, have become untenable to a group too strife-ridden; the order of the performance is dissipated, along with the importance of the man-of-words.

CHAPTER TWO

Traditions of Eloquence in Afro-American Communities

The importance of effective speaking in Afro-American communities has been testified to repeatedly by outside observers. In such communities, the eloquent speaker is capable of garnering a great deal of power, respect, and in many cases admiration through his artful speaking. Men-of-words are given respect and approval for quickness of wit and for eloquence. In general, these two capacities are observable on separate occasions, and in different types of performances and speaking codes. What I have called, for convenience sake, "broad talkers" are the ones who rely primarily on wit and other economical verbal devices, and who commonly use creole as their medium. "Good talkers" are those who rely on elevated diction and elaborate grammar and syntax, and who speak in the local version of Standard English.

Both types of verbal performance are to be found, and in abundance, in working-class or peasant Afro-American communities, but with different focuses and functions due to differing historical, geographical, ecological, and demographic social forces. In Philadelphia, for instance, I noted among my young male informants that high importance was placed upon the capacity to contend with witty and argumentative play (though "good talking" was carried on by preachers in that neighborhood) (Abrahams, 1970). In the West Indies such wit has achieved high artistic form in song traditions like calypso and other types of scandal songs and rhymes; the more fully developed aspect of the speaking repertoire is in the area of eloquent speechmaking.

Furthermore, recent descriptions of African village life and expressive .culture encourage us to look to that continent as the primary source for the Afro-American valuing of eloquence. There has surely been a continuity between New World speechmaking practices and African expressive patterns.

An earlier version of this chapter appears as Traditions of Eloquence in Afro-American Communities in *Journal of Inter-American Studies and World Affairs,* Vol. 12, No. 4, © 1970 University of Miami Press, with permission of Sage Publications, Inc.

Ethel M. Albert's work is characteristic of the literature on African groups, though her account of a speech economy is fuller than most. She notes that

> speech is explicitly recognized as an important instrument of social life; eloquence is one of the central values of the cultural world-view; and the way of life affords frequent opportunity for its exercise. Sensitivity to the variety and complexity of speech behavior is evident in a rich vocabulary for its description and evaluation and in a constant flow of speech about speech. Argument, debate, and negotiation, as well as elaborate literary forms are built into the organization of society as means of gaining one's ends, as social status symbols, and as skills enjoyable within themselves. (Albert, 1964, p. 35)

Similarly, Ruth Finnegan notes in her fine study of Limba (Sierra Leone) tale traditions that

> the ability to "speak" well is continually given as an essential quality of anyone with authority, especially a chief; without a chief, it is often said, there would be fighting and quarrelling everywhere; and, in practice, chiefs do seem to spend much of their time in formal speaking with and between their people. (Finnegan, 1967, p. 13)

Many novelists of African life draw on these speechmaking traditions as a means of dramatizing village conflict. (See, for instance, Laura Bohannon's *Return to Laughter* and Chinua Achebe's *Things Fall Apart*.)

In its New World manifestations, however, the maintenance of such oratorical skill has not received the approving notice of observers, perhaps because it flies in the face of the white image of blacks as linguistically and culturally deficient. Such oversight has led investigators to ignore evidence for Afro-American cultural vitality and to argue that, in effect, any cultural attainment of the Afro-American was due to European rather than African origins — except in cases like *vodun* (the syncretistic religion of Haiti), in which the stereotype of savagery and superstitions may be reinforced. It therefore seems important to review some of the reasons why, even in scholarly discourse, this stereotypical reaction has been maintained, and to survey some of the counterevidence provided us by travelers and journal keepers.

Studies of Afro-American cultures and societies continue to be haunted by the shape-shifting, pursuing spirit of ethnocentrism. Those who stress cultural deprivation and social pathology are but the latest incarnations of this spirit in relying on mainstream Western values and practices as norms. Stigmatization arises from the imputation that blacks have no culture, that is, no shared sense of order exhibited by the members of the group. We can discover through most of the literature on Afro-Americans that the model of acculturation employed is much the same as that used throughout the period of enslavement as a rationale for what was done to blacks. It is argued that Africans were savages, animals, superstitious creatures in need of civilizing. Moreover, any elements of "culture" that survived the middle passage were to a great extent eliminated by the plantation experience.

This attitude has led to some current statements such as one made in a widely used reader:

The American Negro comprises the largest segment of this country's disadvantaged and ethnic-minority-group population. While differing languages and identification with cultures different from that dominant in the United States serve to isolate as well as insulate certain of our ethnic minority groups, such is not true of the Negro. While not afforded full social acceptance in American society, the Negro ideationally and culturally is Anglo-Saxon. (Webster, 1966, pp. 4-5)

The logic of this argument is that whatever culture Afro-Americans have is based on Western values and practices, misunderstood and improperly carried out. This misperformance is accounted for in terms of some kind of cognitive disability or the continuing subordinate and marginal social status that mainstream society accords Afro-Americans, a situation that makes it difficult or impossible to internalize the real meaning of these values and practices.

It was just such a point of view that Melville Herskovits argued against in his now-classic *Myth of the Negro Past*: by surveying the ethnographic literature (as well as relying on his own field experience) he concluded that the most stereotypical of all arguments was that African culture had been eliminated by the New World experience (Herskovits, 1941). Herskovits recognized a tremendous number of African culture traits that remained in practice in one or another Afro-American community and observed that there was an interplay between African and European cultures in the New World setting. Hence he argued that a more meaningful acculturation model would describe this coming-together process without assuming that European practices were either dominant or normative. Observing African traits as they became a part of New World culture, he saw three kinds of persistences: thoroughgoing African retentions; reinterpretations of African practices; and syncretisms, traits in which certain behaviors shared by both Old World culture areas were embroidered upon.

The history of the controversy that attended the publication of this book provides us with a case study of what may happen when a consistent argument is waged against stereotypical logic. It disquieted many, who accused the author of special pleading, of thesis-pushing. Thus, when E. Franklin Frazier elaborated an effective argument against one facet of the Herskovits hypothesis, it was seized upon by the disquieted and used by them to reject the entire perspective. That was a generation ago, and it is only now that we witness an open reassessment of the Herskovits position by students of Afro-America. Characteristic of this tentative development is the introductory statement by historian Sterling Stuckey in his "Relationships between Africans and Afro-Americans":

American historians have displayed a pronounced ignorance of the work on Africanism which has been done by ethnomusicologists, anthropologists, musicologists, and folklorists. Despite the studies which have been conducted in these fields since the 1940's, historians have been, with very few exceptions, oblivious to what these disciplines have to offer. It is quite possible that the culture deprivation syndrome, which has long influenced the thinking of American historians toward Afro-Americans, militates against the use of findings from these disciplines, thereby contributing.to a general tendency to ignore the cultural contributions of black people in the U.S. (Stuckey, 1969, p. 4-9).

What Stuckey says of his colleagues might be noted of nearly all academic disciplines, including anthropology; even in that culture-based discipline the findings of the few who have been interested in Afro-American communities have generally been ignored, and the area of New World Afro-American studies regarded as a way station into esoteric cultural investigations of more exotic groups.

There is, however, a major weakness in the Herskovits perspective that has made it difficult for scholars in other fields to accept his way of arguing: though Herskovits avers that he is describing an ongoing process of cultural retention, his documentation (in *Myth of the Negro Past* more than in his ethnographies) is heavily oriented toward specific culture traits. With the growing disenchantment in anthropology with trait orientation in general, the Afro-American culture hypotheses has been ignored rather than refuted. It seems necessary to refocus the argument away from traits and place it more firmly upon descriptions of observed social processes and expressive and in-strumental systems.

The systems approach is forcing us into a reconsideration of past assump-tions especially in the formulation of strategies of collecting data, changes that have led a number of these observers to postulate the integrity of the life-style of these communities, an integrity attributable not only to the shared slave and plantation experience but also to traditional practices that are preservations and adaptations of African expressive styles and techniques.

One of the few steps taken in this direction is Alan Lomax's musical per-formance profile, derived in great part from his cantometric and choreo-metric analyses. As he notes of the African, and by extension the Afro-American:

> The regional profile is dominated by the style features of the Bantu-African core. The major approach to song is choral and antiphonal, with the characteristic use of overlap, so that at least two parts are frequently active at the same time. A well-balanced, rhythmically tight, often polyphonic choral performance is the norm in most areas. The major vocal style is clear and unconstricted, but with playful and intermittent use of high register, yodel, nasality, rasp, and forcefulness. . . .
>
> Everything contributes to an open texture, inviting participation fostered by a rock-steady beat, and by clear, liquid voices singing one note per syllable. The rhythmic formula is a playful use of simple four-square meters with rhythmic unison in the chorus, but in the orchestra independence of parts gives African music its most unusual characteristic—polyrhythm, or metrical conflict between two or more levels in the orchestra—frequent elsewhere in our sample only for India. Vocal polyrhythm, quite rare in sample, occurs as an important feature of the specialized African Hunter style. The overall impact of the African style is multileveled, multiparted, highly integrated, multi-textured, gregarious, and playful-voiced. (Lomax, 1968, pp. 94-95)

Lomax's profile has not only been testified to on both sides of the Atlantic, but some of the features to which he has pointed have been fruitfully related to other, nonmusical expressive forms with specific reference to their social uses. John Szwed, for instance, has demonstrated that the "soul music" of the 1960s represented a return in great part to selective elements of this African pattern after the popularity of the blues, which he argues is an atypical form:

> The blues . . . are almost unique among traditional American Negro forms. First they are sung solo, without the typical vocal call-and-response pattern . . . the blues are completely personalized . . . [and] are the least redundant of all American Negro forms. There is greater concern with textual message and meaning: they are information oriented. (Szwed, 1969, pp. 117-118)

After surveying the social forces to which the blues responded, Szwed argues that soul music revives the basic African pattern, a move that was possible because church singing had retained these features of performance, and this tradition became the basis of the "roots" movement.

In a seminal work on African patterns of dance performance (with special reference to Yoruba style), Robert Farris Thompson provides a perspective that suggests this development of blues is perhaps not so much a departure from the African pattern as a specialized development of one unique feature of West African practice. Thompson notes that a number of West African traditions exist in which there are songs and dances of derision that depart significantly from the modal pattern of the "cool" community-focused performances, a departure commonly occasioned by some special social problem calling for a licensed behavior.

> Indigenous critics of art may characterize the dignity of . . . expressions as "cool." When Tiv (in Northern Nigeria) dance satirically . . . the flawless seal [of cool] shatters. . . . But in the aggregate, West Africans dance with a mixture of vigor and decorum.
>
> Multiple meter essentially uses dancers as further voices in a polymetric choir. The conversation is additive, cool in its expressions of community. The balance struck between the meters and the bodily orchestration seems to communicate a soothing wholeness rather than a "hot" specialization. . . . Call and response is a means of putting innovation and tradition, invention and imitation, into amicable relationships with one another. In that sense, it, too, is cool. . . . [However] the [hot] dance of derision sometimes breaks these rules in order to mime the disorder of those who would break the rules of society. (Thompson, 1966, p. 98)

By this, I do not mean to argue that blues are satirical or even "hot." Rather, within West African performance traditions, a type of song and dance exists in which individuals present themselves as social commentators permitted, even encouraged to play with "heat." The individual, representing the norms of value of the community, is commonly regarded, as a low-caste or marginal person himself—such as the blues man is in America. Whether a griot from the Sudan or a Maroki in Hausaland, such praise- and scandal-singers, though often wealthy, have very low status within the community. Their singing carries with it the power of contamination, resulting in a condemning of the singer to a marginal status when not performing.

Lomax's and Thompson's profiles, which so nicely complement each other, are characteristic of efforts to apply a cross-cultural systems approach to African expressive culture. Furthermore, Lomax explicitly and Thompson implicitly demonstrate the usefulness of the systems that they describe in showing the depth of cultural persistences in the Afro-American communities. Although the Lomax musical profile is more readily demonstrable in Afro-American performances, there is little doubt that the "cool" aesthetic operating in dance and drama and other expressive forms, as well as in the plastic arts, can be shown to have persisted with equal intensity in Afro-America—including the oratorical events, and other items in which eloquence and decorum are called for.

Even more directly related to the immediate problem of effectively describing the relationship between African and Afro-American oratorical traditions are the studies we have of attitudes toward speech and ways of speaking. The so-called "creole language hypothesis" is of direct reference here, in that it postulates a creole language already developed as a trade language in Africa (perhaps derived from the Mediterranean, Portuguese-based Sabir); a sufficient number of arriving slaves knew that they had a mode of communication shared between otherwise linguistically disparate groups. This "basilect" provided two models out of which developed the various New World creole tongues. The principle of the formation of these creoles, it is argued, is a "relexification," a switching only on the level of vocabulary from that used in the African milieus to that supplied by the culture of the enslavers.

This chapter provides some evidence that just as there may have been a relexification of an African creole language in the complex New World setting, so also many speech events called for the substitution of certain European forms because of the slaves' identification of the plantocrat's power with his European tongue. But this substitution was a selective one. The language of everyday discourse remained essentially creole for the majority of the lower class and peasantry. Only on certain ceremonial occasions was the European tongue called into play, and then only the most formal style of that speech system. This was often judged, when viewed by whites, as being a misunderstanding of the uses of their European speech system; to the contrary, it was, I would argue, a misunderstanding on the part of the observers. They could not see the forest for the trees; surface similarities and the arrogance of ethnocentricity made them unable to recognize what an artful presentation was in process. The performance seemed a corruption of the European practice because whites were experiencing a different system of performance and verbal behavior.

Accounts of slave life and slave practices made by travelers and by missionary or plantocrat journal-keepers during the eighteenth and nineteenth centuries looked on slave life from the perspective of those interested in whether African ways were being retained or not. These people were primarily concerned with whether the enforced cultural experiment of civilizing the Africans was working. But, unlike our twentieth-century social scientists, they saw a remarkable persistence of African traits in spite of continuing contact with European ways. Because these descriptions were made by racists, the observations were never brought to bear on the deculturation hypothesis because of a supposed unreliability. But often the most racist literature is replete with accurate, if highly selective, descriptions of cultural practices of the stereotyped group; as racist arguments generally equate cultural difference with inferiority, "liberal" scholars in general have ignored their observations as well as their interpretations, thus throwing the baby out with the bath water.

If we adopt a strategy, counter to both racists and antiracists, that insists cultural differences do indeed exist but that difference does not mean inferiority, then we may more meaningfully approach these rich documentary sources.

THE VISITORS SPEAK

In his reminiscences of twenty-five years in the New World, the Reverend Henry Kirke goes on at great length about the elaborate letters and speeches written by his Guyanese parishioners. He notes among other things that "their speeches are as wonderful as their letters. At a black wedding one of the guests delivered an oration":

> My friends, it is with feelings of no ordinary nature which have actuated my inmost heart on this present occasion, for on such festivities so full of mirth and aggrandisement, when the Bridegroom and Bride in all their splendour repair to the house of reception, and there we find familiar friends and neighbours which otherwise would fail to draw out our congratulations. . . . And now I must close, and take the phrase *No Quid nomis*—"too much of one thing is good for nothing." Trusting these few remarks may be found *multum in parvo*, as I am now attacked with *caoethes loquendi*. I shall resort to my *ex cathedra* asking the ladies present melodiously to sing for me a verse of the hymn—
>
> How welcome was the call,
> And sweet the feast day. . . . (Kirke, 1898, p. 91)

Given the evolutionary and progressivist bias of their model of acculturation, observers like Kirke saw such speeches as examples of simple people attempting to copy the ways of the dominant whites. However, from our contemporary perspective, the highlighting of this type of elaborate speechmaking is somewhat ironic, given the continuing arguments about the inability of Afro-Americans in the United States to learn to speak effectively. Specifically, the great majority of lower-class blacks here are portrayed as verbally deficient and as incapable of making the most elementary distinctions between different kinds of talk, different levels of language appropriateness because of a socially pathological (or genetic) condition among ghetto-dwellers.

The attribution of this pathological condition to Afro-Americans in the United States is a comparatively recent addition to the inventory of stereotype traits. The most ironic feature of the argument is that it is almost diametrically opposed to the ways in which the stereotypers of blacks in the eighteenth and nineteenth centuries described the linguistic habits of blacks. Afro-Americans were constantly subject to *misusing* language; nevertheless, even the most bigoted whites were willing to admit that verbal talents of Afro-Americans were widely observable and, as in the case of W. S. Cash, saw this as a reason why traditions of eloquence held no longer in the American South among whites.

> In the south there was the daily impact upon the white man of the effect of the Negro, concerning whom nothing is so certain as his remarkable tendency to seize on lovely words, to roll them in his throat, to heap them in redundant profusion one upon another until meaning vanishes, until there is nothing left but the sweet, canorous drunkenness, nothing but the play of primitive rhythm upon the secret springs of emotion. (Cash, 1941, p. 53)

> Both in Africa and in America the Negro seems to find a decided pleasure in altiloquent speech. Perhaps this bombast is partly due to the fact that the long and unusual word has a sort of awe-inspiring almost fetishistic significance to the uneducated person, and with the Negro, at least, it indicated a desire to approximate the white man in outward signs of learning. As it is, the Negro is constantly being lost in a labyrinth of jaw-breaking words full of sound and fury but signifying nothing. (Puckett, 1926, p. 396)

Rather than noting verbal lacks, these earlier observers could talk about little else than the drive of Afro-Americans to make speeches or dramatize on any occasion. Mrs. Lanigan, the plantocrat-journalist, pointed to just this of her Antiguan charges: "The negroes are indefatigable talkers, at all times and in all seasons. Whether in joy or in grief, they ever find full employment for the little member, the tongue" (Lanigan, 1844, 2: 45). She was here repeating a cliché of travel literature.

It must be pointed out, however, that though the deficit theory of Afro-American language behavior is comparatively new, Western Europeans, especially the English, have long used linguistic deviation as a means for proclaiming cultural deficiencies, constructing a stereotype by which they have engineered and rationalized domination. We can see this stereotype operating in the numerous journals and travel accounts written by whites about plantation life, especially in the West Indies. As the movement toward emancipation developed, these visitors or part-time residents were actively seeking evidence as to whether Afro-Americans were human, with special focus on the presence or absence of black culture. Consequently, there was a good deal of note taken of the manners and social ways of the slaves, including a number of reports concerning Afro-American attitudes toward words and word usage.

These accounts, though seen from a stereotypical point of view, are remarkably accurate in noting an important segment of the range of speech activities. Revealed is the importance attached to all manner of speech: the use of talk to proclaim presence of self, to assert oneself vocally in the most anxious and the most unguarded situations. We are shown the importance of arguing in daily life, as one technique of self-dramatization. And we are, in terms of certain special occasions, permitted a view of the importance of a highly formal and decorous approach to language in both the intercultural exchanges and in intra-group activities.

This is something of a confused picture of blacks, for they are presented as being both chaotic and overly formal in their use of language. This confusion arises primarily because of an area of cultural difference that existed between the European and the slave concerning the value of words and the way in which effective verbal performance was used in Afro-American groups for the attainment of status. Little did the white observer understand that Afro-Americans had brought with them a sensitivity to a wide variety of speech activities and a highly systematic sense of appropriateness in regard to content, formality, and diction.

Most books concerning the West Indies in the eighteenth and nineteenth centuries contain discussions of some aspect or another of the behavior of the slaves, including certain aspects of their use of language. Most commonly noted were the "noisy" aspects of Afro-Americans in public, their tendency toward overdramatization, and their trait of talking to themselves. Typical of this approach was Charles William Day, Esq., who throughout his work betrays a disgust at Afro-American behavior, especially of the verbal sort:

> The Negro is very fond of talking to himself or herself, or at least of publishing in the streets his private opinions on his own private affairs for the benefit of the public at large, and he goes stumbling along in sweet colloquy with himself, seeming every now and then to "put it to you" whether he has been fairly dealt with. The women are particularly prone to this. They appear to have no idea of keeping their thoughts to themselves, and in fact their character is the strangest melange of childish simplicity and low cunning it is possible to imagine.
>
> Surely no fiends can be more clamorous than Negroes. The whole place resounds with cries—no time is sacred to quiet—even Sunday is desecrated by the yells and bawling, whistling and singing, and he cannot understand the advantages of quiet. Shrieks of laughter also, or of rage, as the case may be, are all very well now and then, but when ringing in one's ears *sans cesse* the whole day, they absolutely become "wearing." From the systematic thieving, swindling, or quarreling, in some shape common to the Negroes, there was a "row" in our street every five minutes throughout the day; and our street was but an epitome of every other street. . . . Their language is horrible in the extreme. (Day, 1852, 1:23; 2:61)

Not all such commentators were so deeply offended by this exhibition of a different attitude toward language (and noise). For instance, Bryan Edwards wrote perceptively of the difference in modes of address and petition:

> Among other propensities and qualities of the Negroes must not be omitted their loquaciousness. They are as fond of exhibiting set speeches, as orators by profession; but it requires a considerable share of patience to hear him throughout; for they commonly make a long preface before they come to the point; beginning with a tedious enumeration of their past services and hardships. They dwell with peculiar energy (if the fact admits it) on the number of children they have presented to *Massa* (Master) after which they recapitulate some of the instances of particular kindness shown them by their owner or employer, adducing these also as proofs of their own merit; it being evident they think no such kindness can be gratuitous. This is their usual exordium, as well when they bring complaints against others, as when they are called upon to defend themselves; and it is vain to interrupt either plaintiff or defendant. Yet I have sometimes heard them convey strong meaning in a narrow compass: I have been surprised by such figurative expressions, and (notwithstanding their ignorance of abstract terms) such pointed sentences, as would reflect no disgrace on poets and philosophers.
>
> One instance recurs to my memory, of so significant a turn of expression in a common labouring Negro, who could have had no opportunity of improvement from the conversation of White people, as is alone, I think, sufficient to demonstrate that Negroes have minds very capable of observation. It was a servant brought me a letter, and, while I was preparing an answer, had, through weariness and fatigue, fallen asleep on the floor; as soon as the papers were ready, I directed him to be awakened; but this was no easy matter. When the Negro who attempted to wake him exclaimed in the usual jargon, *You no hear Massa call you? Sleep,* replied the poor fellow looking up, and returning composedly to his slumbers, *Sleep has no Massa.* (Edwards, 1793, pp. 78-79)

In the hands of a spectator such as Edwards, language usage was observed to be different but nevertheless artful. And it was such that we find first noted the propensity of certain slaves to flavor their everyday discourse with set speeches, effusive patterns of movement, and proverbs. This led to the notation of proverb usage in other situations in further works by travelers.

Some of these commentators had interesting features to note in regard to proverb use. For instance, James Stewart notes that the Negroes'

> ideas cannot be expected to extend to abstract and metaphysical subjects. . . . They cannot dilate and subdivide their conceptions into minuter distinctions and more abstract combinations; yet they will often express, in their own way, a wonderfully acute conception of things. These conceptions they sometimes compress into short and pithy sentences, something like the sententious proverbs of the Europeans; to which many of them bear an analogy. Their sayings often convey much force and meaning, and would, if clothed in a more courtly dress, make no despicable figure even among those precepts of wisdom which are ascribed to wiser nations. When they wish to imply, that a peaceable man is often wise and provident in his conduct, they say, "Softly water run deep"; when they

would express the oblivion and disregard which follows them after death, they say, "When man dead grass grow at him door"; and when they would express the humility which is the usual accompaniment of poverty, they say, "Poor man never vex." (Stewart, 1823, p. 257)

But he, too, claims boredom at their use of these proverbs as part of a longer mode of appeal:

> Although the proverbial sayings of the Negroes have often much point and meaning, they, however, no sooner begin to expatiate and enter more minutely into particulars, then they become tedious, verbose, and circumlocutory, beginning their speeches with a tiresome exordium, mingling with them much extraneous matter, and frequently traversing over and over the same ground, and cautioning the hearer to be attentive, as if fearful that some of the particulars and points on which their meaning and argument hinged should escape his attention. So that by the time they arrive at the peroration of their harangue, the listener is heartily fatigued with it, and perceives that the whole which has been said, though it may have taken up half an hour, could have been comprised in half-a-dozen words. (Stewart, 1823, p. 264)

Stewart describes the proceedings in terms of a structured oration and also sees that the proverbs function much like the *copia* of European oratory style; but because of the cultural distance between his time values and his sense of occasion and those of the Afro-Americans, he is unable to see the importance and the extent of the conventional artistry of such pleadings. He also finds it difficult to give the slaves credit for any kind of verbal acumen, especially if this calls for a recognition of their abilities to think and express themselves in terms of abstractions, in spite of the evidence he himself gives to the contrary.

The reason note was taken of this kind of elaborate speech behavior was certainly more than just shock at the existence of Afro-American oratorical ability. More important, this behavior elicited a sense of embarrassment on the part of those toward whom the speech was directed, because it seemed inappropriate to the occasion. These observers recorded, then, a recurrent interpersonal situation in which a failure of communication arose because the speaker and the hearer operated on different systems of speech decorum. Speech of the sort recorded here is, in the European system, regarded as inappropriate in a person-to-person communication, no matter how great the social distance that exists between the two. Thus, the observer took note of the oration both because of its similarities to British practices and its inappropriateness; he can only fall back on his stereotyping habits to handle his sense of embarrassment by suggesting that these Afro-Americans were trying to copy their master's verbal practices but misunderstood and therefore imperfectly reproduced them. Once we recognize this dimension of embarrassment and accept that the orator operated in terms of a behavioral system (albeit a different one) there is little difficulty in separating actual behavior from stereotypical judgment of it.

The problem of dealing with data of this sort extends, however, beyond contending with its stereotypical presentation. We are told about the uses of oratory in these situations of contact between master and slave, but from the evidence given it is difficult to place such speeches in the total repertoire of speaking devices existing within Afro-American communities. With this limitation one tends to see such speechmaking not only as an imitation of white man's ways but also as being developed primarily to direct an appeal to the plantocrat. This kind of speech is regarded as a borrowing from British sources, rather than as an adaptation of African style to New World language, setting, and occasion. For this reason it is important to survey the other existing speech occasions in which this type of elaborate and formal oratory arises.

Unfortunately, here the evidence from the travel and journal literature is somewhat meager. However, the quotation from Henry Kirke about wedding speeches indicates it was recognized that not all such ornamental and elevated speechmaking was (and is) directed toward *buckra man* (the master). To the observers, nothing seemed quite as ludicrous as Afro-Americans using large words and elaborate formalities; this sense of absurdity was probably more occasioned by a feeling of *non sequitur,* that these children were trying to act like adults and failing at it, just as children do in play situations, because of hypercorrections and overposturing. Exhibiting such a perspective is, for instance, Hesketh Bell, who wrote of the wedding customs of his Grenadian black neighbors in the West Indies:

> Everything having been pretty well cleared off the table, the moment for speeches and toasts has now arrived. The health of the married couple is proposed by one of the guests in certain set phrases which are never departed from. Allusions to the happy connubial state of turtle doves, and the well-known adventures of Isaac and Rebecca are never omitted, and this speech once over, the other more amusing and original toasts begin. One of the groomsmen will get up and propose the health of the bridesmaids. The more polysyllables and highsounding, senseless phrases he can remember, the more will he and the company be pleased. Passages from any book containing very long words, though having no earthly reference to the occasion, will be learnt by heart and retailed to the admiring guests, who would disdain to listen to a sensible speech made up of commonplace, every-day words. Verses from the Bible are frequently pressed into service, and seem to afford much satisfaction. (Bell, 1889, p. 139)

Bell identifies these speeches, as did Kirke, with the epistolary style of blacks, thus giving us a comparative description of the two practices:

> Quashie has an intense love for long words of which he does not know the meaning, and delights in using them on any occasion. In his love letters especially does he express his feelings in the longwinded polysyllables. Sense is a secondary consideration, and his position in the affection of his lady love very much depends on the number of jaw-breaking words he can cram into an epistle. (Bell, 1889, p. 140)

The assumption by some of these observers that unions between blacks were so easily and quickly entered into and dissolved is one of the primary reasons for seeing such a dislocation between performance and behavior, thus regarding such speeches and letters as ludicrous. Only those who are capable of living with some manner of decorum and discretion can be accorded the pleasure of ornate words, it would seem. But Bell and Kirke and the others provide us with a record of the perseverance of an essentially oral, African attitude toward eloquence.

The reason for this oversight goes beyond the stereotype, however. Most investigators of Afro-American societies have presumed that African institutions were eliminated from the cultural repertoire of most blacks in the New World. All behaviors, including speech, can then be described in terms of a spectrum of acculturation running from behaviors in which European forms are imperfectly understood and reproduced to a total ability to understand and reproduce these European forms.

Although there is a good deal of data that does indeed make sense viewed in this way, there are a number of misunderstandings that also arise. Certainly, for instance in the United States, linguistic performance does gravitate toward the norms of Standard American English regionally defined. Furthermore, the more middle-class a black community becomes, the more its observances tend to conform to white norms (because it is whites who dictate the middle-class forms of behavior). However, when dealing with features of lower-class or peasant behavior, this approach can be misleading and wrong-headed. In such cases, there is often a superficial resemblance to European practices, while the manner of performance, especially of interactional expectations, is more characteristic of African performance patterns.

CREOLE ELOQUENCE

Although these observers obviously saw the stream of culture running the other way, we can hypothesize that these documents provide us with evidence of the continuity of African attitudes toward eloquence and the adaptation of selected European forms into this value and performance system. The reason why the African elements seem dominant, in spite of the forms, is that the base patterns of performance in which these speeches arise are more characteristic of African modes than European ones, and these performance elements determine both tone and function. It seems useful to survey the argumentative strategies and the speech events in which such eloquence arises to see its uses both within the structure of the performance, and in value and behavior systems in general.

Not only courtships and weddings but baptismal fetes, send-offs, church services, Christmas serenades, some Carnival performances, and many other occasions call for such speechmaking from one or more performers, and sometimes from everyone in the group. Once it is recognized that the community engages in these numerous ceremonies in which eloquent speechmaking is called for, it becomes possible to note that the occasions revolve around times of transition. Eloquence, then, is regarded as appropriate to all ritual occasions and some festival ones. Furthermore, when speechmaking like this occurs it is judged by the community as good and beautiful and is seen in contrast to everyday creole talk. In many parts of the West Indies, for instance, creole is referred to as *talking broken* or *bad* or *broad,* whereas highly decorous eloquence is regarded as *talking good* or *sweet.* The West Indians themselves, in other words, recognize that they have two codes—one high (*H*) and one low (*L*), to use Charles Ferguson's "diglossia" distinctions. If *H* happens to be an approximation of formal Standard English, this is due not only to the British investment of a high value to such usage; it is also attributable to a willingness to take whatever word power exists within one's social environment and to convert it to one's own performance uses (Ferguson, 1959, pp. 325-340).

H arises, for the most part, in these ceremonial occasions, as the most important marker of the performance system. Ornamental diction and a certain kind of delivery indicate that the performers and the community are emphasizing their ability to apply decorum—a self-conscious order—to their proceedings. Decorum is the key word to many of the West Indian speeches uttered on these occasions, and the audience response, "sweet, sweet," means not only beautiful but also truthful and discreet. To fully understand the force of these self-conscious orderings, it is necessary to understand the range of speaking (especially performance) alternatives, especially those in performance *L.*

Performance *L* relies upon a series of techniques that emphasize wit through word play. The most common and dramatic techniques by which this is accomplished are by emphasizing dialogue, and even contest punning and other ambiguities, and by centering on rapid-fire delivery. Performance *L* is commonly the language of license, a set of devices by which a release from social and linguistic order is sought. This code is therefore used by one playing the role of some kind of trickster—for example, a fool, a clown, a devil—the enemy of order and social constraint.

H emphasizes order and the ability to make discretions and distinctions, to reveal the real world in terms of observed or received truths. It is usually brought into play at those times when transitional experience sparks an intuition of a possible social disordering among members of the family or community. There seems to be a functional relationship between the imposed order of speaking (which is paralleled by movement restrictions as well) and these intuitions. Furthermore, in the case of most of the occasions in which eloquent speechmaking arises, there is an intensification of the social order by an underlining of the roles played by the speakers and by those to whom the oration is directed. The importance of performance H therefore seems to reside in the conventional formalism of the language that underscores the ritualistic nature of the occasion.

The occasions in which eloquent speeches are made are of three types, two of which we have already noted. The first (and least common) is the *appeal* directed by one occupying a lower status position in the social structure to one of somewhat higher status. This kind of speech is not just to be found in begging occasions, such as those described by the travelers, but also during certain performances, such as the Christmas serenading. In this a person steps out from the group that travels from the yard of one larger house to another and asks for some kind of contribution. Before doing so, however, he commonly makes a speech on the season, with proper biblical references, finally blessing the house, the inhabitants, the crops.

The second type of occasion for such speechmaking is during a fete related to a rite of passage or some other crisis time in the life of the individual. This includes, then, not only wedding and baptismal feasts but also *thanksgivings* after a trip or an illness and *send-offs* before trips. Such informal ceremonies are generally held in the privacy of a home. Although one person is generally the acknowledged leader, all present are called on to make a speech (or sing a song) directed at the person or couple for whom the feast is being held. These speeches often call for the same sentimental commonplaces found in letters and autograph albums, the central features of the performance being the encomium and the advice.

The third type of occasion is connected with seasonal festivities, such as Carnival or tea meetings—those occasions in which the most elaborate performances are observed. In keeping with the licentious nature of the celebrations, they are commonly performed competitively, the eloquence and the control over *facts* becoming devices by which one performer attempts to outperform the others. These are competitive; thus the proper place for their performance is in a public hall or on the street. Furthermore, the licentiousness generally means that the speakers depart from their usual social roles, taking on characterological names—like the calypsonians—and often wearing masks or costumes to signify this change of identity.

These three types of occasion are paralleled by three different persuasive techniques: the strategies of appeal, of praise, and of impressiveness. Most oratorical performances use all three strategies, but in varying degrees. Quite obviously, the eloquent plea calls for stressing devices of appeal, and the fete speech primarily involves praise. But as the following wedding toasts from Nevis demonstrate, the speaker seems to impress his audience through his knowledge:

> Behold me standing at the D-double O-R door,
> Behold me pleading M-O-R-E, more.

So with my heart suppress within me,
May I come in?
Yes!! [*answer all*]
Bride and bridegroom,
Ladies and Gentlemen,

As I stand on this happy occasion giving my best wishes to all Mr. Bride and Mrs. Bride—when I look around at this domicile it make me feel *Homa Doma*, which is to say it make me feel like a new girl. Mr. and Mrs. Bride, this feast reminds me of the feast of Belshazzar. Belshazzar made a great feast before a thousand of his lords and he drink wine before the thousands. Belshazzar while he drink wine he commanded a man to bring his gold and silver vessels, which his father, which was Nebuchadnezzar, had taken out of the temple, which was in Jerusalem. Mr. and Mrs. Bride, I will not take up any more of your precious and your valuable time. Ima dance *pasear de boca* come and take—a kiss from the lips all time touch the heart.

To the Ladies and Gentlemen, inside and outside. Please to listen to my melodious anthem, which is to say, my beautiful voice, to Mr. Bride sir.

Please to take Mistress Bride and care her well.
Her most tender love for you you cannot tell.
I do hope the earth will be in need a few drops of dew
Before her love will be ever changed from you. (Rosalie Jeffers, Brick Kiln, Nevis, August 1962)

This blending of techniques becomes even more observable in the longer speeches, especially those made during festival occasions. Here, for instance, is just the introduction into a tea meeting speech from St. Vincent in which the whole range of techniques is utilized. The oration begins with an address to the chairman, who runs the meeting, the judges, who decide who has given the most fluent and knowledgeable speech, and "Mr. Presenter," the choirmaster.

Ladies and gentlemen of this social assemblage, a pleasant evening to you all. Likewise to these great men of justice, whilst not omitting Sir Presenter and his melodious choir.

Mr. Chairman, sir, the facts of which I shall deal this evening are mainly old and familiar. Nor is there anything new in the general use I shall make of them. If there be any novelty, it will be in the mode of presenting the acts and the inferences and observations following the presentation.

Sir, when I entered this hall this evening, I was touched at once by the feeling attaching that compelled me to choose a subject through the English prose that would bring light out of darkness, and for the edification of my audience. The subject of my discourse tonight is one fraught with momentous importance, not only to the citizens of this community, but to every Negro lover of liberty and ambition, and of every free institution throughout the West Indies. I invite your closest attention to my topic, for it concerns your personal, social, political, and religious welfare as much as it does mine. It concerns your children's children's welfare in the future.

Mr. Chairman, sir, I was informed that you were the orator of scope. To whom must I compare you? Should I say that you are like Jeremy Bentham from the school of political philosophy, the principles of morals and politics, who expounded utilitarian system with great facility? Should I say that you are like Jeremy Bentham, founder of this school of political philosophy? Or shall I say that you are like Nicholas Copernicus, the famous astronomer who became doctor and canon of the Chapel of Frankfurt? No, I think you are greater, I shall now compare you to the great illustrious statesman Abraham Lincoln, a man whose name is immortal and stands as a shining light to mankind, for he believed justice must be done to all, even to the servants and all.

Your honor, the judges, I see that you are fully impregnated with love for your people. I see that you are willing to fulfill the great duties of teachers, as spiritual guides. I see your love for your country. Your motto, sir, is to let those who have light give unto others. Sirs, tongues fail me, to consult my Webster for words to compare you, but I do hope that you will give justice unto whom justice belongs, when this meeting shall have come to its close.

[*Turning to Mr. Presenter and to the choir*] Sir, as I came around the road this evening I was listening to the singing of birds skipping from tree to tree, calling their mates in a language no one can understand but themselves and their recourse. Looking at the beautiful landscapes of the Rockford Mountains, folding their arms at the command of nature, then I knew that I was coming here to listen to Jubal's harp. So, to whom must I compare your choir? Should I say that you are like Mendelssohn, who was director of concerts in Leipzig? Should I say that you are like Mozart, that celebrated composer of the imperial courts of Europe? No, I shall now compare you to Walter Damrosch, head of the American Conservatory of Music, he who toured the European countries and was honored by nobility.

Mr. Chairman, your honor, the judges, ladies and gentlemen, fearing that the time would keep me away from my darlings so long, I shall now turn your attention to my topic, which is on the birth of Christ. (Charles Jack, Yambou, St. Vincent, August 1968)

Looking at the content of a speech such as this, it is clear that most of it is ultimately derived from books, and British ones at that. Yet the pattern of the performance, the uses of this material, the manner in which the performer interacts with his audience, and many other features are not British at all. The idea of a speech, as with almost any other kind of performance, is to enlist the attention and response of the audience. Karl Riesman pointed to just such a pattern in his study of Antiguan talk, noting that, because there is an equation between creole, argument, disorder, and noise, a speaker who orates effectively is demonstrating contrary values—order, harmony, "good talk," and decorum. But

> people take great joy in making noise. . . . [Indeed] this is the basis of the symbolism of most village rituals. Meetings begin with a call for Conduct, and descend into "noise" and Creole via argument. (Riesman, 1970, p. 1941)

Furthermore, the good speechmaker does not really feel that his talents have been demonstrated unless he is able to contend in the midst of noise, thus giving order to random sound.

In many cases throughout this area, the noise itself is ritualized by inserting into the proceedings a traditional debate—often a heated one. Riesman mentions that at Antiguan christenings this is done by putting two plates at each end of the table in which money is deposited—one representing the principle that the cake in the middle of the table should be cut, the other that it should not be. Similar techniques found in the Caribbean are the Jamaican mock bidding (DeCamp, 1968), a well-planned audience jeering, and many other subjects for mock disputation.

This argumentative framework is perhaps less central to the household feasts like weddings; but it is the dramatic focus and the raison d'être of the tea meeting and Carnival speechmaking events. Here the contest element comes to the fore and, as indicated with tea meetings, there are judges who award prizes for the most articulate performance. Furthermore, the contention in these ceremonies is not just between performers but also with hecklers in the audience. And it is clear that the idea is to demonstrate for the moment the primacy of decorum and of *H* in these confrontations, for the language of the hecklers is performance *L* and therefore utilizes wit, ambiguity, and derision.

The ascendancy of *H,* however, should not be read as a total acceptance of *H* values and norms. Rather, the existence of both codes is attested to, the strengths and weaknesses of both systems fully demonstrated. These oratorical contests, then, are not simply demonstrations of the ability of the community members to speak performance *H* effectively. It is a community celebration of speech of all sorts, a revelry of talk in which the entire range of speaking acts and events are put on view and enjoyed.

These oratorical events are, then, part of a system of performance and language behavior that continues to place effective speechmaking as a central notion to being a good person and a good community member; the centrality of oratory in contest is a clear instance of the carry-over of an attitude and approach to language, from the African experience. Whereas the content and *H* variety are obviously derived from European sources, the style and mode of use are not. Although performance *H* is primarily derived from oratorical style in Standard English, it is recognizably a substitution for similar codes of eloquence found in Africa. In its use within the environment calling for a high degree of voice overlap and interlock, it is closely tied in with the African performance pattern described by Lomax and Thompson. Most important, though the *H* code exists, and many members of the community can speak it, *L* nevertheless remains the primary means of both entertainment and communication. Just what the explanation for this is, or what its implications are, is not clear. It does seem significant that performance *H* is just one variety of many, primarily relegated to ceremonial occasions, but in such situations it is certainly a code substitution for African eloquence speaking, in parallel with the kind of relexification going on throughout the creole world of Afro-America.

CHAPTER THREE

After the Myth: Studying Afro-American Cultural Patterns in the Plantation Literature

(with John F. Szwed)

How easily have we continued to accept the notion that, in the coming together of different peoples within the expanding world economy, the group that dominates politically will also prevail culturally. That this is not necessarily so in all culturally plural situations is only commonsensical. That it is especially not so with regard to the coming together of Africans and Europeans under the plantation system seems self-evident, given the large-scale influences of black expressive cultural forms and practices in all New World creole cultures, including that of the southern United States. Nevertheless, the notion of the deculturalization of Africans persists despite the fact that the more we look at what historical records we have—predominantly of the informal sort, to be sure—the more cultural maintenance and development we encounter.

No case undercuts our received model of acculturation so clearly as that of Afro-American peoples, as so many of the basic features of plantation and modern New World life have been obviously influenced by the Afro-American cultural presence. For instance, Africans often possessed a more highly developed agricultural technology than Europeans, especially in tropical gardening, so that the Europeans often found themselves in an environment more alien than did their slaves. In line with this, planters found it convenient not only to allow African practices to be maintained but actually to encourage them, especially in such noninstitutional areas of culture as work practices, play, and systems of magic and curing. These could be encouraged because they assisted directly or indirectly in the workings of the plantation and did not attack the stereotypical concept of blacks as perpetual children or as animals.

Wherever Afro-Americans could interact with one another (whether or not in the presence of Euro-Americans), shared expectations, attitudes, and feelings emerged, drawing upon the common features of past experience in Africa and in the New World. Wholesale carry-overs of community-based culture need not be posited to argue that African cultural continuities are obvious and long-lasting. Many Euro-American observers recognized this cultural persistence from the earliest plantation days and provided a large, if selective, record of African and Afro-American cultural practices as filtered through their stereotypical rationalizations.

In *African Civilization in the New World,* Roger Bastide states that "the current vogue for the study of the African is a comparatively recent phenomenon. Before the abolition of slavery such a thing was inconceivable, since up till then the Negro has simply been regarded as a source of labour, not as the bearer of a culture" (p. 4). Afro-American communities could not be studied in a methodical and systematic manner, because the techniques for analysis of cultural continuities and discontinuities are comparatively recent developments. Nevertheless, there has been an ongoing debate for at least two centuries on the issue of whether or not Africans have a culture.

To anthropologists, the idea that a group could be forcibly divested of their culture, yet maintain themselves and even proliferate, seems a strange argument indeed. Yet this deculturation argument is still an article of faith for many scholars studying Afro-Americans. Perhaps Euro-Americans are still unwilling to consider the ways of black peoples as authentic manifestations of culture unless these ways are close enough to European practice to appear as misunderstandings or corruptions. The deculturation argument is perhaps only one outgrowth of our notions of modernization—an unexamined set of assumptions applied equally to other groups who came, for better or worse, to the New World under industrialization and a cash economy. It is implied that loss of culture happens to all agricultural peoples when they are forced off the land in search of wages. This divestment provided the raison d'être of sociological study and appears as a constant rationalizing thread of argument from Tönnies and Durkheim through Parsons and Merton, even to Fredrik Barth. This is not to say that anthropologists have been blameless in their treatment of "the dispossessed." Redfield's folk-urban continuum is an obvious extension of Tönnies's *Gesellschaft-Gemeinschaft* distinction; and Oscar Lewis's conception of a "culture of poverty" is directly related to such "negative pastoral" arguments as are found in Durkheim and Marx—the pastoral operation as a literary castigation of city life while extolling simple country existence (see Williams, 1973) was widely rejected, and two types of counterarguments arose. On the one hand, specific Africanisms were postulated, debated, and largely rejected, a classic "baby and bath water" problem. On the other, some scholars demanded that the putative African elements be demonstrated as retained from a specific African ethnic group. The Africanness of traits was not so much rejected as ignored as being incapable of adequate testing.

The frustrations of defending the cultural continuities argument have not diminished since the famous Melville Herskovits-E. Franklin Frazier confrontation after the publication of the former's *Myth of the Negro Past.* The basic lines of argument have not altered very much since the early 1940s, as Afro-Americanists have found to their sorrow. The following recorded conversation between Frazier and Herskovits catches the direction of the arguments and the sense of frustration:

Mr. Frazier: I have not found anyone who could show any evidence of survival of African social organization in this country. I may cite a concrete case. You will recall that in reviewing my book, *the Negro Family in the United States,* in the *Nation,* you said that the description I gave of the re-union of a Negro family group could, with the change of a few words, be regarded as a description of a West African institution. But it also happens to be equally adequate as a description of a Pennsylvania Dutch family reunion. What are we to do in a case like that? Are we to say that it is African?

Mr. Herskovits: Methodologically, it seems to me that if in studying a family whose ancestry in part, at least, came from Africa I found that something they do resembles a very deep-seated African custom, I should not look to Pennsylvania Dutch folk, with whom this family has not been in contact, for an explanation of such a custom. I may be wrong but that seems elementary.

Mr. Frazier: But where did the Pennsylvania Dutch get their custom that resembles the one I described? Did they get it from Africa too?

Mr. Herskovits: May I ask if the methodological point at issue is this: is it maintained that if we find anything done by Negroes in this country that resembles anything done in Europe, we must therefore conclude that the Negroes' behavior is derived from the European customs, the inference then being that the traditions of their African ancestors were not strong enough to stand against the impact of European ways?

Mr. Frazier: No, I wouldn't say that, but I believe it should be the aim of the scholar to establish an unmistakable historical connection between the African background and present behavior of Negroes, rather than to rely on *a priori* arguments.

Mr. Herskovits: We will be in agreement, if you will add to your statement that neither should the scholar deny any such connection on *a priori* grounds. (Herskovits, 1941, p. 85)

Even when such arguments emerge today among social scientists, M. G. Smith's call in 1960 for the tracing of specific cultural practices to a specific ethnic group in Africa is still heard; never mind that highly cognate forms of behavior exist between West Africa and the New World. There is considerable evidence of direct and specific retentions. For instance, Sea Island basketry can be shown to be made with the same techniques and similar materials as those used in Senegambia (Thompson, 1969, pp. 139-140; Perdue, 1968).

Similarly, Bascom has surveyed the wide range of retentions of Yoruba and Dahomean deity names in such New World cult religions as Vôdun, Candomblé, and Shango, even while he demonstrates why such continuities have been maintained in so many culturally distinct parts of the New World (Bascom, 1972). Many other practices can still be observed in Afro-America, such as dancing, drumming, and funeral rituals, that are obviously close to African antecedents.

Richard Price has noted, however, that there is greater potential in seeking such "development within historically related and overlapping sets of . . . ideas" than in restricting our search to "direct retentions or survivals" (Price, 1970, p. 375). Or as two students of Herskovits, George E. Simpson and Peter B. Hammond, commented:

> Both past records and an examination of the contemporary situation in the New World indicate that beneath the relatively superficial level of form there is a significant, non-conscious level of psychological function. On this level there is an important basic similarity [for instance] between varieties of religious practices both throughout West Africa and in the various New World Negro communities. (Simpson and Hammond, 1960, p. 48)

In their subsequent discussion of spirit possession, they account for its cultural tenacity through its basic commonality with West African religious behavior. Finally, rejecting M. G. Smith's assertion that continuities can only be established through common forms found in specific places in the Old World and the New, they state that

> form is the most superficial level of cultural reality. Since it is consciously realized, it is often much quicker to change than the profounder philosophic principles and psychological attitudes which are frequently more persistent and tenacious because they exist beneath the level of consciousness. (Simpson and Hammond, 1960, p. 50)

Such opinions are, however, all too rarely encountered in Afro-American scholarship. Although less strident than E. Franklin Frazier or M. G. Smith, a number of recent commentators maintain the deculturation argument while carrying out some impressive ethnographic reporting. Diverting attention from African continuities in the New World and the professed intent of the slavers to strip the slaves culturally, these scholars argue instead that if there are New World Afro-American cultures, they must arise for the most part from the common experiences of blacks of enslavement and social exclusion. For example, Sidney Mintz argues that

> enslaved Africans were quite systematically prevented . . . with few exceptions . . . from bringing with them the personnel who maintained their homeland institutions; the complex social structures of the ancestral societies, with their kings and courts, guilds and cult-groups, markets and armies were not, and could not be

transferred. Cultures are linked as continuing patterns of and for behavior to such social groupings; since the groupings themselves could not be maintained or readily reconstituted, the capacities of random representatives of these societies to perpetuate or to recreate the cultural contents of the past were seriously impaired. Again, the slaves were not usually able to regroup themselves in the New World settings in terms of their origins; the cultural heterogeneity of any slave group normally meant that what was shared culturally was likely to be minimal. . . . [However,] the slaves could and did create viable patterns of life, for which their pasts were pools of available symbolic and material resources. (Mintz, 1970, pp. 7-9)

Certainly African institutions were vulnerable to elimination in the New World, at least when they were incompatible with slavery. Still, too much contrary evidence exists for one to accept Mintz's argument without some real qualifications. One thinks, for instance, of the widespread West African practice of *susu*, which has not only been encountered under the very name in several places in Afro-America but also provides insight into the importance of such Afro-American voluntary associations as Friendly Societies, lodges, burial societies, rent parties, and the like (Crowley, 1953; Bascom, 1941; Reid, 1927). The religious domain also continues in modified form in a variety of cults in Brazil, Cuba, and elsewhere (Landes, 1971, p. 1310; Herskovits, 1955; Cabrera, 1968; Bascom, 1952). Numerous expressions of apparent African nationalities occur in such festivals as the Nations Dances of Carriacou (Smith, 1962), "the dance in Place Congo" in New Orleans (Latrobe, 1951), the "jubilee" in Washington Square in eighteenth-century Philadelphia (Watson, 1857, 2:261), and many other places. Admittedly, the intricate African kingship organizations could not be widely maintained in the Americas, but the relatively independent and complementary positions of men and women widely observed in the slaving areas of Africa must be considered a formative force in the development of the "matrifocal" household system (Herskovits, 1941, pp. 167-186). This is what we mean by the deeper forms of culture that seem to bind Afro-Americans together.

EXPRESSIVE CONTINUITIES

Just such expressive continuities are crucial to an understanding of the institutions developed by blacks in their various New World situations. The great diversity of New World settings in which Africans found themselves — plantations, cities, mining areas, escaped slave outposts, and so forth—makes it impossible to demonstrate parallel developments in such areas as religious practice, community governance, economics, and even the family, simply in terms of the shared experiences of plantation slavery. These similarities reflect a common conceptual and affective system of which the slave could not be stripped—shared practices, beliefs, and behavioral patterns that not only survived but were developed further in the New World setting. The importance of performance in the stylization of individual and group relationships cannot be overemphasized. These patterns of performance of simplified models of social organization in the Old World provided the basic groundwork on which African-like community interactions would be generated in spite of the loss of the details of their institutional renderings.

If one uses only the literature of white journalist and traveler, the area of black life most fully documented for continuities from the African past are folk beliefs and practices and ghost lore. In the United States, under the name of *hants, hags, rootwork, conjuring,* or *hoodoo,* and in the West Indies as *duppies, jumbies* (among many others), and *obeah men* or *wanga,* accounts of plantation life include large sections devoted to the depth and persistence of such "superstitious" beliefs and practices.

The reasons for this interest are various. The most obvious one is that such practices were evidence of maintaining the stereotype of blacks either as simple-minded heathen nature-worshipers or—even worse—as pawns of the devil. But each observer had a different reason why this subject was of interest. For the planters, these practices were seen as a threat to their operation, and they tried sporadically to militate against them, though one suspects that the folk medicine practices and ceremonies were encouraged or overlooked as a way of keeping the slaves alive and happy. For abolitionists or their foes, the strange practices were proof of the presence or absence of human feeling and culture; for missionaries, they provided evidences of what had to be fought. For whatever reason the observations were made, they form a large body of data that has not yet been utilized effectively in the study of cultural continuities.

As noted, the Africans brought to the New World were often master tropical gardeners. The journal keepers noted again and again the remarkable abilities of the slaves not only in working the cane fields and melting houses, but also in providing their own foodstuffs, even to the point of marketing the excess on their one day off, Sunday. John Luffman's account of Antigua life of 1788 is typical of such often begrudging descriptions:

> Every slave on a plantation, whether male or female, when they attained their 14th or 15th year, has a piece of ground, from twenty five, to thirty feet square, alloted to them, which by some is industriously and advantageously cultivated, and by others totally neglected. These patches are found to be of material benefit to the country, their produce principally supplying the "sunday market" . . . with vegetables. They are also allowed to raise pigs, goats, and fowls, and it is by their attention to these articles, that whites are prevented from starving, during such times of the year as vessels cannot come to these coasts with safety. (Luffman, 1788, pp. 94-95)

Although the contribution of the slaves to the development and operation of the plantation is yet to be studied extensively, suggestive work has been done by Peter H. Wood (1975) on South Carolina; he shows Africans to be the source of rice agriculture, new forms of cattle breeding and herding, boat building, inland water navigation, hunting and trapping, medicine, and other skills. Indeed, the agricultural success of South Carolina seems more a function of the slaves' knowledge and technology than it was of their masters'.

The slaves often found themselves in a position to teach their masters and to carry out their agricultural tasks in agricultural time or tempo. Numerous European observers recounted with amazement the coordination of activities in Afro-American work gangs and recorded the songs sung while carrying out the work tasks. "Their different instruments of husbandry, particularly, their gleaming hoes, when uplifted to the sun, and which, particularly, when they are digging cane-holes they frequently raise all together, and in as exact time as can be observed, in a well-conducted orchestra, in the bowing of the fiddles, occasion the light to break in momentary flashes around them" (Beckford, 1790, p. 225). Observers noted that this work was carried out through the use of songs in classic African call-and-response pattern, by which the work gangs both coordinated movements and created and maintained a sense of common purpose. Such descriptions as this, from J. B. Moreton's *West Indian Customs and Manners* (1793), are a commonplace of the genre:

> When working, though at the hardest labour, they are commonly singing; and though their songs have neither rime nor measure, yet many are witty and pathetic. I have often laughed heartily, and have been as often struck with deep melancholy at their songs:—for instance, when singing of the overseer's barbarity to them:
>
> Tink dere is a God in a top,
> No use me ill, Obisha!
> Me no horse, me no mare, me no mule,
> No use me ill, Obisha.

Such activities were, of course, given as indications that the slaves were a happy, childlike people who loved their work. As one especially light-hearted observer describes it, the harvest provided "a scene of animation and cheerfulness" in which the ear and the eye are suffused with evidences of "the light-hearted hilarity of the negroes," in which "the confused clamor of voices in dialogue and song, present a singular contrast to the calm response which nature seems to claim for herself in these clear and ardent climes" (Wentworth, 1834, 2:66).

It was not, however, just the cooperative working style that made Africans the ideal slaves in the plantation system. As a *gardening* people, they already measured time and apportioned energy by the cycles of the crops. They understood the necessity of working long hard hours during planting and harvesting seasons, but they were also used to working considerably less hard during the other seasons. This disparity was often noticed, but without much comprehension of the system of time and energy allocation that lay behind it (Genovese, 1974).

From the perspective of racial stereotyping, this cycle was particularly convenient. When the blacks worked very hard in the sun or in the heat of the building where the sugar was boiled, they could be portrayed as brute work animals. But during other seasons, when they resisted what they regarded as senseless work, they could be accused of being lazy. One way or another, the stereotype could be applied.

WORK AND PLAY

Continuities of African work practices are, then, relatively easily accounted for, because they fit the needs of the planters while in no way challenging the European image of blacks. The aspect of play is more problematic because of a longer history of black-white relations and imaginings involving a range of behaviors viewed by some as anathema to enterprise. For centuries before colonization, Europeans had associated Africans with festival entertainments; and music, dance, and other forms of public entertainment were ideal opportunities to judge whether or not blacks could acquire culture. The existence of a great many detailed descriptions of play activities enables us to explore the deeper levels of cultural continuity and may thus help in understanding the creation of Afro-American culture. Play materials tell us about patterns of behavior going far beyond the realm of play, because play involves a selective stylization of motives also found in other domains of activity. For instance, Alan Lomax and his associates' studies in choreometrics (Lomax, 1968) have demonstrated a high correlation between work and dance movements within specific groups and culture areas. Equally important, however, in discovering deeper cultural patterns is how and to what play activities are contrasted.

Even before there was direct contact between Europeans and Africans, black peoples from the south held a special symbolic importance for Europeans. As Henri Baudet pointed out, this interest was occasioned by a pre-Rousseauvian primitivism that included all non-Europeans, who were envisaged as simpler people living closer to nature, and therefore closer to a state of primal innocence and harmony. As travel increased, black Africans were contrasted positively with Muslims, who had become feared enemies during the Crusades.

With the beginning of the Renaissance, however, Europeans became more knowledgeable about Muslims and came to admire them and their culture. Baudet describes the consequences of this change:

> Unlucky Negro: our culture has always presented him in unequivocal opposition to the Muslim. But now, quite suddenly, Islam is found to merit admiration. Rapidly and unexpectedly, its star moves into a new orbit and the traditional

contrast between Negro and Muslim is reversed. For a century or more Islam and not the Negro, has been the subject of scientific interest. . . . A new reputation for the unfortunate Negro has its origins here, and he approaches the next two centuries as typifying the lowest stage of human development . . . an altogether inferior creature, a slave by nature, lacking all historical background. (Baudet, 1965, p. 47)

Europeans were brought together in huge numbers, at a time when the negative image of the primitive was convenient for rationalizing enslavement. However, during the earlier period, the fascination with Africans had caused Europeans to associate "Moors," "blacks," and "Negroes" with parades and other kinds of festival behaviors. Eldred D. Jones's *The Elizabethan Image of Africa* (1971) brings together a number of illustrations of this fascination: blackface characters identified with Africa appeared in medieval mummers plays or in the courtly "disguises" of the sixteenth century; Henry VIII and the Earl of Essex marched with such "Moors" in 1510; blackface figures led the pageants and cleared away crowds during the same period; Edward VI took part in a Shrovetide masque in 1548 in which the marchers' legs, arms, and faces were all blackened; and Queen Anne appeared as a Negro in Ben Jonson's *Masque of Blackness.* Numerous other Elizabethan dramas—most notably *Othello*—also contained important black roles.

Later, after the beginning of the slave trade and the increasing presence of "real" Africans in Europe, the cultural impact became even greater. For example, black drummers were popular in European military and court bands in the late eighteenth and early nineteenth centuries (Pierpoint, 1916; Hunt, 1973, p. 72). Their music, style of performance, and costumes had important and lasting consequences for Europeans and Euro-Americans. And though it has been recognized that African and Turkish drum corps were the inspirations for compositions by Gluck, Mozart, and Haydn, it is not so well known that the source of the "Turkish music" (seventh) variation of the "Ode to Joy" theme of Beethoven's *Ninth Symphony* was not Turkish drummers (Cooper, 1970, p. 33), but more likely the African drum corps active in Germany at that time, who played what was called "Turkish music" (Pierpoint, 1916, p. 303). Surely, part of the shock value of Beethoven's last movement for Europeans lay in its images of African drums and drummers gathering with the heavenly hosts around the throne of Heaven!

This association of blacks with public entertainment is characteristic of how marginal groups are stigmatized. One of the few roles available to outsiders in European culture is that of the performer, because it does not undermine the stereotypes. Performance abilities are utilized as one of the few ways they can survive economically. For instance, among Gypsies in Europe, this performer role has been developed into an entire way of life, as it is with the Bauls in Bengal and the Arioi society in Melanesia.

In any case, black parades and festivals were encouraged by the plantocracy and used by them on most important occasions of entertainment. Such Euro-American interest and occasional participation simply gave an unofficial stamp of approval to practices that came to fill a central role in Afro-American communities throughout the New World. Afro-American carnivals, processions, and street parades have been performed annually for many years in Bahia, Rio de Janeiro, Havana, Port of Spain, New Orleans, and, in past times, Mexico City, Philadelphia, Wilmington, North Carolina, Hartford, and other cities. Although such events often have been dismissed by puritanical members of Euro-American societies as licentious bacchanals, they are highly structured performances based on religious cults and social clubs, many of which have existed for more than three hundred years. The characteristics of these events are well known: clubs of maskers organize around a variety of exotic themes, elect kings and queens, make banners, and focus on such special performances as stick fighting, baton twirling, and group dancing and singing on the streets and roads. In some areas, sacred and secret symbols are displayed on this day, while in others group spirit possession occurs before the clubs make their appearances. On these days groups and their symbols are moved from the privacy of *favelas* or ghetto neighborhoods, whose street life they have been part of throughout the year, into the public areas where Euro- and Afro-Americans come together. The significance of these events is well recognized and feared by the guardians of public order, the police, because they know these "back-street" social organizations rule their streets after dark.

Some have dismissed these arcane and "Africa"-like institutions as the results of partial and incomplete acculturation, as way stations on the road to national homogeneousness; in other words, blacks attempting to join or parallel Euro-American festivities with whatever cultural resources they can muster. We might better take our lead from the sociolinguists who speak of multiple codes in language systems. In the case of festivals, the codes are not linguistic ones, but instead are performance rules governing musical, motor, and religious behaviors that are the legacy of a wide variety of African peoples brought to Spanish-, Portuguese-, French-, and English-America. These Afro-American processions and carnivals might best be described as rites of passage, not between positions in single societies, but between the performance rules and social hierarchies of two different segments of single societies. These festivities exist because of the cultural dualities present in New World societies, and they have survived through the distinctions between public and private areas of urban life. During those festivities the boundaries are broken down (Marks and Szwed, 1971), and the performances become more creole, more "country," more "down home," more African as the effects of license take hold.

Certainly the organizations that give life to these Afro-American festivals in no way approximate the complex institutional arrangements that characterize West African societies, but their existence illustrates the ways in which identification with the African homeland was maintained and how this contributed to a sense of ethnicity and cultural identity in these various Afro-American societies.

Carnival, *Jonkanoo,* and other such festivities are regarded as the most public, unrestrained, and most African of all of Afro-American performance occasions, with the possible exception of Shango and other religious practices. While it is easy for Euro-Americans to be carried into the spirit of such occasions, to be able to understand how very different these performances are for Afro-Americans it is necessary to understand the world order of black communities, especially their contrasts between *work* and *play,* and between *private* and *public.* To relegate such expressive behavior as JonKanoo to the periphery of culture is to ignore the centrality of interpersonal performance in black communities, and its use as a countervailing force against enslavement. In this context, an institution-centered definition of culture must give way to a study of micro-behaviors and the larger interactional system, which provide the formal and informal rules by which these groups live on a day-to-day, minute-to-minute basis.

Basic cultural differences exist between Euro- and Afro-American attitudes and behaviors in play and work—or seriousness. Because play is a departure from everyday behavior, especially with regard to the intensity and self-consciousness of its stylization, it is crucial to note to what it is contrasted.

Play generally has been used by Euro-Americans to describe activity free from the need to be productive within the so-called real or serious world. Although this freedom to be unproductive is often confused with freedom from rule-governed constraints, the most casual observer of play knows that the opposite is true—that to play is to act in accord with a self-consciously articulated and tightly circumscribed set of rules. Although less apparent in contest games, in which winning takes precedence, the rule-governed and stylistic dimension of games nonetheless remain paramount. This concept of play is apparently characteristic of all groups, not just Euro-Americans, but Euro- and Afro-Americans differ in their use of the term and in their practices.

Euro-Americans employ the term *play* primarily in contrast to *work,* and Afro-Americans use the same terms, but what is meant by them differs sharply between the two groups. In Euro-America and elsewhere in the Western world, work is what one does to distinguish oneself as an individual. One learns to work successfully by most fully applying one's individual intelligence to a presented task. One proves one's worth by one's works, as it has been voiced until recently. However, play is the activity by which one progressively learns how to cooperate with others. One's values emphasize that the older one becomes, the more one must learn the importance of "team play." In an admittedly simple rendering, then, working comes to mean, as one grows up, developing one's individual abilities, while playing during the same period comes to represent the subordination of individuality in favor of coordination and cooperation with others. Work is one's most *public* set of behaviors, and play is as private as one can maintain, unless one chooses one of the two most deviant of all acceptable roles: the entertainer or the athlete, he who plays in public. Even here, one attempts to redefine his behavior as work. Thus, the most individual of all behaviors, work, is also the most public.

Almost exactly the reverse characterizes Afro-Americans. Work tends to be identified with family and, by extension, with home and its relative privacy. Work is learned within the home as the most important feature of extended family living and is identified with the maintenance of the familial order of the household. Commonly under the direction of the mother, children learn to work from older children in the household. Work is thus defined as a cooperative activity. Conversely, play, which is used to refer primarily to performance in this context, is learned from one's peers, commonly outside the home, and comes to be *the* activity by which Afro-American individuality is asserted and maintained. Thus, *playing* or performing is associated with public places, while work begins in the home and remains a kind of private or at least guarded range of behaviors. This accounts in part for the relative lack of discussion of work by blacks, especially in those public circumstances in which oral playing is regarded as more appropriate.

The distinction parallels that between the female-dominated household world and the male street-corner way of life, in terms of the difference of orientation, activity, and value systems between female respectability and male reputation maintenance (Wilson, 1969). In the Afro-American sense of the term, *play* is not commonly practiced in the house, being more appropriate in public, where masculine, crossroads, reputation-centered values may be celebrated. In this sense play means highly unruly behavior, noisy oral dueling, and using a dramatic speaking style known in the West Indies as *talking bad or broken*. When the noise, unruliness, and speaking style are brought together, the result is called *nonsense* or *foolishness,* evaluative terms derived from household values but usually accepted by the male speakers themselves. Because it is public and individual, play is regarded as inappropriate in areas dominated by respectability values, especially the home (Abrahams and Bauman, 1971; Abrahams, 1972, 1976).

Undoubtedly, the term *play* is used by Afro-Americans with many of the same meanings as other speakers of English. But in black communities in the United States and the West Indies it has developed another range of meanings that points to an important social feature of Afro-American public behavioral style. Specifically, play describes situations of style- and code-switching, changes that have consequences reaching far beyond more stylistic or aesthetic dimensions of culture to the assertion of value- and culture-difference in performance terms.

Although these generalizations derive from contemporary ethnographic research, old travel literature indicates that the differences have long existed, both in the use of the word *play* and in the concept of what playing is and how it should be properly carried out. As early as 1729 A. Holt mentioned that the slaves in Barbados had gatherings on Sunday, "which they call their plays . . . in which their various instruments of horrid music howling and dancing about the graves of the dead, they [give] victuals and strong liquor to the souls of the deceased" (cited in Handler and Frisbie, 1972, p. 14). Peter Marsden similarly noted in 1788 that "every Saturday night many divert themselves with dancing and singing, *which they style plays*; and notwithstanding their week's labour, continue this violent exercise all night" (p. 33; our emphasis). Such festivities were more commonly associated with the major holidays, especially Christmas. Another commentator, William Beckford, noticed that

> some negroes will sing and dance, and some will be in a constant state of intoxication, during the whole period that their festival at Christmas shall continue; and what is more extraordinary, several of them will go ten or twelve miles to *what is called a play,* will sit up and drink all night, and yet return in time to the plantation for their work the ensuing morning (Beckford, 1:392; our emphasis).

This different approach to time, this all-night and unrestrained performance of play, seems to have most troubled these spectators, because, almost formulaically when they mention the term, they discuss its nocturnal aspects: "The dance, or play as it is sometimes called, commences about eight o'clock . . . and . . . continues to daybreak with scarcely an intermission" (De la Beche, 1825, p. 40).

Nothing troubled the planters more than the nighttime activities of their slaves, relating to a whole group of stereotype traits such as diablerie and supersexuality. Every effort was made to cut down on excessive nocturnal ceremonies, burials and wakes, the practice of obeah, and, of course, these *plays.* Yet, as anyone knows who has worked in the West Indies, the high value placed on playing any celebration all night remains to the present. Whether it is a wake, *Christmas sport, Carnival, tea meeting,* or *thanksgiving,* a celebration that cannot be sustained all night is a disgrace to the performers and the community.

The designation of these all-night performances as plays was only one of the black uses for the term, possibly fastened on by whites because it departed so fully from their own usage. In *A View of the Past and Present State of the Island of Jamaica,* James Stewart gives us some glimmer of the Afro-American domain of the term when he mentions that "plays, or dances, very frequently take place on Saturday night" and also suggests that *play* is their term for any licensed nonsense occasion (Stewart, 1823, pp. 269-72). Any holiday was called a *play-day* (Lewis, 1836, pp. 45, 97)—as was a wake (Scott, 1833, p. 204).

This set of practices, although persistently defined as bad and often illegal, has been maintained and even recently intensified throughout the anglophonic West Indies. Significantly, the most licentious of these celebrations are still referred to in play terms. One "plays" wake, Carnival *mas'*, Christmas sport, or any of that range of performances generally termed nonsense or foolishness.

Playing, then, means the acting out of behaviors regarded as *bad,* yet that provide a means of channeling the energies of all those in the performance environment. This acceptance of a negative self-image by at least one segment of black communities during such "licentious" occasions has been widely noted by ethnographers. Karl Reisman (1970) has pointed out the "duality of cultural patterning" between positive (usually European) forms and negative (usually old-fashioned, country, or African) ones. It is an integral part of this performance system to seek power by playing out in public these negative roles. These *bad* performances, regarded as appropriately masculine, embody male reputation values. This kind of nonsense behavior is acted upon constantly by the *sporty fellow, bad johns,* and *rude boys,* but only when playing is sanctioned are the *sporty* ones permitted to perform before the community as a whole, and then only by dressing up or dressing down, taking unaccustomed roles into which they channel their antinormative (i.e., antihousehold) nonsense.

Thus, playing in Anglophonic Afro-America means not only switching styles and codes characteristic of all types of play, but also switching downward to roles and behaviors regarded from household (and Euro-American) perspectives as "bad" or improper. Furthermore, as Morton Marks has noted of this switching in other parts of Afro-America, it is "always from a 'white' to a 'black' style" and in music and dance at least, "from a European to an African one" (Marks, 1972, p. 5). The juxtaposition of the implicitly "good" household-based norms of the black community with the "bad" activities produces the kind of mass release of energies noted by all observers of Afro-American celebrations. Playing then means playing *bad,* playing black, playing lower class. It is no coincidence that playing Christmas often led to insurrection, as was noted by the planter-journalists and travelers. The play world, with its nonsense and its masculine, defensive, and regressive black motives, simply began to break down the boundaries and rules of play, spilling out over the fences into the yards of the great houses.

Play is used in an analogous but somewhat more restricted sense in black talk in the United States. Here playing, *playing the dozens,* and other similar locutions refer to code-switching into *baaad* varieties of speaking and acting that call for the same kind of performative acceptance of the negative role to obtain the power inherent in such behaviors. Thus, throughout Afro-America, playing is equated with a powerful but negative image of the performer. The power in the liminal world is a means of *getting into it,* setting up *the action,* but such playing provides a constant threat to the household world.

This speaking frame of reference acts both positively, in establishing the street environment as an appropriate place of witty and inverted performances, and negatively, in restricting speaking behavior within the household and other places dominated by respectability values (Abrahams, 1970). In the Afro-American order of behaviors, "play" is not distinguished from the "real" or "work" but from "respectable" behavior. Play is thus conceived of in a very different way in Afro-American communities than it is in Euro-American ones. It is an important element of public performance of black communities, by which men-of-words are able to establish and maintain their "reputations." The descriptions of West Indian plays indicate the depth of interest given such entertainments. Through these accounts we can gain insight not only into the alternative attitude of playing but also into the ambivalence of Euro-Americans to such energetic practices, and the ways in which the slaves gradually incorporated European play occasions and in the process developed an Afro-American creole culture.

In the process of exploring Afro-American cultures through material such as these journal accounts and histories, our object should not be simply to search out "Africanisms" as survivals of African traditions but rather to use Africa as a base line, as a starting point, as it was historically. The numerous Afro-American cultures of contemporary North and South America provide important points of comparison. Instead of searching out the *sources* of this or that pattern of behavior, parallel processes and functions must be searched out in Africa and Afro-America after European colonialism and slavery. As Hortense Powdermaker pointed out long ago in *After Freedom,* her study of a Mississippi community, in taking on new cultural values from the whites, the blacks did not simply replace older "African" values, but rather added new patterns to older ones. This is what Paul Radin meant when he suggested that the "Negro was not converted to [the white Christian] God. He converted God to himself" (1968, p. ix). Both implied that African sensibilities were the starting place and that European values were selectively adapted to the specialized needs of Afro-Americans. While all of this is rather elementary anthropology, in taking up the politically charged subject of the roots and nature of Afro-American culture, we must remind ourselves of the universal principles operating in the most diverse groups of the earth's peoples.

The demands of Afro-American students for a cultural history that is relevant to black people—that is, one that considers both the past and the present of blacks—have often been dismissed as lacking substance. Such dismissals depend entirely on the view that no unique Afro-American cultural past exists beyond that of the institutional systems of either Africa or the New World plantation. This connection between the two is at best considered more discontinuous than continuous, and at worst nothing more than (to use Ralph Ellison's phrase) "the sum of a people's brutalization."

Herskovits recognized this view for what it was—the myth of the Negro past. We would add that it also constitutes the myth of the Negro present, and it is to this myth and its debunking that we have addressed our arguments here.

CHAPTER FOUR

Joking: The Training of the Man-of-Words in Talking Broad

One of the dominant features of life in most Afro-American communities is their continuing reliance on oral expression. This means that, among other characteristics, there is still a good deal of social value placed on oral abilities, and these can often be best exhibited in a contest fashion, contests that are waged in creole or street language rather than Standard English. Discussing the role of such verbal abilities in one Washington, D.C., ghetto neighborhood, Ulf Hannerz noted that

> the skill of talking well and easily is widely appreciated among ghetto men; although it is hardly itself a sign of masculinity, it can be very helpful in realizing one's wishes. "Rapping," persuasive speech can be used to manipulate others to one's own advantage. Besides, talking well is useful in cutting losses as well as in making gains. By "jiving" and "shucking," ghetto concepts with the partial denotation of warding off punishment or retribution through tall stories, feigned innocence, demeaning talk about oneself, or other misleading statements, a man may avoid the undesirable consequences of his own misdemeanors. . . . However, all prestige accrued from being a good talker does not have to do with the strictly utilitarian aspect. A man with good stories well told and with a quick repartee in arguments is certain to be appreciated for his entertainment value, and those men who can talk about the high and mighty, people and places, and the state of the world, may stake claims to a reputation of being "heavy upstairs." (Hannerz, 1969, pp. 84-85)

The ability to contend effectively with words is, then, a social skill and highly valued as such. Furthermore, it seems significant that these contests bring black talk (or, as most West Indians refer to it, *patois,* or *bad, broken* or *broad talk*) to a high art. One might hypothesize that the ongoing importance and usefulness of such practices may contribute to the retention of creole speech patterns as the major code for in-group black interactions and entertainments. This argument seems even more plausible as one investigates the crucial place that certain of these verbal contests, like *playing the dozens,*

55

take in the socialization process of young men in widely scattered black communities.

The importance of these skills in actively contending is amply testified to by many who have grown up in the ghetto environment in the United States, including Malcolm X, Dick Gregory, Claude Brown, Jr., and H. Rap Brown. Brown says of the whole language "problem":

> I learned how to talk in the street, not from reading about Dick and Jane going to the zoo. . . . The teacher would test our vocabulary each week, but we knew the vocabulary we needed. They'd give us arithmetic to exercise our minds. Hell, we exercised our minds by playing the Dozens. . . . We played the Dozens for recreation like white folks play Scrabble. . . . Though, the Dozens is a mean game because what you try to do is totally destroy somebody else with words. . . . Signifying is more humane. Instead of coming down on somebody's mother, you come down on them. But, before you can signify you got to be able to rap. (Brown, 1969, pp. 25-27)

Playing the dozens is, as Brown explains here, just one of a number of oral contest traditions that ghetto boys learn and use as the basis of their entertainments. However, this kind of joking activity is not unique to ghetto blacks. The practice of mother-rhyming has also been observed in various other Afro-American communities, as well as in a number of groups in Africa, including the Yoruba, Efik (Simmons, 1962), Dogon (Calame-Griaule, 1965), and several Bantu tribes. Peter Rigby, for instance, notes among the Bantu Wagogo that "the abuse between age-mates is of the strongest kind. . . . Grandparents . . . may be freely included in 'the verbal banter, as well as references to each other's 'parents,' particularly 'mothers'. . . . Completely free conversation, which therefore includes references to sexual matters, is characteristic of relations between age-mates" (Rigby, 1968, p. 150; see also Zahan, 1963, p. 73-77). Philip Mayer similarly reports among the Gusii that "the true measure of the unique unrestraint of pals and the climax of their intimacy is to exchange pornographic references to the other's mother and particularly to impute that he would be prepared for incestuous relations with her" (Mayer, 1951, pp. 31-32).

These reports are all but unique because they make a reference to content features as a part of the process of joking. There has been a good deal of discussion concerning the social form and functions of the "joking relationships" in various African groups. But these discussions (other than those noted) focus primarily on who can joke with whom, not how jokes are generated or learned and for what reasons they are employed. Thus, it is difficult to tell how widespread such mother-rhyming is, and what alternatives there are, in joking situations in Africa. We do know that such specially licensed behavior is very widespread on that continent and that it plays an important part in its various speech economies and expressive repertoires.

In the New World, such play is one aspect of a special kind of aggressive joking calling for oral quickness and wit. This highly aggressive joking domain is known by a number of names in the United States, such as *rapping* or *signifying,* whereas in the West Indians it is called *giving rag, making mock,* and *giving fatigue.* These joking domains, whether in Africa or the New World, are always described in terms of the giving of license because of special relationships or festive occasions. Joking is in this way related to the entire tradition of scandal performances and the various practices of clowning or playing the fool. These scandalizing practices are equally widespread and important in African and Afro-American communities. And we can infer from the range of practices and their importance in community life that when mother-rhyming is practiced by adolescents it is part of the training procedure for adult performances.

JOKING AT THE CROSSROADS

Peasant and lower-class communities in the West Indies and the United States share this attitude toward effective use of words. The range of this verbal repertory includes the ability to joke aggressively (in some groups this includes riddling), to "make war" with words by insult and scandal pieces, to tell Anansi stories (any kind of folk tale), and to make speeches and toasts appropriate to ceremonial occasions. Community status is designated in the West Indies by making the man-of-words the chairman at wakes, tea meetings, or service of song, and the toastmaster at weddings and other fetes. Few, of course, achieve such distinction.

There tends to be something of a separation made between two kinds of artful word use: one emphasizes joking and license, the other, decorum and formality. The former emphasizes bringing the vernacular creole into stylized use, in the form of wit, repartee, and directed slander. The latter is a demonstration of the speaker's abilities in Standard English, but strictly on the elaborate oratorical level. From this distinction two types of man-of-words have been posited: the *broad talker,* who, using license, brings creole into stylized form; and the *sweet talker,* who emphasizes eloquence and manners through the use of formal Standard English.

Artful broad talk may occur at any time, most commonly in public places; it is not considered appropriate in the yard or the house. This is almost certainly because it involves *foolishness* or *nonsense* behavior, which is regarded as a frontal assault on family values. Therefore it occurs on the streets and at places where the men congregate apart from the women. As a rule, only on special occasions like Carnivals or tea meetings is this type of performance carried on in front of women, and, on such occasions, women may involve themselves in the by-play, especially if they are masked in any way. Further, on such occasions there may be a confrontation between such broad-talking performances and ones that call for *sweet* speechmaking. In such a case, the community dramatically presents the widest range of their performance styles.

Both types of speaking are not only useful for individuals seeking special performance status within the community; they also fit into the system of social control. Speechmaking is an overt articulation of the ideals of the community. The sweet talker achieves his position of moral authority not only by invoking these ideals but also by embodying them in a formal rhetoric. In contrast, the broad talker achieves license to joke because he commonly focuses on behavior of others that is in gross violation of these ideals. His scandalizing therefore acts as something of a moral check on community activities.

The broad talker does a good deal more than this, however, especially on ceremonial occasions. He is licensed to play the fool or the clown and, as such, may enact behaviors that would be regarded as improper on any other occasion. By playing the fool or by describing the antics of the trickster Anansi, the broad talker therefore enacts something of an antiritual for the community; he produces a needed sense of classless liminality and serves as a creative channel for antisocial community motives. Furthermore, by giving him this power, the community provides itself with a set of people who bring a sense of liminality upon the entire participating group, permitting them to forget themselves under special circumstances (like Carnival or Christmas revels) and to enter into the licentious occasion. The importance of this lapsing of the social order for its eventual reorganization is crucial to an understanding not only of the festival but also such licentious ceremonies as wakes.

For both kinds of verbal performer there are, of course, training procedures that have been developed by the community. These differ in their particulars from one Afro-American enclave to another, but some general comments can be made about them. Throughout the West Indies (and, to a certain extent, in the United States), there is an identification of talking sweet with family occasions, especially ceremonial rites of passage. Certainly talking sweet embodies values that focus on the family as the modal institution in which proper, responsible behavior is learned and carried out. But there is also a feeling that parents or grandparents should be responsible for a child learning how to talk sweet. Therefore, if parents or grandparents do not know speeches that they can teach their children for those occasions in which such talking is necessary, they send the child to someone in the community who is an expert in such matters. This person either trains the child orally or, more commonly, writes out a *lesson,* which the child memorizes. When it is learned, the child returns, recites it, and receives help on his or her delivery.

Learning to talk broad artfully, however, is not developed within the family. Rather, there is an identification of dramatic and stylized broad talk with values that run counter to those of the family and that are associated with public life, the crossroads, rum shops, and markets. Artfully talking broad is therefore a technique developed apart from the yard and the family environment, as a function of the friendship system on which masculine identity relies. As such, a certain degree of antagonism develops between the values implicit in talking broad and those of the family, because friendships take men (especially young ones) away from the yard. This antagonism is complex and often ambivalent because friendship values in their most important expressions develop from those of the family, especially in the positive valuation and practices of sharing and trust. In a sense, the sharing dimension of friendship actually creates an area of potential conflict because there is just so much to be shared and families and friends therefore vie for what they regard as their due. But the deepest distrust that family people have of friendships arises because drinking is carried on among friends and this often means a breakdown of decorum and the possibility of any number of assaults on family values.

Nevertheless, even the strongest of family people acknowledge, openly or by implication, that both friendships and license are important for the continuing vitality of the group. This is why such value is placed on *keeping company* and why social pressure is often brought on the *selfish* (shy) person or the *garden man* (loner), who are distrusted because of their lack of sociability. Often being selfish is equated with *getting on ignorant* and means an inability to take a joke and reply in kind. A joking capacity is therefore one of the key behavioral manifestations of group membership extending beyond the family and the yard. The young, especially males, are expected to get out of the yard and the garden and to develop friends, both as a means of broadening the network of people upon whom they can rely in times of need, and as a technique for creating some kind of interlock within the community by which the problems that arise within the family may be taken care of.

The most important of these problems are related to the antagonisms arising from the distribution of power and responsibility within the family. Whether the family is headed by a male or a female, West Indian peasant groups find themselves confronted with the need to maintain an age-based hierarchy and forcing the young into observing continuing respect for their elders. This naturally creates problems with those seeking autonomy, problems that are greatly increased when opportunities that may provide employment for the young exist outside the family. Whether or not these wage-earning positions exist, there is a strong feeling of shared needs and experiences among male peers in these peasant communities, a sharing that results in a mutual and supportive friendship network in the face of common problems.

Because the focus of these problems is on the social institution that most constrains them—the family—they tend to channel their performance energies into antifamilistic forms. As a licensed role (or roles) that provides a model of performance for these motives already exists, a number of broad-talking traditions may be observed, mostly joking forms. Appropriate to the peer relationship, these serve both as a training ground for future nonsense performances and as a device by which friendship can be put into action. Thus, as in many groups, joking is an index to the type and intensity of a relationship.

In such situations, learning to be verbally adept is part of the process of maturation. For the adult performer, the man-of-words provides a model of on-going masculine abilities, especially in a contentious and economically marginal world. Consequently, in the practice of the rhyming insult found through this culture area there is an element of masculine role-playing that is one facet of an informal initiation practice. It is, at the same time, a technique by which young men may voice their peer identification and, in so doing, achieve license within that segment of the community to try out their talents. Just such an orientation toward this peer-group joking practice has been exhibited by a number of those commenting on similar practices in Africa. But such verbal practices do much more, for they permit a trying-on of mature roles in the safety of the peer-group confines while arming the young men with weapons useful in adult life.

The relationship between adolescent practices and adult ones is clear in most cases because of the different subjects and formulas used to embody joking aggressiveness. Thus, in the West Indian community in Panama, the most common subject of adolescent rhyming is the same as that of adult joking—the attribution of homosexuality to the other (a focus probably borrowed from Latin American neighbors), while references to the other's mother—except to start a fight—is prohibited for the most part.

RHYMING ON TOBAGO

Rhyming in Plymouth, Tobago, however, permits this focus on the maternal figure, a focus that is shared with the numerous songs and *ring play* (singing games played by adults and children) and verbal routines in Tobagonian bongo (*wake*), as performed by adults in the community. Some of the wake dance songs address this theme, illustrating its intensity and licentious playfulness:

> An' de bull take 'e pizzle an' he make his mama whistle,
> De bull, de bull, de bull jump 'e mama.

> An' de bull, de bull, de bull jumped 'e mother.
> De bull, de bull, de bull jump 'e mama.

An' de bull take a whistle and everybody whistle,
De bull, de bull, de bull jump 'e mama.

An' de bull down Carrera with some peas and cassava,
De bull, de bull, de bull in de savannah.

An' de bull jumped 'e mama and he bring forth a heifer,
De bull, de bull, de bull jump 'e mama.

An' de bull jump 'e sister in a open savannah,
De bull, de bull, de bull jump 'e sister.

An' de bull in de savannah, he make your sister partner,
De bull, de bull, de bull in de savannah.

An' de bull take de pizzle an' 'e make your sister whistle,
De bull, de bull, de bull jump 'e mama.
[*Repeat ad lib*]

Rover dover, roll body over,
Pam palam, knock 'em palam.
T'row way me breakfast an' gi' me de moon-a
Pam palam, knock 'em palam.

A little, little woman carry a big, big moon-a
Pam palam, knock 'em palam.
A big fat woman carry a small, small moon-a
Pam palam, knock 'em palam.

Them small, small woman, bottle neck moon-a,
Pam palam, knock 'em palam.
Them big, big, woman got a small, small moon-a
Pam palam, knock 'em palam.

Dem bottle neck moon got lard at de corner,
Pam palam, knock 'em palam.
Big fat woman serve like a sugar,
Pam palam, knock 'em palam.

This fascination with incest and female genitalia is exhibited in any number of other ways during the bongo. One example that stands out in my memory is a fifteen-minute exercise in metaphor in which a woman's genitalia were compared to a water well, the major point being the pleasures attendant upon digging and finding water.

The practice of adolescent rhyming is more easily understood in the light of these adult performance pieces. For purposes of comparison of content, I shall report one ritual argument, which I heard in November 1965, in a group of six male peers, all of whom were ages fourteen and fifteen. They punctuated each rhyme with punching motions and foot-shiftings. Each rhyme was followed by hilarity and a fight to see who would give the next, so that the underlying impersonality of the invective was even more pronounced than if only two had been trading insults. (This may have occurred because of my presence and because I was recording their contest with a promise of playing it back. They indicated that this often happened when the first assailants ran out of ready rhymes.)

1. Ten pound iron, ten pound steel.
   Your mother' vagina* is like a steering wheel.
2. I put your mother to back o' train.
   When she come back she porky strain.
3. Christmas comes but once a year.
   I fuck your mother in a rocking chair.
4. Ten crapaud† was in a pan;
   The bigger one was your mother' man.
5. If aeroplane was not flying in the air,
   Your mother' cyat wouldn't get no hair.
6. If snake was not crawlin' on the ground‡
   Your mother' cyat would not get no tongue.
7. Beep bop, what is that?
   A tractor falling a tree in your mother' cyat.
8. Beep bop, what is that?
   Thunder roll in your mother' cyat.
9. Tee-lee-lee, tee-lee-lee, what is that?
   A tractor stick in your mother' cyat.
10. Voo, voo, what is that?
    A blue fly worrying your mother' cyat.
11. Your mother fucking a old pan,
    and bring fort' Dan.
12. A for apple, B for bat.
    Your mother' cyat like alphabet.
13. Me and your mother in a pork barrel,
    And every word a give she porky quarrel. §
14. Me and your mother was digging potato.
    Spy under she and saw Little Tobago.
15. Sixty second, one minute,
    Sixty minute, one hour.
    Twenty-four hour, one day,
    I fucked your mother on Courland Bay.‖
16. A little boy with a cocky suit
    Fuck your mother for a bowl of soup.

*Pronounced "vá-ji-na."
†Inedible frogs.
‡Pronounced "grung."
§Made noise.
‖Plymouth's main beach.

17. Me and your mother was rolling roti;*
    I drop the roti and take she porky.
18. I put your mother on a electric wire,
    And every wood I give she, porky send fire.
19. I put your mother on a bay leaf,
    And every word I give she was a baby free.
20. I eat the meat and I t'row away the bone.
    Your mother' cat like a saxophone.
21. Forty degrees, the greasy the pole.
    That was the depth of your mother' porky hole.
22. Three hundred and sixty-six days, one leap year.
    I fucked your mother in a rocking chair.
23. Me and your mother was two friend.
    I fucked your mother and bring forth Glen.†
24. I fucked your mother on a telephone wire,
    And every jerk was a blaze of fire.
25. Me and your mother was cooking rice,
    And she kill she cat and frighten Chris'.‡
26. Up into a cherry tree,
    Who should come but little me.
    I held the trunk in both my hand
    And I fuck your mother in a frying pan.
27. Ding-dong bell,
    Pussy in the well.
    Your mother' pussy like a conk shell.

These rhymes cannot, however, be fully understood only in terms of content features. Rhyming is just one of many contest performances that until recently were very common in Tobagonian festivities, especially Carnival.

In the past two types of performance have been fostered by the community (in line with practices throughout Trinidad and Tobago): performances by the group as a whole or by individuals within it; and performances by individuals addressed to the group, generally while engaged in competition with other individuals. The primary occasions for these are bongo, Carnival, and St. Peter's Day (29 June), which is a special event for Plymouth. Other occasions are christenings, Emancipation Day, and Christmas. All of these occasions present opportunities for both types of performance. For instance, Carnival commonly calls for the town to get together for some *Costume mas'*, a group enterprise in which a theme of decoration is agreed upon and many dress in line with the theme. Then, on Carnival Tuesday, the entire mas', along with the local steel band, goes to Scarborough to *jump up* together, to show off, in a sense, their community solidarity and strength. A great deal of

---

*A curry dish introduced by the East Indians.
†The name of one of the boys.
‡She burned her vagina and hollered.

time and money is expended on this enterprise (so much so that in a bad fishing season such as 1965-66 Tobagonians did not have the resources or spirit to put together a mas').

In the past, Carnival has also offered an opportunity for the individual performer to have his day. There were a number of traditional ways in which he could dress and compete with other such performers. One of these was the *Caiso Mas'*, groups led by a *chantwell*. Another such competition was *Speech Mas'*, which involved composing boasting and deprecatory speeches of inflated rhetoric and pungent invective. A further activity of this sort was the well-known *kalinda* stick-fight dance (E. T. Hill, 1972).

Lately, in Plymouth, these competitive exercises are being rejected by the younger members of the community and are dying. The young men still admire the good competitors, but not enough to emulate them. The one remaining chantwell in Plymouth no longer performs at Carnival and the one Speech Mas' performer comes from another community and must go to yet another village to find others to form a troupe. It is difficult to understand why this is happening, but one possible explanation is that such competitive expression is no longer as highly valued as the more cooperative performance, or the fully solo activity that takes the calypsonian off the street and places him on the stage.

This retreat from competitive expression is seen in the need for excuses and explanations that is felt by the competitive performers. They self-consciously insist that they are involved in a harmless game of words, though the contest of the speeches, songs, and stick fights is totally aggressive and destructive.

The same rationale has been used by adolescents in their rhyming sessions. Those who play today insist that a nonviolence pact must be made before beginning:

> We made an agreement that we can rhyme on your mother. Then we start. I say, "Go and rhyme." He might say, "Okay" or something like that. Then he first will start. The person who first to ask to rhyme, he won't give a rhyme first in case they break the arrangement. (Daniel Dumas, age fifteen, Plymouth, Tobago, March 1966; he aided me in gathering the rhyme texts)

Yet the idea is clearly not to play but to hurt as much as possible, to "come back with a hurtful one to make more vex; something like when two persons cursing." The rationale of play arises because the value of this invective contest has been challenged and is to an extent undermined. This defensiveness seems a recent phenomenon, judging by the reminiscences of men in Plymouth.

Whether this development is an indication that rhyming will go the same, say, as Speech Mas' and *Caiso Mas'* is unclear; it is more important to understand that this self-conscious reaction does not mean a rejection of all of the licentious and joking traditions that surround these practices. Rhyming is just one technique of exhibiting verbal wit and directing it toward persons outside one's own peer group. There are numerous other such traditions, some of which provide the primary entertainment forms and themes for adolescents. Most important in this regard is a series of short legendary jokes and songs about local happenings, especially those involving ogre-fool figures. These compositions are very much in the scandal-piece tradition, for they focus on activity regarded as foolish and inappropriate. Any kind of action that elicits laughter because it is a disruption of the expectations of the group may become the subject of such scandal pieces among the boys. For instance, when a local boy, Egbert, found a ring in the road, he wore it on his penis and made an exhibition of himself. His father then compounded the indiscretion by giving him a public beating for it, and so the boys sang this song:

Egbert, he busting [he was so happy]
An' he t'ought he get a ring,
But Uncle Darnell
Pitch 'e big wood on him.

Another such song sung by the young is not only a scandal piece but also involves many of the same motives as rhyming. It is a formulaic composition into which can be fit the names of any couple who have recently been caught at illicit lovemaking. Then, however, the song sometimes is performed as a rhyming boast in which the singer becomes the fornicator. Here is an example of such a song:

People, if I hear de fix
Charlie eat up Miss Vaughnie' chicks.
People, if I hear de fix
Charlie eat up Miss Vaughnie' chicks.
Den I [or 'e] gi' she one
She started to run.
When I gi' she two
She buckle she shoe.
When I gi' she three
She cut down tree.
When I gi' she four
She break down door.
When I gi' she five
Now I started to drive.
When I gi' she six
She break up sticks.
When I gi' she seven
She t'ink she was in heaven.
When I gi' she eight
She lay down 'traight.
And I gi' she nine
She started to whine.
When I gi' she ten
Den my cock ben'.

As with rhyming, these songs are similar in content and focus to some of the song games performed at bongo by adults. In the case of the bongo pieces, however, it is assumed that everyone knows the story and therefore many little details, rather than the narrative, are given. Here for instance is the saga of Jean-Louis, a man from the town of Lescoteau [le-ki-to] who made a determined pass at a young girl, who promptly ran away and was said to have bawled out this song:

> You know Mr. Jean Louis
> Tim bam.
> Come out a Lescoteau
> Tim bam.
> You know wha' he hold me for?
> Tim bam.
> You know Mr. Jean-Louis
> Tim bam.
> He hold me for pom-pom soir,
> Tim bam.
> He hold me for pom-pom soir,
> Tim bam.
> He know me a very long
> Tim bam.
> You never hear a trus' before,
> Tim bam.
> Well you know Mr. Jean-Louis
> Tim bam.
> He come up from Lescoteau,
> Tim bam.
> He born in Tobago,
> Tim bam.
> He ain' never call me yet.

Rhyming on Tobago is, then, one of a number of traditional devices by which adolescents group themselves on a peer-group basis and learn how to perform while joking about their shared problems and perspectives. Although one of these problems certainly is in displaying their masculine identities —which is attempted in part by the combination of boast and taunt in rhyming —this focus on female symbols is not the only means they have of asserting this generational unity and independence from the constrictions of the extended family. License is given them to focus on the generational split as well as the sexual one.

RHYMING ON NEVIS

On Nevis, rhyming is also practiced and for many of the same reasons, but here the boys rely almost entirely upon the scandal-piece tradition, or they use the closely related techniques of the taunt. As on Tobago, the focus of their joking is on females and on older people, but the rhymes never use the strategy of indirection and impersonality to make their point. Rather, in keeping with the sense of strong interpersonal antagonism, discussed in chapter one, the rhymes are directed at individuals and usually refer to the names of those present. These are primarily formulaic rhymes in which names may be substituted. Others simply make fun of a class of outsiders—for example, young girls, older men—or make specific reference to an item of gossip. Here is a series of rhymes as performed by a group of fourteen- and fifteen-year-old Nevisian males during the summer of 1962. As explained to me, the idea was to attack some close relative or friend or one boy, to which he might or might not make a bantering reply. Once the rhyming begins, there is apparent license for any rhyme to be performed, whether it happens to be directed at someone's familiars or not, and thus later in the series there are a few rhymes that are scandal pieces about people who live outside the social world of the boys.

1. Just for the sake of a box of matches,
   Rose can't put in common patches.*
2. Just for the sake of a banana,
   Jim knocked Sam from corner to corner.
3. Twenty boobies on a rock,
   Sonny catch them by the flock.
   Bobs put them in the pot
   And Mirie eat them piping hot.†
4. The sweetest pumpkin ever born
   Mirie turn some‡ in the corn;
   The pumpkin was so sweet
   It knocked out three of Audrey's front teeth.
5. I went to Dolly' house last night
   To tell you the truth I didn't sleep all right.
   I got up in the night to make my pee,
   I found bug all over biting me.
   Bug is a t'ing don't have any respect
   It walks from my chin to the back of my neck.
   I bawl, I bawl,
   For the dogs, fleas and all.
6. I went down to Booby Island§
   I never went to stay.

---

*Rose, the sister of one of the boys, does not even know how to sew, something that all girls are expected to learn.

†The idea of eating boobies, black pelicans, is ridiculous; the rhyme also makes fun, on occasion, of a boy and girl who are courting.

‡Mix and fry.

§A small rocky island between Nevis and St. Kitts.

I rest my hand on Dinah
And Dinah went away.
7. Just for the sake of a root of cassava,
That's why some of those young girls don't know their pickny' father.
8. Young bee meck honey,
Old bee meck comb.
Those young girls get their bellies
Because they won't stay home.
9. I went up the lane,
I met the parson kissing Jane.
He gave me a shilling not to tell,
An' that's why me suit fit me so well.
10. When I was young and in my prime,
I used to jump around those young girls no less and a time
Now I am old and feeble,
They call me "Dry Sugar Weeble."
11. Just for the sake of Mr. Kelly's bell*
That's why Halstead and Berdicere† kisses so well.
12. Racoon‡ was a curious man,
He never walked till dark.
The only thing could disturb his heart
Is when he hear old bringle dog bark.
13. Penny, ha'-penny woman
Sit down on a pistol.
Pistol leggo boom boom
Knock off Miss Wallace hairy poom poom.
14. Miss Pemberton has a landing.§
The landing work with spring.
The wind blow her petticoat
And then you see her magazine.||
15. Miss Budgeon# has a pepper tree,
Jennifer hang she panty dey;
When the pepper tree begin to bear
It burn off all of Jennifer' pussy hair.
16. The longer I live, the more I hear.
Bullwiss bite of Rose Pig ear.**
17. When Mr. Clark falls asleep
George Baker run with the sheep.††

*Mr. Kelly was a teacher at a local school.
†These two were "friending."
‡Racoon was a "selfish" man who lived alone, had never had a wife, and constantly chased dogs.
§Porch, balcony.
||Genitalia.
#The name of any mother and daughter may be inserted here, but especially those who have recently been observed fighting.
**They are brother and sister; biting another's ear is a common practice in fights.
††A court case the previous year.

As on Tobago, on Nevis there is a great similarity between these adolescent rhymes and adult entertainments both in content and form. In fact, a number of the same rhymes are used both by adolescents and adults; the latter only use them as part of the licentious clowning performances found in certain Christmas sports and tea meetings. In their adult uses, the rhymes are commonly associated with songs in some way, either as an introduction or within the text spoken between stanzas.

A number of Christmas troupes perform ribald and scandalous inventions, each of which portrays a powerful figure in broad comic terms. Politicians, kings and queens, preachers and schoolteachers, landlords and overseers— none are spared. One of these groups, performing a set of plays called *Nigger Business,* takes a piece of scandal that has come to its notice, and reenacts it while also performing a song with veiled references to the socially disapproved doings. This group first plays in the yard of the miscreants to see if its members can exact a bribe, but even if they are able to, there is no guarantee that the show will not be given in other yards as well.

Groups such as the Saguas or the Buzzards or the Schoolchildren do not have such a unity to their performance, but rather a series of comic routines that comment on human nature or on recent noteworthy events heard through gossip. It is this type of group that most performs rhymes and songs that are closely related to those of the adolescent boys.

The idea of the Saguas group is, for instance, for a group to dress up in broadly rendered cutaways and other formal wear and to go from yard to yard at night alternating songs and dances with rhymed speeches. These rhymes are often similar to those of adolescents, although they are performed with a great deal more liberty and are more often centered around an item of scandal. Here are some of the songs and speeches performed by a group of Saguas from the community of Brown Hill.

(*Sung*)
Monday morning, break a day,
When the old folks got me goin'.
Saturday night when the sun goes down
All those young girls are mine.
[*Repeat ad lib*]

(*Spoken*)
Here we are, the higher classes,
Of all the pie asses,
Straight from Missy Wallace, Limited and Company.*

(*Spoken*)
I've got me business organized and planned.
Dis year when de next boat land.†

* A clothing store on St. Kitts.
† Gets wrecked, as happened recently.

Luther got 'e paddle ready.
Charles Ward got he saw.
Shorty* got 'e pickaxe,
And me, Steel, got me clawhammer.

(*Spoken*)
One Monday morning, I went up the lane.
I met the parson fixing a Jane.
He shove me six pence, told me not to tell.
That's why me sagua coat fit me so well.

(*Sung*)
Dollars again, dollars again,
I put me hands on dollars again.
[*Repeat ad lib*]

(*Spoken*)
Out of the hollow tree I came,
Calabash is my name.
So long me get me long hungry gut full,
Calabash still remain.

(*Spoken*)
Hark, hark, the dogs do bark,
Beggars are coming to town.
Some give them white bread,
Some give them brown.
But I just give them a big cut-ass
And send them out of town.

(*Spoken*)
By golly, you that man Mr. Clifton from Churchground?
He motor bike gi' in' him one fall, land him 'pon ground.
So when get up he say, "That won't be all.
I goin' to collect sufficient money and buy Mr. Abbott' Vauxhall."

Similar alternations of speeches, including rhymes and songs, occur in a number of other licentious Christmas sports, such as the following routines from the Schoolchildren. Here the antisocial content is more pointed.

The setting is a Sunday School, and most of the jokes are directed at specific local Sunday School teachers, who are scored for their pomposity and mock erudition. The characters are dressed up as scholars in black robe and mortarboard, and they invariably carry a very large book, which they can barely handle but constantly refer to with great mock solemnity. The other characters are dressed as little children or, in the case of Robin (the one who scares all of the bystanders as the group goes from yard to yard—and thus stands in the same position as the Devil does in many other groups) in motley,

*Members of the community.

or Father Christmas in the Mummies (St. George) Play. (Abrahams, 1968, pp. 176-201). These scenes can go in any sequence, and are more or less ad-libbed. Between each scene, the fife and drum group plays and everyone dances, including members of the audience. Robin tries to scare some of the children.

Robin.   Now here we are, Robin speaking. Yeah!
Christmas come but once a year, yeah heh!
When 'e come, it bring good cheer (I'm glad, you know),
All what I see happ'nin' this year
Is the minister dem a breed off all de young girls dat come in here.
[*Music and dancing*]
Ward.   I'm Godfrey Ward speaking, but I would not like do do anything before the captain reaching, which is Samuel Daniel.
[*Music and dancing*]
Ward.   Hello!
Daniel.   Hello, man.
Ward.   A book here.
Daniel.   I ready to meet you.*
Ward.   To your exclusion.
Daniel.   Damned confusion.
[*Music and dancing*]
Ward.   Madam, come inside here.
Bradshaw [*man dressed as woman*].   Inside?
Ward.   Inside. All you all time out to make confusion.†
Bradshaw.   Fix me good. [*Acting seductive*]
Ward.   Is all right?
Bradshaw.   Sure.
Ward.   Dat right? [*Goes up next to her*]
Bradshaw.   Is me, Miss Bradshaw.‡
[*Music and dancing*]
Daniel.   Well, den, I want fifty thousand men take up a me book of a dictionary. Well yes, fifty thousand men to lif' de book of a dictionary. Tha's right. So now I look [*leafing through the book*] from the fif' to de six of June, never too late and never too soon, from six o'clock in the afternoon. Blessed assurance after three. One, two, three. . . .
(*Song,* to the tune of hymn "This Is My Story, This Is My Song")
Send them a pasha§ dey wouldn't go.
Take up my cat whip and leggo one blow.

*To contest who knows the Bible better.
†A mispronunciation of confession.
‡The late Prime Minister Bradshaw, former labor leader.
§Pasture.

Well dem dey reverse back, dey wouldn't go.
Dem dey reverse back, well-a chooka pooh-pooh.
[Let them have it with whip, acted out, scaring children in audience.]
Going on a mountain, no walk with no bread.
I going use potato, dasheen and tania head*
Worser me boy we, de dasheen dems sprout.
I wouldn't buy no tania head to scratch out me mout'.†
Daniel.   Now look in the back of the hymnbook for them, boy. Four-nine-nine.
All.   Four-nine-nine.
Daniel.   Last verse, "We going on mountain" after three, One, two, three.
[*Repeat "Going on the mountain. . . ."*]

Ward.   Boys, open your hymn book. Four-nine-two.
All.   Four-nine-two.
Ward.   Las' time I speakin' to you; not again. I hope everyt'ing will come true. You heard me? De las' time we sang a proper program:
My sister had a penny pork.‡
She bind them wid a twine.
She po'k 'em in a doving§ pot.
An' make my water shine.‖

The joking humor presents nonsense as if it were sense, putting together dialogue and song in a continuous fashion but without the usual logic that determines continuities. Thus, the laughter is directed at the nonsensical aspects of these characters. But this is just one dimension of the occasion's license, for, in addition, the high are made low and the virtuous revealed as lecherous and dishonest charlatans. The conventions of this kind of humor turn on dramatizing discontinuities and inverting the ascribed characteristics of everyday roles. Laughter arises with the introduction of the unexpected, though in this setting, such introductions are really expected (though their content is not known in advance). The mock-hymn and the rhymes all rely upon the disruption of expectations derived from the usual uses of these specific items (the hymn, the "Christmas comes but once a year" rhyme) to elicit laughter and to add to the irreverent tone. In such a setting, however, as soon as a device is introduced into the performance, an expectation of disruption arises on the part of the audience. This is also true of the adolescent

---

*Types of taro root.
†Tanias scratch unless cooked properly.
‡A penny's worth of pork, but also slang for female genitalia.
§Cook.
‖The pun here is on pot water, which shines with fat when pork is put into it, and semen, which is referred to as water.

rhymes, which trade both on such humorous conventions and their expectations, and the discontinuities associated with openly attacking others in the protected and licensed confines of peer groupings.

Significantly, the focus of the nonsense is on the symbols of the "sensible" world: school and church. The use of broad talk to confound talking sweet is thus all the more pointed, for nothing represents family-based ideals more fully than teacher and preacher, their books, and their usual manner of formal speech. In these mock speeches then, especially in those of the Schoolchildren, we witness a direct (but licensed) confrontation between family ideals and friendship values in which the latter, for the moment, win the day.

WHY RHYME?

The importance of license is that it permits a playful restructuring of the world. The recognized community order of things, actions, and especially interactions has a deeply felt sense of logic to it, simply because it *is* ordered and provides comfort and control to those who share this perspective. But everyone at some time feels contradictions or tensions arising from within or without the system. One way of handling this shared problem is for the community to get together ceremonially and reenact or recite in its most basic terms the condition and the genesis of the world's order. Another way is to provide license to community members to impose a new sense of order upon the social and natural environment, an order that is so different from that of the everyday that it produces laughter through manipulating discontinuities and contrasts. Masking is, of course, one of the most extreme examples of this effect, because it permits an overturning of the usual social order and the imposition of new status and power arrangements based upon assumed roles.

Joking is in many ways like masking because of its reorganization of the social order on the basis of different logics. But joking often establishes continuities on only a verbal level, through the use of puns and other *non sequitur* juxtapositions. This is essentially what produces the response to rhymes of children and adolescents on both Nevis and Tobago. Further, in both traditions, the potentially disruptive implications of the *non sequitur* and antitaboo arguments are rendered harmless not only by insisting that what transpires is only play (and verbal play at that), that there has been a joking about the most discontinuous things by virtue of the most elementary restricted verbal formulas.

This perspective is an extension of Freud's thesis that wit exists as an arbitrary order that permits a freeing of otherwise restrained motives. Or as Mary Douglas expressed it:

> A joke is a play upon form. It brings into relation disparate elements in such a way that one accepted pattern is challenged by the appearance of another which in some way was hidden in the first. . . . any recognizable joke falls into this joke

pattern which needs two elements, the juxtaposition of a control against that which is being controlled, this juxtaposition of being such that the latter triumphs ... a successful subversion of one form by another completes or ends the joke for it changes the balance of power. . . . The joke merely affords opportunity for realizing that an accepted pattern has no necessity. Its excitement lies in the suggestion that any particular ordering of experience may be arbitrary and subjective. It is frivolous in that it produces no real alternative, only an exhilarating sense of freedom from form in general. (Douglas, 1968, p. 365)

There is no joking, then, unless there is an order that can be overturned or at least challenged by the establishment of new continuities and relationships. But simply because a joke relies upon this previous social order indicates that it acts in response to certain pressures already existing within that order, tensions that are shared by the group who participates in the joking.

Joking thus helps to give the community the feeling that such situations are under control. But when we look at joking from a performance-centered perspective, we see that the joke seizes on such subjects because they already have tremendous potential to attract attention, for they deal with restricted matters. From this point of view, joking induces everyone's participation, because a potentially embarrassing situation is commonly depicted and drawn upon, but in such a context of social and verbal control that relief rather than embarrassment occurs. Laughter arises in response to the failure of expectations in a patterned situation, but joking occurs only when there has been an assent already given to articulating this failure, this abrogation. Joking uses embarrassment and other social dislocations, but puts the disruptions under a social control by framing them, by conventionalizing the behavior as play.

Social anthropologists argue that joking is essential akin to antiritual because ritual underlines and reenacts social order and cosmology, while joking and clowning challenge this for the purpose of channeling off antisocial tendencies. However, E. R. Leach has suggestively argued that there is an intimate structural relation between rite and antirite masking and that, simply speaking in regard to their occurrence, "they are in practice closely associated. A rite which starts with a formality (e.g. a wedding) is likely to end in masquerade; a rite which starts with masquerade (e.g. New Year's Eve, Carnival) is likely to end in formality" (Leach, 1961, pp. 135-136).

Furthermore, as Victor Turner has effectively argued, it is necessary to achieve a "liminal" state for the formal ritual to be effective (Turner, 1969). This seems equally true of antirituals. Liminality is the acceptance, by the group and especially the participants, of a sense of *communitas* in which social distinctions are rejected in favor of a classless state commonly symbolized by the assumption of garb and mien of the lowest social creatures. The costumes of festivals of this sort often "joke" in the same way, combining unusual materials and colors—that is the original meaning of "motley." Joking is similar in almost every sense, given its antisocial thrust and its totally participative strategy in which the joking group coheres on an egalitarian basis.

Joking arises, at least among adolescents, as a ritualistic behavior in which hierarchical order is challenged, and something like liminality occurs in which it becomes possible—in fact necessary—to assert a new order on a peer-group basis. Thus the conventions of joking are crucial not only because they provide a sense of artificial ordering (of words) in the face of disorder (of concepts or themes), but also because the conventions are regarded as the insignia of the peer group. the adolescents' performance is therefore a statement of group solidarity in the face of those who must be considered the common enemy, the actors of hierarchically established roles and relationships within the community. This means that such jokes can be looked to as indications of where adolescents see constraint asserting itself socially. But it does not mean that these jokes focus on *all,* or even on the most important, of these problems. As I have tried to show, adolescents on Tobago and Nevis are given the cues to what subjects may be discussed licentiously in the content of the songs and rhymes and stories that arise during adult ceremonies of license. The sense of liberation is short-lived, for no real social transformation occurs in such playful occasions. Rather, a ratification of common feeling occurs in performances, which also enters into the performance preparation for adult nonsense-making.

The success of this system depends on the peers' casting off these ways after a certain period and using their talents for the entertainment of the entire community. On many West Indian islands, however, there are indications that to do so would be an act of incorporation into an extended family system, which the young are not willing to go through. Because of the occasional availability of employment on the island, or the possibility of emigration to places where employment is to be found, the hold that the family exerts on the young has weakened. Consequently, this kind of grouping on a peer-group basis tends to continue, leading the older members of the community to sense that the system is falling apart, a disruption that they attribute to the rudeness of the young. Essentially, this indictment must be read not as a rejection of youthful license but as a charge that the young do not understand the proper occasions on which license is permitted. It would seem that joking has spilled over from the joking relationship into other performances and communications, and this is read by those who have lived with the system as a social disruption.

The elaboration of this kind of rude joking behavior is furthermore paralleled with some loss of respect for other parts of the speaking repertoire—specifically the ceremonial "sweet" speechmaking. Significantly, this kind of ceremony generally discusses overtly the most important features of household values in which the aged (and the ancestors) are given great respect. Thus, in a sense, this gravitation is away from an acceptance of Standard English as well as from a hierarchical, extended-family ideal. Surely this is not the only explanation of why broad-talk créole has persisted in spite of the obvious opportunities for employment and mobility accruing to those who learn

Standard English. It is simply to urge that we must more fully understand the relationship between speech acts and events, the varieties used by different segments of the community and the social order that is given articulation through the interactions between and among these segments. For then we can discover why these stigmatized ways of talking have been maintained and used as the basis of linguistic and social experimentation.

CHAPTER FIVE

A Performance-Centered Approach to Gossip

Gossip, like joking, takes place between individuals who have a special relationship to one another. We can therefore discern a good deal of a community's formal and informal social structure by noting those categories of people who joke or gossip with each other. Furthermore, both the content and form of gossip are traditional, as are those of joking, and it is these conventional aspects that define and restrict communication. It would thus be instructive in studying both joking and gossip to investigate the communications exchanged in regard to what limits there are to the license given by the community and by the individuals involved, and how judgment is made on violations of decorum. This means that the observer must take note of the qualities of the specific performance that give rise to these traditional gossip and joking relationships. To do this, however, it is important not only to see what other forms of conventional conversational interchange exist within the speech community under investigation, but also such other deliberate, licensed performances as occur. In other words, to understand gossip within the speech economy of a community, it is necessary to investigate the features unique to gossip and those that are shared with other speech acts and events.

The functionalist perspective has made us sensitive to the elements of social control that underlie so much of what people say to and perform for one another. Most public performances call for some highlighted display of the ideals of the group. Theoretically, performances discuss how to act and how not to act under set conditions, expressive acts that provide patterns of emulation and avoidance. But an increasing number of ethnographers have come to regard this approach as lacking subtlety and explanatory vigor. There are other dimensions and uses to such performances that are difficult to account for through the use of any equilibrium model.

Commonly the arguments against the functionalists' position have stressed individual or factional competitive usages of performance devices. Taking the longer view, it seems almost obvious that many of the traditional devices that argue in terms of a public morality, such as proverbs and myths, may also be applied in the pursuit of personal or factional ends. Indeed, it has been elegantly demonstrated by Leach and Firth that just such a process is to be observed in the use of myths, at least among the Kachins and Tikopians (Leach, 1954; Firth, 1961). The nature and function of gossip provided important materials for this ongoing discussion.

Analyses of gossip by students of culture and society have commonly focused on the practice of talking about other people's business as a technique for maintaining community control through the elucidation of a public morality (Gluckman, 1963a, 1968). Arguing from a slightly different perspective, Vidich and Bensman (1968) see gossip in the small-town setting as a means of maintaining some kind of community-held public image in the face of internal conflicts and external pressures from the city. These social concerns have been countered by other arguments that emphasize the importance of gossip for the gossiper, either in the increase of the gossiper's base of esteem, or in the articulation of interactional channels, especially friendship networks (Paine, 1967; Szwed, 1966; Hannerz, 1967). Standing somewhere between these positions, Faris sees the practice as a means of constantly attempting to maintain and renew the fluidity of communications relationships in a small community (Faris, 1966).

Common sense tells us that in gossip these features may be present at the same time. Furthermore, the practice in one community may emphasize ideals, while in another it may stress the personal power that is acquired by being able to tell stories about others. There has been, therefore, some recognition of the relationship between gossip and other types of performance, both in rhetorical strategy and in function; but no one, to my knowledge, has systematically examined this dimension of the subject. To this end, this chapter focuses on the native typology of speech acts and events as expressed by peasants in Richland Park, St. Vincent. I show that there the continuities between gossip and the more public modes of performance are explicitly recognized.

Although Vincentian speakers of English creole do not have the term "gossip," they use in an almost synonymous fashion the French creole *cŏmmess*. In this community there is a great deal of talk about talk, and, because of this, much judgment is passed on communicative behavior. Not only is cŏmmess judged in this way, it is also related in the minds of Vincentians with such other traditional devices as person-centered joking (*ragging, making mock, giving fatigue*), arguing (*making boderation, giving vextation*), and ceremonial performances of a more intense and ritualized sort. In other words, Vincentians seem to say that gossip may be discussed as an expressive act, employing many of the same terms of description and judgment that one would draw upon in discussing the making of a song or a speech, or the conducting of a verbal contest.

I find only Edmonson (1966), among the previous commentators on gossip, hinting at other communities employing gossip in an artful context. Both deal with Middle American Indian languages and both approach gossip as one native form of self-conscious expression among others. Edmonson points out that these categories are somewhat at variance with ours (a possibility that Gluckman seems to ignore in his reliance on a too restrictive dictionary definition of the practice). Edmonson says that

> at first glance the linking of games with gossip and humor may appear both arbitrary and misleading. . . . Taken together, however, the three topics have a certain coherence peculiarly relevant perhaps to the Middle American Indians: in many languages of Middle America they are called by the same word. To "laugh with" (or "at" or "over") somebody is to play with him, to mock him, or to amuse him (Nahuatl uetzca, Yucatec cheech). (Edmonson, 1966, p. 191)

Going somewhat farther in this direction, Gossen indicates that gossip is not only regarded as a form of play or performance among the Chamula but is also categorized as a narrative form, embodying stories about the doings of people in the fourth (contemporary) creation world (Gossen, 1974, pp. 29-33).

A TYPE OF NONSENSE

Among Vincentian peasants cõmmess is judged, as are all verbal performances, in terms of the performer's appropriate use of words. It is thus related in the minds of the group to a number of other types of verbally stylized encounter, both in terms of content (where it is associated with other genres that focus on scandal) and form (where it fits into other types of licensed narrative, such as trickster stories). Gossip is therefore judged in the same terms as a story or a song, according to whether it is judiciously performed in the right setting and under the properly licensed conditions. Because it is regarded as one form of *rudeness* or *nonsense,* a good deal of license from the (restricted) audience is called for if it is to be carried off successfully. Vincentian cõmmess does elucidate publicly approved behavior by condemning departures from norms. It is also used by a number of judicious performers to build up their bases of esteem within the community. This we must infer from the failure of some gossipers to use the device appropriately, and from the ensuing discussions of the consequences of such actions in terms of community division.

As mentioned, on St. Vincent there is a good deal of talk about talk. Indeed, the basic institutions of the peasant family and friendship networks are defined as much in terms of speech behavior as by action (see chapter six). One reason for this focus on talk is that control of words and speaking events continues to provide the key to community status and personal power. As control devices, words are greatly admired when effectively used, but greatly feared when controls are absent or when the expectation patterns established by convention are abrogated (Abrahams, 1967, 1968). In short, Vincentian peasants retain an essentially oral culture in spite of the high degree of literacy in the community, one in which word power is seen to reside more in controlled speaking than in the mastery of writing and reading. Books do, indeed, enter into Vincentian life, but mainly as a source for developing recitations and instituting glosses.

Activities such as making cōmmess and vexation occur constantly but are nevertheless feared because they lead to a feeling of loss of control over the most powerful words of all—one's personal name. One therefore attempts to manage one's own identity by acting sensibly, expecially within the family, and by being judicious in the choice of friends, picking those to whom one may talk without one's words being "stolen" and publicly dramatized.

There is, however, an ambivalence in Vincentian life arising from the feeling that one can fully manage one's own identity only by keeping silent at most times; not even friends and family are really trustworthy in keeping counsel. Yet silence on many occasions is a sign of lack of trust and is strongly resented. The strong, silent type is regarded as strange and unnatural in this community. Furthermore, the same motives embodied in gossiping and arguing, when they are channeled into appropriate ceremonial (play) performances, are encouraged by the community. Although there is a fear of having one's name used in scandal pieces, there is a contrary notion that prestige may result from having one's name used (and therefore known) by so many people. In some cases, because one becomes known (albeit notoriously), community scorn is accepted and taken advantage of by individuals. Here the implication is that people would rather be feared as deviants than ignored.

This contradiction seems due to the presence of contrary motives. One motive dictates that one should live decorously, earning respect for oneself and one's parents. The implication is that one's role in the community is under one's own control or that of one's family. The contrary motive is that community role perception and typing procedures accord one a place and that one must learn to accept and capitalize on this. These contrary aspects are not the subject of much discussion or worry because they are not directly perceived. Rather, the Vincentian sees certain elements of his identity that he may control through developing the expressive capacities consistent with certain roles. There are, however, other features of the role-casting over which he has little control, which he therefore learns to accept and even capitalize upon. This is especially evident in the stigmatization of the physically or mentally defective person.

Everyday communicative behavior is judged on the same terms as more stylized performances. Little distinction is made between those formally and obviously structured expressive performances—such as singing a song, dancing, or telling a folk tale—and ordinary expressive interactions. Thus while there would be no confusion in the minds of the community between a Carnival song and an everyday argument, they would be recognized as being related to each other as controlled contest forms and evaluated as performances.

In short, any public activity (i.e., one that goes beyond the family or a pair who are *friending*) is regarded as a performance; public life is seen as a continuity of experience, from the most casual everyday interaction to the most stylized ceremony. Gossip is therefore seen as simply one of the many inevitable performances of everyday life.

This does not mean that gossip is regarded as good. Indeed, if the Vincentian is directly asked whether he approves of gossip, he will respond that it is of no value whatsoever and that it leads to fights and hard feelings and to family and community divisions. But he will also reply that gossip is inevitable, an inborn proclivity in people, especially blacks. The stereotype here provides a convenient rationale for a type of behavior regarded as potentially disruptive but vital to the life of the individual and the community. Through being talked about, one risks having one's activities disapproved of; but one stands to gain much by such talk—a sense of community identity and involvement. Indeed, there are many individuals who, if their activities have not been public enough, utilize the gossip network to talk about their own business and thus to feel more fully members of the network and of the community—a process called *nigger business* by Vincentians. Gossip is only denigrated when discussed in abstract—therefore ideal—terms, or when it leads to divisive or destructive public actions.

Because of gossip's relation to these ideals, however, it is regarded as *nonsense* and is therefore one of a number of performances—everyday and ceremonial—so designated. Being placed in such a category is, in a sense, a value judgment. Nonsense activities are those that are potentially divisive from the community point of view. They exhibit traits that are regarded as nonfactual, *ignorant*; and those who fall into nonsense are often described as *ignorant fellows*. Consequently, behavior is being condemned when qualified as nonsense. But in the actual operations of the group, nonsense provides the major motive for a number of important ceremonial entertainments such as wakes. In wakes, license for making nonsense is given so that the social confusion of death may be articulated, brought playfully into the open, played out. Licentious play brings the group together and allows it to rehearse confusion and embarrassment in a context that is under control. On such occasions nonsense is a community focus in channeling creative energies in socially useful directions.

Nonsense is a contrast term for *sensible,* and sensible performances are those that are regarded as embodying the highest ideals of the community. A sensible performance is one in which *decorum* (often the key word in such a ceremony) is boldly stated and acted upon; it is one in which the familistic ideals of the community are openly discussed. It is looked upon as a model of behavior not only because of its order but because of its *sense,* its factual and reliable content. Being sensible means being well-spoken and knowledge-able—the two traits are regarded as synonymous—and anything weighed against sensible enactments is seen to be of little or no value. The sensible performance is one that emphasizes the order and decorum afforded by knowledge; in nonsense one focuses upon the energetic and the licentious ambience that accompanies *lies.*

Language usage, which is associated with sensible performance, is referred to as *talking sweet* or *talking good.* Speech that is congruent with nonsense occasions is designated as *talking broad* or *talking bad.* Talking sweet generally means approximating to formal Standard English in diction, grammar, and syntax. There is a natural congruence felt in both principle and practice between the use of this level of language (especially in diction) with the highly decorous stylized ceremonies that are designated as sensible. Indeed, they are more often referred to as sweet than sensible. Furthermore, when nonsense occasions are denigrated, it is often because they are not only full of lies but also expressed in creole language, or talking broad.

Related to the sensible-nonsense dichotomy is the distinction between being *rude* and being *behaved* or *besaid.* Being behaved is regarded as an attribute of being sensible; being rude is associated with nonsense. Moreover, the behaved are regarded as those who have words under control, whereas the rude are those who do not and who therefore cause embarrassment, fear, and anger in others. Thus, the Vincentian has three sets of terms by which he comments upon and judges a performance according to its conformity to his conscious speaking ideals. All these terms are applied both to everyday and to ceremonial performances.

Vincentians regard talk about the doings of others as a device by which these others' names are *called.* By this is meant the ability of a speaker to refer to someone by his familiar designation, and through such reference to use the naming as a means of, on the one hand, increasing one's base of esteem and, on the other, controlling the person named. The *calling out* of names occurs in all performances. But it is taken note of only in those cases in which it is regarded as illegitimate or badly done. The rudeness of such calling out draws attention to itself most commonly in those recurrent failures of reciprocal communication, which are situations of embarrassment.

For instance, when I was in St. Vincent, certain acquaintances would yell out my name as I would pass on the road, and I noticed that my Vincentian companions would suck their teeth in displeasure—a sign of disapproval throughout the West Indies—or suddenly become very quiet. Naturally I asked why this was wrong, and I was told that it was improper for anyone, even my closest friends, to call out my name. The true sign of friendship in such circumstances would have been to wait until our eyes met and then to raise our eyebrows, or to say "How, how?" or "Wha' 'appening, man?" The inappropriateness of calling out my name, especially in the diminutive form, was that when someone names you they imply that you are a friend, that is, engaged in an ongoing relationship in which more than words may be exchanged. Moreover, the calling of a name in public is strongly associated not only with rudeness but with *cursing*—name-calling of the more virulent sort. A person's name epitomizes his private world, and when this intimacy is violated by the inappropriate calling of his name, the victim may say, "You t'ink me and you is sex and size?" or accuses the offender of "playin' man before 'e time." The implication here, of course, is that the namer has mistakenly assumed a peer-group relationship with the one to whom he has called.

Calling name means more than one person yelling out another's name when he passes. It also refers to naming a person when discussing his activities in conversation. Vincentian ideas of cōmmess are included in this concept, and someone who is always talking about others is described as having a *fas' mout.'* This term is significant, for being *fas'* means being thievish, and having a fas' mout' is thus regarded as *t'iefin* someone's good name; that is, betraying trust.

GOSSIP: MALICIOUS AND OTHERWISE

Because it has so many referents, cōmmess is contrasted with at least two other terms, and it is in these contrasts that we see the range of meanings defined. In the sense in which the term is usually employed, it is virtually synonymous with calling someone's name while face-to-face. But on another level, if a person wants to point out who has done the talking about whom, a distinction is made between cōmmess and nigger business. In this context, cōmmess means talking about someone else while he is not present, whereas nigger business refers to talking about someone's business that he himself has instituted, but that is on the same subjects and in the same terms as cōmmess. Nigger business is discussed abstractly, as is cōmmess, as a moral weakness characteristic of the community. One informant explains, for instance, "You know we Negroes are *broad-minded* [talkative] people, bla'guard [bad because of talking too much]; we just feel that if we have any worry on our mind, we couldn't keep without explaining somet'ing [talking about it]."

This rationalization is exactly the same as the one given for calling out a name and for cōmmess. The rationalizations are grouped together as examples of nonsense, *ignorance,* the inability to organize one's thoughts and present them in effective language. One often hears blacks call themselves "a ignorant people—we have no sense atall, atall, atall."

One of the reasons why there is such a strong feeling that both cōmmess and nigger business are wrong is that privacy, especially in family affairs, is highly valued. The quiet person, who keeps most of his communications within the family, is someone who, in principle, is admired. But in actual interpersonal relations, he may be reacted to as an unfriendly person and his reticence may be held against him. This attitude may be shown by members of his own family; he is then termed a *garden man* (one who keeps to himself in the fields). Not only is this lack of communicativeness held against him, b⸱ ⸱ imputations of greed and lack of cooperativeness may also be voiced, for these traits are those associated with this widely recognized Vincentian social type. A similar attitude is maintained in regard to another social type, the bashful person (as noted, the Vincentian term is *selfish*, meaning not covetous but inward-looking). The shy individual is regarded as a somewhat undesirable type, especially because he is said to have no sense of humor and to become easily irritated by those who make fun of him.

PERFORMING CÔMMESS

This ambivalent attitude toward gossip is dictated by conflicting systems of association within the social structure and, by extension, by conflicting values. The disparity can best be summarized by the conflict between the value conferred on a close-knit extended-family unit, on the one hand, and the importance placed on having a large network of friends, on the other. Cômmess and nigger business are naturally associated with friendships, for such talk is one way in which friendship may be demonstrated and maintained. However, this kind of talk often involves clear violations of the kinds of privacy that are associated with the family.

A further reason for the ambivalent attitudes toward talk about people is that in many ways the small community's social system demands cômmess and even more extreme publications of others' business for the maintenance of social order. The subjects discussed or gossiped about commonly deal with the proper maintenance of the household and the appropriate practice of relationships within the family and among friends. Talk about such matters constantly serves to remind those involved of the importance of community norms, but also rehearses the necessity of working within the decorum system by which such relationships are maintained. In a very real sense, cômmess and nigger business establish bases of communication that play an important part in holding the community together.

But, as the members of the community recognize, there are strong dissociative potentials in any speech act that involves the calling out of a name. Thus a distinction is sometimes made between cômmess, which is gossip of any sort, and *melée,* which is malicious gossip. When contrasted in such a way, cômmess is regarded as permissible because it is harmless, whereas melée is frowned upon, especially in principle.

Cômmess in all of its uses provides an active way of guaranteeing a certain level of homogeneity of ideals and even of social practices. This is clearly seen in the common topics of gossip. Men talk about each other primarily in terms of how well they demonstrate their masculinity (in athletics, with women, by getting work and learning a trade, but the number of babies that they have *made*), how well they cooperate with others, and how many friends they have. Men talk about women in terms of who is *wild*; that is, who violates the ideals of trust that are supposed to hold sway in male-female relationships. This ideal of trust primarily means that a girl is never supposed to *talk with* or *friend with* more than one man at a time. (These terms may refer simply to courting, *gossing with,* or to engaging in sexual intercourse.) Women gossip about other women in regard to their abilities to keep their households in order, either in terms of tidiness or in regard to the personal behavior of family members. The poor upbringing of another's children is one common topic of melée, as is the way a woman treats her man in terms of keeping him under control.

To view còmmess only in terms of normative content is, however, to ignore certain features of its practice. Còmmess is subject to a variety of uses. Not the least of these is the maintenance of one's esteem by using stories about others both to demonstrate the extent of the network of people whose business one knows and to solidify a reciprocal trust-and-gossip relationship with the person with whom one is gossiping. This can only be done if certain rules of còmmess are observed. One must not talk badly of others if they are very close friends or family, for then one is subject to a rebuff that leads to a failure of reciprocity in the exchange. One must never give another person the impression that one is interested only in gossip, unless the subject of the information is news; that is, a very startling recent occurrence. But if còmmess arises in a conversational context, it must preserve the appearance of the spontaneous utterance. Furthermore, còmmess is rejected if the initiator conveys the information in too heated a way, thus betraying a coercive or biased purpose in an ongoing argument. the communication is then potentially *molês'* (libel, from the French creole) and therefore is of a different intensity and involves a different strategy than còmmess.

To view còmmess in this way is to see it as contributing to both a sense of community—by articulating ideals and by providing a patterned and expected sanctioning procedure—and to an individual's sense of esteem. But to argue that it should be judged in terms of one or the other is to ignore the way gossip actually operates. Like so many such expressive devices, còmmess is a feature of interpersonal behavior that mediates between conflicting principles. This suggests, then, that one of the keys to understanding gossip, at least on St. Vincent, is to understand the nature of the internal conflicts and to see how expressive devices of all sorts, including gossip, are used to mediate the contradictions that arise in the form of public situations that are problematic.

This survey of the use of talk about others' business suggests that though gossip is a device that is available both for social control and the pursuance of individual aims, it is also profitable to look at the practice from a more performance-centered perspective. This enables us to focus on the folk recognition and evaluation of telling stories about others' business, and thus to perceive the place of gossip in the native system of communication. Further, at least in regard to Vincentian peasants, there is a felt continuity between speech acts, such as commess, and speech events, such as riddling or storytelling sessions. Like Anansi stories and Carnival performances, commess is classified as permissible rudeness, as licensed nonsense—licensed because of the need to embody antisocial motives and to castigate them.

Once the continuity between the more casual mode of the commess performance and the ceremonial "rude" performances is recognized, however, it is necessary to notice the differences between them. Commess is a conversational genre; it must therefore follow the dictates of conversation, which means that it must, among other things, appear spontaneous. Just as there is a structure to overall conversations, there are standard casual storytelling patterns into which this conversational device fits. And there are certain times when the item of gossip is regarded as most appropriate. Furthermore, though there is an art to commess, we recognize the artfulness of the practice not so much through the apparent abilities of the gossip (as we do in more stylized performances), but through the inabilities of those who do not understand the rules, and who therefore cause embarrassment and the attribution of making melée. In this, too, the practice is an aspect of general conversation, because in all such small, casual, and spontaneous personal interactions, we learn about the rules of performance primarily through failures, commonly registered on the interacting group as embarrassment (see Goffman, 1968). The patterns of oral composition and improvisation are not as evident with commess as they are with the more self-conscious performances, but it is this very appearance of spontaneity that, in large part, provides the license for gossip.

Gossip must follow certain lines of argument. It makes a statement of approval or condemnation that reiterates the approved behavioral limits of the group. But it is also a tool by which the gossiper exercises personal control over the talked-about person, if only because he is licensed to call the person's name. The most important rules of commess are that the stories must be told in small groups, ones that include neither the talked-about person nor anyone who would report the conversation to him. It is judged in terms of its success as nonsense, as a device by which friendship values and often friendship networks may be maintained without seriously challenging the moral authority of the family. One is given license to talk about others by judging behavior in terms of the ideals of family life. But by judging all behavior in terms of inevitability and human fallibility, including commess itself, flexibility is maintained even while condemnation goes on.

Commess is one of many devices by which one may use the behavior of others as an occasion to demonstrate one's own oral ability. But unlike storytelling and song-making, it is a technique available to everyone, and all but social misfits (poor performers) may "make cōmmess" to sustain their position in this speaking community, for they are not judged on their stylized handling of words so much as on the validity of their claims to knowledge of personal doings and thus the idle use of someone's name in such a familiar fashion.

The function of gossip in specific groups cannot be fully understood until it is related not only to the system of ideals and the techniques of achieving power but also to the system of performance. This involves an understanding of the rules governing interpersonal decorum and the procedures by which license is accorded to an individual to perform. It also necessitates a consideration of modification, or refusal of audience participation, because of ineptitudes and failures in performance, especially those involving failure to recognize the norms and conventions appropriate to the occasion. In this way, gossip may not only give us cues as to the dictates of public morality but also indicate the native criteria of a good performance (in this case, through performance failures rather than successes).

CHAPTER SIX

Sense and Nonsense on St. Vincent: Speech Behavior and Decorum in a Caribbean Community

(with Richard Bauman)

One of the more nearly universal attributes of mankind is a propensity for minding the other person's business. Few activities absorb more of our time and effort than the observation, judgment, and discussion of other people's behavior, as every ethnographer discovers. On the level of specific cultures, however, the kinds of behavior that are subject to scrutiny by one's fellows, and the principles and standards by which they are judged, are highly variable and distinctive. It is gradually being recognized that one of the principal tasks of an ethnographer is the determination of the relevant categories of behavior for the people he or she is studying. Practical considerations, however, as well as sound analytic tactics, dictate that there must be priorities in such an investigation, and in this light it appears highly worthwhile to address oneself first to those behavioral categories the people themselves most observe and talk about, for these are entrées into the spheres not only of behavior but also of values and decorum.

If one were to follow this strategy for the Afro-American peasantry of St. Vincent, one's attention would very soon be directed to the realm of speech, for speech behavior is unquestionably a principal focus of attention for the Vincentians themselves, and the amount of talk one hears about talk on the island is truly striking. Talking bears all the earmarks among the Vincentian peasants of a cultural focus, in the classic sense of the term (Herskovits, 1955, p. 485). Speech behavior is one of the most crucial keys to social life in every culture, but such is the degree of interest and self-consciousness concerning speech among the Vincentians, and such the degree of cognitive importance that speaking assumes, that the ethnographic elucidation of the use of language in Vincentian peasant society can yield insights of the most direct and immediate kind into the Vincentian culture as a whole.

Systematic interest in the role of speech in particular societies, based on the premise that "language is not everywhere equivalent in communicative role and social value" (Hymes, 1967, p. 3), is a fairly recent development within the field of anthropology. This work has advanced of late under the rubric of the "ethnography of communication," identified with the work of Dell Hymes and John Gumperz (Hymes, 1968; Gumperz and Hymes, 1964; Bauman, Sherzer, and Sherzer, 1974). Hymes's use of the term "ethnography" is a very considered and self-conscious one (Hymes, 1968, p. 133n., 1964b, pp. 94-97); the ethnography of communication, both in its programmatic statements and its substantive investigations, has advanced hand-in-glove with a relatively recent approach and commitment to the practice of ethnography that calls for the construction of a theory of the nature, organization, and workings of a culture in terms of the people's own categories of knowledge and experience, the criteria they themselves employ as a basis for action (Goodenough, 1964a, p. 36; 1963, pp. 258-259; Conklin, 1964, pp. 25-26; Frake, 1964, pp. 111-112. For a discussion of the usefulness of this perspective in folkloristics, see Ben-Amos, 1976).

Accepting this orientation, this chapter is an account of a significant segment of the speech economy of Vincentian peasants as a means of illuminating Vincentian ideas concerning proper and improper behavior as well as the realm of speech itself. Our point of departure is the requirement of "discovering the major categories of events or *scenes* of the culture" relative to decorous and indecorous speech behavior (Frake, 1964, p. 112; cf. Adams, 1962, pp. 1-2, and Keesing, 1966, p. 23), and attempting to indicate their ramifications in other areas of Vincentian peasant culture.

Structural semantic analysis has been part of the basic analytical repertoire of practitioners of the new ethnography, based on the fundamental premise that language itself represents the major available key to a people's cognitive organization of their universe (see Sturtevant, 1964; Colby, 1966; Hammel, 1965). Thus far, however, structural semantic analysis has found its most frequent application in the analysis of folk categories of things, objects broadly conceived—for example, kinsmen, firewood, diseases, plants—in which the structuring of the semantic fields tends to be more directly related to traits and conditions of objects or recurrent relationship than it does in the realm of acts (Hymes, 1964a, p. 169). As such, it can be directly related to a testing and reformulation of the Sapir-Whorf hypothesis concerning the relationship between vocabulary and cultural focus or condition. The technique has not found as much use in the analysis of native categories of events or scenes, even though the discovery of them is one of the major instrumental goals of the practitioners of the "new ethnography" (but see Faris [1968] and the structural analyses of Tenejapa Ladino weddings by Metzger and Williams [1963] and Subanun drinking occasions and religious occasions by Frake [1964, 1964a]). As of 1962, Hymes stated that he knew of no structural analysis of native terms for speech acts (1968, p. 110); we are not familiar with any published subsequently. However, this chapter is based in significant part on the elucidation of a folk taxonomy of a particular domain of speech acts (we follow Adams [1962, p. 2] in defining an act as "a segment of a human behavior continuum such that the segment is distinguished from the preceding and following phases of the continuum by formal attribute differences recognized by the *actors*"). We also take into account certain more extensive activities identified by the Vincentians, which we designate performance occasions, ceremonies, and, following Hymes (1967, pp. 19-20), speech events.

The preoccupation with speech on St. Vincent is part of a wider concern with decorum in general, a constant and conscious focus on the maintenance of (or departure from) standards of behavior and comportment. This concern is certainly related in part to certain disruptive factors now affecting Vincentian culture and the felt need to shore up the defensive aspects of the system, but it is also owing to a continuing belief in the power of effective word use, and the consequent ability of a person who is an effective talker to attain a measure of special status within the community because of these abilities.

Given this focus on word power and the high value placed on decorous behavior, it is not surprising that the most highly valued speech acts are most obviously those in decorous and deferential language. These speech acts are often the most ceremonious in tone and manifest what has been the conscious linguistic ideal of the community. Their salient attributes are an elevated diction, an elaboration of stylistic features, and an approximation of standard English speech patterns, with an emphasis on the demonstration of fluency and knowledge, both in the form of facts and effective arguments. The folk designation for this type of speech act (as discussed in chapter five) is that it is *sensible*, which is contrasted in folk terminology with *talking nonsense*. Talking nonsense means a number of interrelated things: self-consciously departing from a logical or factual basis of argument; talking in creole; being hesitant or indecorous; or being totally out of control of the language; that is, *making noise*.

The sensible-nonsense opposition is both denotative and evaluative: it designates two basic kinds of speech behavior; but it judges as well, for the sensible acts represent the conscious linguistic ideal and the nonsense ones depart from this ideal in perceptible ways. *Nonsense*, therefore, is often used as a term of disapproval, but nonsense acts are not necessarily regarded as always and altogether useless or disruptive. The community recognizes the need, on certain occasions, to channel certain of the motives implicit in the nonsense behavior in predictable directions, in the form of performance occasions, even though this behavior is regarded as courting chaos and is therefore feared.

Closely related to the sense-nonsense dichotomy as applied to speech behavior is the opposition between *talking sweet* (or *good*) and *talking broad* (or *bad* or *broken*). This opposition represents a contrast between both codes and styles. Talking sweet refers to speech that exhibits elevated, formal diction and patterns that are believed to approximate Standard English. It is applied by extension, on certain occasions, to a display of performance control. Talking broad refers to talking in creole, with a minimum of stylistic elaboration and an economy of phrasing.

This strongly felt and often articulated distinction between two varieties and levels of speech indicates that we are involved in a situation of "diglossia" (Ferguson, 1959); that is, even though for descriptive purposes we must consider West Indian creole and Standard English as two language systems, they are not so considered by the Vincentians. Rather, the Vincentians recognize each of the two systems as being part of the speech economy of their community, and they assign relative values to the two, corresponding to Ferguson's *H* and *L* (high and low); yet they strongly recognize the appropriateness of each with regard to particular kinds of situations (see Reisman, 1970). Although talking sweet and sensible is the approved conscious ideal, it is not regarded as appropriate for general conversations between most members of the community, only those between an older and a younger person in which the older is teaching in some way, setting himself up as an ethical and linguistic example.

The relationship between the two types of speech is an extremely complex one, because talking sweet is regarded consciously as the ideal linguistic behavior, yet it is also seen as only being attainable by certain members of the community. It therefore stands as an ideal that only some people pursue at all, and then only at certain times. *H* speakers are regarded as those members of the community who are capable of competing linguistically in the outside, dominant world (although their performance is not directed to an outside audience).

Adding further to the complexity of the situation, the image of a high language is intimately bound up and contrasted in the minds of the Vincentians with a negative image of themselves as always talking bad as one dimension of *acting bad.* Although the system of social stratification that incorporated this self-stereotype as a rationale has had little day-to-day effect on the lives of contemporary peasants, it has remained part of their social equipment because the argument has been taken over by the older members of the extended families as a means of articulating the importance of authority. The *H* form has therefore come to be associated with the extended family ideals within the community. Heads of families are expected to teach children a few speeches in *H* and, if possible, arrange for education with a local man-of-words that gives their children productive competence in it. The entire public school system on the island has therefore oriented itself toward language teaching of this sort. With the weakening of the family system, a selective rejection of the *H* linguistic standard is emerging as well.

Even though it is tempting to accept the general Vincentian evaluation of the ideal of talking sensible and talking sweet at face value, this would give rise to certain conceptual problems, for actually there are two speaking ideals within the community, one relating to talking sweet, the other to talking broad. The ideals are situation- and occasion-specific, each involving different considerations of appropriateness. This is evident because there are two kinds of adept talker within the community who are admired for their abilities: those who can talk sweet and sensible on the proper occasions and those who can bring broad talk up to the level of performance art. In connection with the latter, it is notable that when a scandal song, written in creole, is judged especially successful because of its wit and economy of expression and its memorability, it may be praised as a sweet. Songs of this kind are appropriate on a number of ceremonial occasions, such as Carnival. It is for such reasons that it seems most consistent to regard *H* as the conscious speaking ideal and *L* as having an ideal dimension that is unconscious but nonetheless discernible and describable, for when it is exhibited in performance it is judged in the same terms as a good performance in *H*. Furthermore, by viewing the speech situation in terms of diglossia the internal dynamics of the community are more readily accounted for.

Perhaps the major reason talking broad is regarded as low is that it is associated in the minds of Vincentians with *getting on rude*. In other words, violations of the standards of appropriateness in regard to speaking behavior occur generally in broad talk, and there are, therefore, a number of associations of impulsive and antisocial activities that are attached to this type of speaking. Thus, talking sweet versus talking broad and talking sensible versus talking nonsense are paralleled by a further dichotomy commonly applied to behavior in general, though with speech once again as the primary referent. This is the distinction between *acting behave* (or *besaid*) and *getting on rude*. Acting behave means acting properly and decorously, knowing when to speak and when to be silent. Getting on rude refers to unruliness and especially to "making noise to annoy"; that is, loud, aggressive, self-assertive speech (cf. Reisman, 1974a).

These three sets of oppositions, then, serve as symbolic classifiers for the Vincentians, marking off broad contrasts between kinds of speech acts and at the same time providing the terms by which specific acts are judged. Not surprisingly, however, it is the kinds of behavior judged nonsensical, rude, or bad that elicit the greatest amount of comment on the part of the community. It is such behavior that most threatens the individuals involved and, by extension, the family and, in extreme cases, the community. This is reflected in the structure of the semantic field relating to speech acts, for there are many distinctions made in reference to nonsense acts, whereas none are made in connection with the sensible. There is, in fact, a folk taxonomy of speech acts within the domain of talking nonsense.

As in all taxonomies, the relationship between levels in an ascending direction is one of inclusion. As befits a taxonomy of acts, the taxa are labeled by verb constructions, either verb + object or verb + complement. All designate segregates of speech acts. It is noted that several of the terms operate on more

TABLE 1

*talking nonsense**

(any kind of broad talking, especially of the combative or quick-witted sort)

calling name					*getting on 'ignorant*	
(any kind of personal interaction)					(uninformed talk, making a fool of oneself)	
cursing (abusive use of someone's name)						
calling (out) name (using someone's name in a public way)	*giving fatigue* (making mock, giving rag)	*making comrness* (talking about particular individuals, including oneself)				
	(jocular use of someone's name)	*making comrness* (talking about others' business)	*making melée* (malign others, talk about, especially that leading to fights)			
			talking rugger business (broadcasting one's own business)			
	making vexation (making boderation, getting on 'rageous)	(loose talk leading to arguments)			*telling story* (discovered false talk)	*talking trupidness* (talking without order or logic)

*Adapted from Abrahams and Bauman, 1971

than one level of contrast: Conklin has noted that "phonemically identical (homonymous) lexemes may designate separate taxa of different ranges of generalization at successive levels." Conversely, in several cases "a single taxon may be labeled by phonemically distinct form" (1968, p. 424).

It is difficult to assess which types of talking nonsense receive the greatest amount of discussion. However, the acts one observes most commonly are in the realm of *calling name*. Outside of the family, the use of someone's Christian name in St. Vincent commonly indicates that one is at least conversant with that person, and probably that he is included in one's friendship network. Friendship in St. Vincent is a well-defined relationship that obtains only among people of the same sex and usually the same age. The closeness of the relationship, among males, young women, and girls at least, is signaled by the degree of familiarity of the name used; that is, whether the person referred to is called by his formal title (Mister _____), by his first name, or by his *pet name* (Jo-Jo). (*Nickname* is also used for a peer-group name, but meaning a designation not approved by the person so called.) Mature women tend to use formal names even with their closest friends when talking directly to them. In discussions of other women not present, it is permissible to use their girlhood names or nicknames to indicate the degree of friendship. But it is not considered calling name simply to use a person's appellation; the term is reserved for indecorous use of the name, such as using a first name or a nickname without first having established a friendship (this is regarded as boasting), or the use of the name in a disrespectful way.

There are two ways in which this may occur, one of which is also referred to as calling name or *calling out name*. In this sense, calling name is the practice of speaking another person's name in a loud voice; that is, shouting it out while inebriated or in some other disordered state, or calling out to the named person as a means of signaling recognition when the two parties are at a distance. Both of these are regarded as terribly rude by the community and are commonly answered by silence or by a sucking of the teeth.

These are rudenesses and examples of nonsense because one does not use a name in a totally public arena without some element of notoriety and unwanted attention and, therefore, potentially, of embarrassment, attaching to it. Using someone's name indicates friendship with him, yet to bring notoriety and embarrassment to a person is to dishonor him, something one would not wish to do to a friend.

It is worth noting that calling name is an act that occurs primarily between males—with the exception of the great arguers, the market women. Loudness results in unwanted attention and embarrassment. Some local women are known for the noise they make, but most women simply do not make the mistake of using names improperly. Men are not guilty of calling name with women unless cursing is going on.

Although calling name is regarded as a socially dangerous phenomenon, there is one form in which it is regarded as legitimate and permissible, if still not decorous: *giving fatigue, making mock,* or *giving rag.* Giving fatigue involves ridicule, the use of insulting names, and the jocular insinuation or accusation of certain kinds of deviant or tabooed behavior. Almost any kind of frowned-upon behavior may be used in giving fatigue, but never attributions of incest, sodomy, bestiality, inducing abortion, or blatant adultery. These are simply not joking matters.

The legitimacy of giving fatigue lies in that it may take place only between friends; if someone attempts to initiate it who is not regarded as a friend by the one to whom the fatigue is directed, a fight occurs, and the action is conceived of as a *molĕs'*, a libelous action for which the actor may be taken to court. In this regard, friendship among the Vincentians is a joking relationship. Indeed, one of the most frequently discussed attributes of friendship is that one may say anything to a friend and he will not take it amiss. Rather than disapproving of giving fatigue, the onlookers, especially the more indecorous among them, look forward to such performances.

Giving fatigue is a form of verbal performance to which certain community members are more inclined than others. These are the *sporty fellows* or *jokers,* who are known both for their predilection for *keeping company* (joining those kinds of gatherings in which giving fatigue is likely to take place) and for eliciting and entering into verbal performance whenever they are in public.

A less public way of calling name than giving fatigue is *making cŏmmess* as discussed in the preceding chapter. As noted there, making cŏmmess in its most general sense means simply talk about particular individuals. A distinction is then made between talking *nigger business,* which is talking about one's own problems, and making cŏmmess, which is discussing the affairs of others. (The word "gossip" is not used by the Vincentian peasants at all.) On another level, making cŏmmess in contrasted with *making melée.* The former designates talk about others that is not harmful to them and does not start fights; the latter refers to malicious gossip, talk calculated to stir up trouble and cause harm. Cŏmmess relationships are commonly between people of the same age and sex, but this is by no means a categorical rule.

The Vincentian peasant fears the threat of arguments, for it is on such occasions that one's name may be called to the greatest public notice. Calling name, cursing, and *making vextation* are all violations of privacy and therefore threats to one's identity and to the maintenance of social order. Vextation produces noise and strains social relationships and is thus regarded quite strongly as rude and nonsensical.

Even with this negative attitude toward them, however, arguments arise constantly. One of the most common remarks one hears about a person not present is "Me an' he [or she] ain' 'gree," meaning that the speaker and the subject have had a loud argument recently, one that has probably been regarded as a molĕs' and therefore wound up in the hands of the local constabulary. Moreover, such arguments, like giving fatigue, are regarded as great entertainments; whenever one occurs, it immediately draws a crowd of eager spectators, seeking both entertainment and a subject about which to make commess. The great interest in verbal battles and contests may be reflected in the number of synonyms for giving fatigue and making vexation; it is noteworthy that these are the only speech acts to receive this kind of lexical elaboration. Still, the same people who enjoy watching arguments and gossiping about them condemn the contentiousness of the participants, speaking of the trait as one of the worst habits of blacks.

Looking around at his neighbors' propensity for calling name and making vexation, as well as their apparent inability to speak well (in the sense of speaking Standard English), the Vincentian rationalizes this ubiquitous rudeness in terms of an innate lack of sense. In line with the other explanations for his own as well as his neighbors' departures from the standards of ideal behavior, he rationalizes this lack of sense in terms of innate racial traits: "We Negroes is a ignorant people." Ignorance is used to account for a wide range of behavior, but *getting on ignorant* refers to the specific range of acts that demonstrates in some kind of public arena that one does not have the requisite knowledge or understanding to pursue a discussion or an argument effectively. Getting on ignorant thus means making a fool of oneself by revealing one's ineffectiveness as a speaker.

There are two ways in which one may be so revealed, through a lack of veracity or a lack of logic. In the case of the former, the person so discovered is accused of *telling story*; in the latter, he is classed as a fool and accused of *talking trupidness*. Neither act is categorically bad; in certain performance situations, such as wakes or Carnival, this behavior is licensed and expected. Indeed, telling story is entirely proper, though still nonsense, in the recounting of a folk tale or a joke. Talking trupidness is expected not only from performers who take the role of fools during ceremonial entertainments, but also from persons who really are *trupidy*—that is, mentally defective, tongue-tied, or insane—and therefore expected to talk trupidness whenever they come into public places. Even such behavior may take on the display of a performance, especially in the rum shops. On one occasion, a tongue-tied man was asked to describe a movie he had seen; the result was a nonsensical, trupidy recounting of some of the dialogue, delivered with great good spirit and animation, for which he was rewarded with much laughter, applause, and a drink.

The range of semantic elaboration within the domain of talking nonsense indicates the recognition in Vincentian culture of a wide range of potentially disruptive and negatively valued speech behavior. At the same time, however, the very naming of these acts may itself function as a means of controlling them and the motives that give rise to them. To be able to recognize and name a social act is to be provided with a cushion against the shock of its occurrence, and with the means to indicate quite specifically the focus of one's disapproval (see Malinowski, 1935, pp. 233-235).

It should be made clear, however, that there is by no means a total derogation of the nonsense. Indeed, there seems a recognition on the part of the Vincentian that because these acts involve the most tendentious and potentially destructive use of words, they are the acts that may contain and release the greatest amount of social energy. This energy release is feared when it arises in a disordered and inappropriate frame of reference, and it must therefore be controlled by expressions of disfavor by the sensible and behaved members of the community. This same energy, however, may be controlled and channeled into performances that then become conventional and appropriate vehicles for creativity. Thus, acts and motives that are feared in everyday social intercourse become a source of pleasure in the more controlled context of the speech event.

CHAPTER SEVEN

Christmas and Carnival on St. Vincent

Rituals and festivals are related if only because they are both unusual but recurrent ceremonies or celebrations. Both involve a spatial-temporal sense of "removal," an establishment of a highly redundant set of behaviors giving witness to rigid rules for the occasion (even when the central rule is to break those of everyday life) and a psychological sense of separation usually referred to as the experience of liminality. Commonly the festival performance has been regarded as the opposite of the formal ritual in function, the latter permitting an intensification for the purposes of establishing or supporting the life process (in the passage of the year or the life of maturing individuals), the former enacting social discontinuity, acting as a "steam valve" for antisocial motives, which inevitably arise but might destroy the orderly life process (Gluckman, 1963; Leach, 1961; Turner, 1969).

I hope to show here that, at least in the Anglophonic West Indies, this steam valve approach is not sufficient to explain the manifestations of such revels and reversals. Rather, I want to demonstrate that this performance complex operates neither as an aesthetic alternative to life nor as a direct reflection of reality, but as a stylized rendering of some of the central expressive practices and moral concerns of the group. As Clifford Geertz points out in regard to Balinese cockfighting, such intense cultural displays are neither an imitation of some pattern of Balinese life nor a depiction of it, but rather "an *example* of it, carefully prepared" (Geertz, 1973, p. 451). In other words, I want to establish certain continuities of everyday activities and more intense acts and events, in terms of subjects, styles, and criteria of judgment.

There are competing values in many parts of Afro-America between the overt household-based *respectability* norms (associated with women and social maturity) and the more covert crossroads or street *reputation* values. West Indian ceremonial occasions reflect this distinction, embodying in their practices the values and ideal behaviors of one or the other competing systems.* Respectability canons revolve around family continuity, home, order, and tradition. In other words, they focus on those elements of life guaranteeing the continuation of the family as a viable economic and social unit. Within the West Indian peasant community, there is little doubt that the oldest woman in the household (except in the case of one very aged) is regarded as the proper keeper of the order of the family, and in her resides all of the powers attendant upon achieving and maintaining respectability. Men are regarded as potential intruders into this world of house and yard. They must be careful not to obtrude too greatly. They are expected to spend most of their time at work or pursuing friendships in male meeting places like the rum shops and the crossroads, the traditional places along the roads where cards and dominoes are played. While women are expected to maintain a multigenerational sense of family (and minimize friendships with peers), men must maintain their reputation by being good and active friends, especially to their peers.

These two worlds coexist in easy complementarity, conflicting with each other only in regard to the distribution of the men's resources or when a man insists on bringing crossroads behaviors into the world of the yard. In such cases, the canons of order and respectability are challenged. A woman may be judged in regard to her ability to control her men when they are in her yard.

This distinctions between worlds and values I found especially strongly stated in Richland Park, St. Vincent. This island in the (former) British Windwards shares many cultural and social characteristics with the other Anglophonic smaller islands, of course with some unique features. Their configuration of ceremonial performances, especially in the playing of both Christmas and Carnival is, for instance, very much like those of the other former British possessions in the southern end of this arc of islands. In the eastern Carribean, where there was little influence from the Catholic (i.e., French and Spanish) islands, Christmas was the traditional time of freedom and license for the slaves—so much so that their other major holiday, Easter, was often called "Pickininny Christmas." Thus, on islands like Jamaica, Nevis, St. Kitts, Antigua, and Barbados, the formal and the licentious type of ceremony was commingled in the observation of the Christmas season, though revelry certainly was the more important activity. In the more southern islands—most of which were at some time under French rule—Carnival is also played, thus creating the situation in which the motives of formality and decorousness can be attached

*Here I use Peter J. Wilson's distinction between female "respectability" and male "reputation" values, though it should be noted that the great majority of the performers in both kinds of ceremonies are men, thus modifying the sex-specific dimensions of his argument. For further development of this argument, see the following chapters, especially chapter ten.

to one celebration; "nonsense" and revelry, to the other. This is the situation encountered on St. Vincent.

Ceremonial life on St. Vincent conforms in a remarkable way to the division between the two life-styles and ideal systems. Indeed, it was the differences between public festival traditions and those of household ceremonies that first called my attention to the contrasting and often contradictory approaches to life. These insights were gathered in discussions on the differences between who *plays* (i.e., gets involved in) Christmas and Carnival. Repeatedly, I was told that only the *rude* play Carnival, for that is the Devil's holiday, whereas everyone may play Christmas, for that is God's son's birthday. But as these discussions proceeded, it became clear that the problem was much broader, for both occasions call for a great deal of road activity, but Christmas provides for an orderly invasion of the yard, where the seasonal performances of singing and speechmaking are carried out. Carnival must be kept to the road, however, because it is an overt and constant threat to the social order, and therefore to yard values. It is the time of the year when the rude ones are permitted the greatest amount of latitude.

These two festivals, observed during the same winter season (usually about a month and a half apart), are both times for a great deal of visiting and drinking. But there is a strong feeling that Christmas is a time of relative restraint when one reaffirms one's place in the community, while Carnival is a time when one loses one's identity through masking and other licentious activities. Christmas is regarded as a time for good behavior and high decorum, into which the mannerly can throw themselves. However, these same people are not likely to play Carnival, regarding it as a time of rudeness and *vextation.* Thus, only the most extreme fun-makers are attracted to playing Carnival; the participation of others, if at all, is by observation. Carrying out this distinction between the two, Carnival is properly played on the street, whereas Christmas performances are given in the yard; this is a physical differentiation of great symbolic importance to the Vincentian, for, as noted, the yard is the family place, the place of privacy, while the street is almost synonymous with sportiness, rudeness, dissension, and trouble.

The patterns of performances and their content underline this difference of approach to, and spirit of, the occasion. Christmas performances emphasize order, respect, and a sense of community; they subordinate elements of strife and display in favor of a formal, knowledgeable, harmonious, and devotional approach. The appropriate speaking code is oratorical *talking sweet.* Carnival is a licentious occasion in which the usual order of society is challenged through institutionalized rudeness and *boderation*; performances center on the entertainment potentials in assault, coercion, argument, and gaudy array. The occasion is one in which creole is stylized, being the most appropriate code for argument, gossip, and other such *nonsense* activities.

Performing groups are shared by the two festivals, especially the various musical ensembles. In keeping with the movement in the rest of the West

Indies, there are a growing number of steel bands that play for these occasions. The steel band, which developed on Trinidad, is made up of three sizes of instruments fashioned by hammering oil drums into certain segments so that the section plays a true tone when hit. These three sizes are bass (rhythm), tenor (harmony), and melody. Optional, but often found as rhythm instruments, are drum, cymbals, scrapers, triangles, or some other pieces of resonant metal, or *shock-shocks,* which are stones in gourds or tin cans.

Older musical groups are the *bum drum* and the string band. The former is comprised of a flute and two small and one large goatskin (trap) drums played with drumsticks. The number of members in the string bands fluctuates. The core is made up of a flute, guitars, and *cuatros* (which are similar to ukeleles). Optional are the rhythm instruments: a *baja* (a piece of large bamboo into which one hums bass notes), an *elbow* (a pipe played like a baja), a *scraper* (a serrated piece of metal—usually a tin can—that is made to vibrate by rubbing a stick or a metal rod over it), and a shock-shock (a maracca).

Each touring group of performers must include one person who makes contact with the audience, but his role is different for the two holidays. On Christmas the person is a speechmaker who presents himself and the group in the medium of inflated and highly decorous rhetoric. The group goes from yard to yard. While in the street they may play anything, but in the yard they must play music that is appropriate to the season—hymns and carols.

After the first piece is played, the speaker steps forward and directs his speech to the household members, whether they have come to the door or have remained inside. (If those inside like the speech, they may come out and ask that it be repeated.) The speech is, of course, in tune with the season, commonly referring to biblical accounts of the birth of Christ. But the emphasis of the speeches is upon the kind of elaborate diction, the "talking sweet," that is most appropriate for this decorous occasion. The speech begins with the recitation and ends with the address to the hosts. The following is an example of such a speech:

> Is showing you now the purity of the teaching of Zoroastrianism. Is not alone to be discovered, but a loftier conception of the attributes of the Divinity is observed there in the hope of a Messiah who would conclude with all the power to reform the world and establish a reign of universal peace.
>
> Pleasant good night to you, past meridian. We the serenading songsters now come to celebrate now the day of Christmas. With Christmas approaching every twelve month, every twenty-fifth of December, including seven day [or however many remain till the day]. Then with this we are look with decent action and behavior. But now turning to my most melodious songsters and songstresses I say, "Now songsters, sing me a song as Miriam sung and the last hymn over Egypt' dark sea; Moses have triumph', his people are free."

Quite often, the address emphasizes even more fully the necessity of maintaining *decorum* on such an occasion, and the way in which the *ban'ers* (members of the band) are able to do so.

Turning to my most melodious songsters and songstresses, I say "Sung me a song!" For when we come to conclude, we may gain B for Behavior, C for Credit, D for Deliberation, and A by our good talk to All.

One of the most notable features about Christmas serenading is that it presents a model occasion for mannerly behavior, one in which there is a demonstration of community cooperation and cohesion. It is the season in which the cooperative ideal of group life is brought into focus. Visiting during this season is governed not only by conviviality but great formality. This is the season when there is a great desire to *keep company* and to observe all of the amenities that ensure that everyone is comfortable. The serenading is considered the model of this visiting procedure, the musicians and speechmakers often referring to themselves as *visitors.*

The visitation is connected by the speechmakers with the Christmas season and its attendant atmosphere of good cheer and sharing; in some cases, the serenaders give this feeling by referring to themselves as those who went from inn to inn at the birth of Jesus, looking for the Holy Family so that they might give him gifts and sing his praises. Their speeches point this out by addressing their hosts:

> A pleasant good evening to the inn dwellers of this inn. We are the bright evening star now come to serenade you the Birth of Christ. Wish you to know that Christmas goes and comes once in every year, in every twelve months. And every twenty-fifth of December, day to date, leaving seven days. So with these few words I will not hesitate, not contemplate, but turn now to my most melodious ban'ers and say, "Now ban'ers, serenade with me while angels are rejoicing."

The essence of keeping company is sharing, especially of money and of food. This is an ideal that is widely practiced throughout the year, but is strongly reinforced at Christmas. Visits call for a conspicuous show of sharing, both in word and deed, for it is strongly felt that when others visit one's yard there is a natural desire to share what one has with them. As opposed to serenaders on other islands (as well as English-style wassailers), Vincentian serenaders neither demand admittance nor beg for money, food, or grog. As one Christmas speechmaker explained it, "While we visiting, it don't do right to ax for anyt'ing. For I have, I give you; you have, you give me—it all the same. But I don't ax."

Nowhere is the distinction between Christmas and Carnival more clear or far-reaching in its social ramifications than in this rejection of begging. Not only is this important within the Vincentian scheme because it is a rejection of a Christmas practice common on other West Indian islands like Nevis and Jamaica, but because it emphasizes that the sharing principle arises from the family rather than the friendship system. Among family one never asks for anything but expects to be given to freely; among friends one asks regularly, as it is one of the major functions of the friendship system to employ friends as resources. Significantly, during Carnival the friendship procedures are carried one step further, and something is not only asked but demanded of passers-by, the masking being used as a means of scaring or intimidating others. Coercion and contentiousness of a humorous sort are the marks of the Carnival performance. However, the keeping of Christmas relates to the birth of Christ, an event in which all people are brought together as one in his eyes and in which rivalry, vexation, and past quarrels must be forgotten.

Just as many provide such a vocally Christian rational for the playing of Christmas, so they find biblical reasons for rejecting Carnival. They focus upon the external condition, the masking, that allows license, lapse of decorum, and the playful character of the celebration. As one Christmas speechmaker expressed it:

> I don't play Carnival. Carnival it come from the crucifixion of Jesus. Through the crucifixion and at the same time in Gethsemane when he was in the garden of Gethsemane and he tell the disciples then, "Pray here while I go yonder." And it come in the form now as great drops of blood when he was praying in the garden. Drop from him. And when he come he meet the disciples, them sleeping. Then he said, "Why can you not watch with me one hour! Pray lest ye enter into temptation, for the spirit is willing indeed, but the flesh is sweet."
>
> And afterward he lef' and go back. And when he come he tell them, "Sleep and be loved. Sleep and take your rest." And at the same time, the people dem were coming. Some disguised their face with tubes and lantern [blackening] and all the way like that. And at the same time, though the moon were full, but the garden of Gethsemane were dark. And then afterwards they were come up and all the way like that. He axed the question, "Who are you looking for?" They said, "Jesus." He say, "I am he," and meanwhile he say, "I am he" they driven backward. And then they come again. And some they formerly put on faces and all the way like that. That is the direction [the reason] why they come now to say they are playing Carnival in that form why they disguise they face. Yes. So with that I don't reach.

Carnival is indeed the time of masking, of disguising one's usual role with a more dramatic one. Masking encourages a direct challenge to the usual order of life. Men may dress and act as women, women as men. Clothes may be worn backwards or upside-down. And men may be transformed into animals, devils, name-callers, or exalted personages—roles not permitted them at other times. Social and sexual restrictions that operate during the rest of the year are dropped because of the license of the season. Whereas Christmas underlines the aesthetic potential of decorum and community solidarity, Carnival explores the realms of aesthetic transport involved in sudden freedom from restraints.

As its focus of entertainment, Carnival exalts individual initiative and builds upon antagonism and egocentricity. Again, the central organization is the touring musical band, but the center of attraction is the one or two maskers who lead the group. Characteristically, the masker organizes the activity and enlists the services of the band. Others in the community decide to follow along with this group by *jumping up* to the music; the band members costume themselves, sometimes using the same theme as the lead figure, but more often simply by putting "lantern" on their faces, painting "rude" words and phrases on newly purchased white pants and T-shirts, wearing *washikongs* (tennis shoes), and fashioning unusual hats.

The most common traditional characters portrayed are the Devil, Wild Indian, Bold Robber, the humpbacked Bruise-ee-Back, a two-headed donkey, a monkey, and a bull. As leaders, they commonly are at the head of the dancers, but there are also performances in which one dances alone, is chastised by some other masker, and attacks members of the audience (especially children) to frighten them.

The group commonly has one song, written for the occasion by the leader, that it performs wherever it goes. In some cases, the song is an advertisement for the group, as in the following one, which was fashioned by the late Glasgow of Mesopotamia to be sung as an accompaniment to the high antics of his Monkey Band.

Only come, Glasgow, come,
Only come, Glasgow, come,
Only come, Glasgow, come,
He favor a monkey more than a man.

How long he come in this land,
How long he come in this land,
How long he come in this land,
He favor a monkey more than a man.

His costume was only broadly simian; he had a coxcomb on his head, a suit of red velvet, a mask with a long snout, and a long tail, which he picked up and tried to lash the onlookers with. He always organized a group that dressed up in the same red cloth, and he was followed by a string band.

A similar group is the Donkey Band. This group is organized around one person dressed as a donkey and another who follows and beats him. The person dressed as a donkey and another who follows and beats him. The *donkey man* goes berserk and scares the crowd. As the group comes to town they sing a song in which one man sings a line (usually the donkey man) and the others repeat it:

Clear de way, let de donkey break away
Clear de way, let de donkey break away
Clear de way, let de donkey break away
Let the donkey break away
On Carnival morning clear the way
Clear the way, let the donkey make his play.

The primary motive of all such groups as opposed to the equivalent Christmas players, is making money. Consequently, the scaring of members of the crowd is generally accompanied by a demand for money. The group has some kind of violent argument as part of its performance. This both amuses and scares the audience, attracting onlookers but preparing them to be coerced out of some coins. In the case of the Monkey, Donkey, or Bruise-ee-Back groups, the conflict is central to the performances, but with the *old mas'* calypso groups, the focus is on the song used to road-march; this has resulted in the addition of players who enact an argument of some sort, such as one between a cowboy and a gambler.

The songs composed by the *washovers* are like topical songs anywhere, concerned with local happenings and local characters. As opposed to the *hangings* (effigy burnings connected with extremely scandalous behavior, like acts of incest), in which the social offense dramatized is extreme, for Carnival slander songs almost anything can be singled out as a basis for a joke. For instance, a song was made by a Richland Park man and performed by a group from there that discussed a woman's faux pas when she first cooked a special kind of fish, the kitty; her mistake was not the disastrous fish tea, but telling others about it. The *tree-tree* mentioned is a fresh water fish that turns soaplike when boiled (and therefore is commonly eaten fried).

> Nanna go to town and she buy some Bequia kitty;
> Nanna go to town and she buy some Bequia kitty;
> And she put de kit' in de pot to cook
> And it turn tree-tree soup.
> "What I doing do fo' the man' dinner tonight
> In dis colony!"
> "You better run in de ship and buy penny saltfish,
> In dis colony."

Quite often it is a subject like this in which a person has talked too much or acted in an obviously foolish manner that provides the situation out of which a song arises. One fine washover composer, Selwyn Teshira of Cane's End, Mesopotamia, St. Vincent, described the circumstances that led to his writing a Carnival slander song one year:

> A gentleman who was playing in the very ban' with us maliciously went somewhere and interfered with a home. According, he used to be friendly with the woman and he make his mouth very fas' an' she set up a little drench for him. An' she have him properly scoured with a basin,* of whatever was in it. . . . An' e have a proper bat'. . . . He go an' talk an' tell a frien' an' de frien' come back and tell the woman an' she set up for 'im. . . . So after 'e get that bat', I never tell 'im not'in until we have three days before everything coming to a final, an' I placed in there. He vex but he have to be please' because every piece for hims to play Carnival.†

---

*Chamberpot.
†Through it he can make some money.

The song he composed on the subject was:

> (*Chorus*)
> Population, the married men start to moan
> Since the plaster Belly Baroan.*
> [*Repeat*]
> 1. This married man was so privileged
>   Miss Jubry take him to makes you rich.
>   (*Chorus*)
> 2. So he was afraid to tell us the truth
>   For the dope† was mixed-up with conjo-root.
>   (*Chorus*)
> 3. This married man was lookin' so nice and game
>   But de bowl of water dat brings him tame.
>   (*Chorus*)
> 4. De reason why se cas' de filt' in 'is face
>   He walk and tell de people 'e fin' a bump around' she wais'.
>   (*Chorus*)
> 5. So if you heard this song an' want to know dis man
>   'E was the only married man in dis ban'.

Not all of the old-time washover songs are scandal pieces, however. There are always a number of songs in praise, encomia to some political leader or a party, to a local product and its producer (especially if there is a competition run by that company that year), or to some person who just happens to be very popular. Here, for instance, is a song that was written about a popular teacher in Mesopotamia who had recently retired. The third stanza refers to the new teacher and, I was assured, was not really directed against him but was a way of praising Mr. Bledman all the more.

> Sweet teacher, Bledman
> Look 'e walk out wit' bat in han'
> And never been bowl' yet in all his days.‡
>
> When you reach up an' teach in grade
> He's as sharp as a razor blade
> An' when he put on a well-press' suit
> Our Big-John call him "the Highland Duke."
>
> The new teacher come with his rule
> An' 'e change up Morocco School,
> Look the children can hardly step
> With the junk of cardboard around their neck!

We have then in the parallel celebrations of Christmas and Carnival a good index of some of the important conflicts of motives and ideals within the

---

* A married man, here called Belly Baroan, becomes plastered (i.e., covered with feces).
† Urine and feces.
‡ *Bat* and *bowl* are cricket terms.

Vincentian peasant communities. By emphasizing group values through visitation, serenading, and speechmaking. Christmas is able to bring some of the community's oft-voiced ideals into the open. It does this by focusing on the birth of Jesus and using that occasion to emphasize a community of love in which internal contention is periodically done away with. With this ceremony one can see an enactment that emphasizes the cluster of attitudes most commonly regarded as ideals, even by the sporty element in the community—sharing, sensibility, concord, family and group harmony, personal and group decorum, a celebration of privacy—through the rest of the year by an opening of the yard to others and, by implication, putting an end to *cõmmess,* vextation, and nonsense. And it is the serenading bands that serve as models of the visitants, especially the attendant speechmakers, who both proclaim and exemplify the proper sense (through knowledge of scripture and therefore the nature of the Christmas occasion) of decorum.

Carnival brings the realities of life to the fore, emphasizing pleasure and freedom from social constraint and not only allowing license and highly aggressive behavior, but bringing it to high performance art. This is precisely the point of the two celebrations: they give an opportunity for those with conflicting attitudes and life-styles in the community to embody their motives in artistic, pleasurable performances. Attitudinal conflicts, which during other times of the year lead to all kinds of failures of communication, are brought into the open and dramatized, and, through embodiment and such performances, become pleasurable to the beholders as well as the participants. The performers of one are the audience of the other in many cases. In this way both achieve license to act out their motives, to use them creatively.

Carnival takes a characteristic of the community that is commonly regarded as negative—the tendency to play nonsense and *boderation*—and uses it for creative purposes. To view these simply as social control devices is to miss their focus and meaning. These seemingly antinormative performances permit the *sporty fellows* in the community who subscribe to these values in their everyday behaviors to bring them to the public's attention. In doing so, this does not mean that the public is just allowing the performers (or themselves, vicariously) to blow off this antisocial steam. License allows these performers to become, at least for a time, the models of behavior, permitting a second look at social restrictions and an alternative of behavior. The "noise" of these activities is a frontal attack on the household family-based ideals of socialization. The values embodied are simply extensions of the principles of reputation maintenance.

For the "steam-valve" theory to work, one would have to see two things: first, that these aggressive performances are regarded as ridiculous, clownish, and nonsensical by all; and second, that by allowing this blowing off of steam, these motives would be eliminated for the rest of the year, except in the activities of deviants and outcasts. But neither of these conditions is met. That these performances are not regarded as totally ridiculous and that they do not expend all this "antisocial" energy is shown in that these motives and actions are reenacted in interpersonal situations by many (indeed, most) members of the community at appropriate times and places throughout the rest of the year.

Why should we assume that a people portray themselves only in ideal terms in their stylized public enactments? Does not art explore the range of the crucial values and motives of a group? Again, to refer to Geertz's masterful analysis of ceremonial cockfighting in Bali:

> Oblique, cautious, subdued, controlled, masters of indirection and dissimulation . . . they [the Balinese] rarely face what they can turn away from, rarely resist what they can evade. But here [in the cockfight] they portray themselves as wild and murderous, manic explosions of instinctual cruelty. A powerful rendering of life as the Balinese most deeply do not want it (to adapt a phrase Frye has used of Gloucester's blinding) is set in the (social) context of a sample of it as they do in fact have it. . . . The slaughter in the cock ring is not a depiction of how things literally are among men, but, what is almost worse, of how, from a particular angle, they imaginatively are. . . . Jealousy is as much a part of Bali as poise, envy as grace, brutality as charm; but without the cockfight the Balinese would have a much less certain understanding of them, which is, presumably, why they value it so highly. (Geertz, 1973, p. 451)

To understand the values and focused motives of a group, we must be willing to look beyond its ideal presentation of itself and its members. Ideals, after all, can appear rigid when embodied in ceremony. Is there not the constant problem of maintaining a reservoir of energy as well as a sense of order within a group? Being sporty on St. Vincent, as engaging in cockfighting on Bali, reminds us of these energies and the pleasures attendant upon focusing them, even at the expense of the most valued ordering principles.

It therefore seems useful to see these festivities as enactments of the polarities of conflicting attitudes and alternative life-styles. Rather than viewing them as revelations of a single concept of social order, we can more profitably regard them as the traditional enactments of individuals in the community who recognize the focus of energies inherent in recurrent social tensions and conflicts of life-style, and who capitalize upon these energies by embodying these otherwise embarrassing nonhousehold nonsense behaviors in their licentious festival performances.

CHAPTER EIGHT

The Training of the Man-of-Words in Talking Sweet

Many groups socially value one variety of language more highly than another, generally because its members associate it with a segment of the community that has high status. With the development of writing and a complex and introspective literature, the language variety so employed often is accorded such high value because of the recorded nature of the medium and the need to be trained to read and write it. But such written varieties are not the only ones accorded value. Indeed, any speaking code used ceremoniously accumulates the sense of power inherent in the occasions of its use.

All of these remarks were either stated or implied in Charles Ferguson's description of "diglossia" (Ferguson, 1959). But as he there pointed out, though the native valuation leads to a desire to use the *high* (*H*) variety as the basis of formal education, there are those egalitarians who argue that the *low* (*L*), the conversational, variety is more appropriate:

> The proponents of L argue that some variety of L must be adopted because it is closer to the real thinking and feeling of the people; it eases the educational problem since people have already acquired a basic knowledge of it in early childhood; and it is a more effective instrument of communication at all levels. (Ferguson, 1959, p. 339)

The creolists studying Afro-American languages seem to have entered this controversy inadvertently. Betraying their egalitarian sympathies, they have ironically turned the tables on the proponents of *H*. They argue implicitly that because the creole *L* has demonstrable connections with the African past and is a systematic language system separate from European tongues—joined to them primarily by lexemic borrowings—that it is the code most worthy of study. Although extremely useful and informative, this exclusive focus on the elements of creole *L* varieties has prevented us from recognizing the full range of speaking competencies to be observed in Afro-American communities.

Although it is incontestable that there has been a consistent utilization of West African creole forms in the speech of those Afro-American communities in the British sphere of influence in the New World, so also there has been adaptive use of levels and varieties of Standard English throughout this area. Without describing these as well as the creole forms, we cannot meaningfully discuss the educational problems and potentialities of Afro-American students.

Much fruitful discussion of linguistic acculturation by creolists has put forth the notion of a continuum establishing a range of code variations from the most creolized (i.e., African) to the varieties very close (or identical) to Standard English or French. As David DeCamp describes it:

> The basic alternatives seem clear enough. A creole can continue indefinitely without substantial change, as Haitian French seems to be doing. It may become extinct, as Negerhollands and Gullah are doing. We say that it may further evolve into a "normal" language, though we are hard put to find documented examples of this, and even harder to define what we mean by a "non-creole" or "ex-creole" language. Finally, it may gradually merge with the corresponding standard language, as is happening in Jamaica. (DeCamp, 1971)

Even though this continuum permits us to fit virtually every New World linguistic code into it, as DeCamp himself points out, "we still have not done much to identify the sociolinguistic factors that determine which of these four alternative courses a creole will take." One reason is that we know very little about the symbolic importance attached to creole of Standard English, and therefore to the value-laden social uses to which they are put. We assume that because Standard English is spoken by those who are socially, politically, and technologically superordinate, universal desire for upward mobility guarantees linguistic acculturation toward Standard English much as we see culture being influenced by the power of economic and political factors. But this approach totally ignores the social forces that encourage the persistence of archaic creole features, even when they are stigmatized, both from forces within the Afro-American communities and from without.

Within Afro-American communities there is often a deep sense of linguistic diversity. One feature of this native linguistic consciousness is the native distinction between creole and Standard English. In the United States, for instance, there are various designations for varieties that are filled with creole features: *kid talk, country talk, talking bad,* and so forth. Similarly, in the West Indies, there is much discussion of creole as *talking broken* or *bad,* and oratorical Standard English as *talking sweet* or *getting on sensible.*

The diglossia model operates successfully here because it assumes that any given speaker within the community has a recognition of, and a variable competence (whether a productive or simply a receptive competence) in, the two kinds of talk. This chapter is an observer's report on a tradition of teaching a variety of speaking regarded as high and sharing many features of formal Standard English in one Afro-American enclave, St. Vincent. Beyond simply reporting a language configuration, I hope to demonstrate the social importance played by the high variety not for inducing commerce between the everyday speakers of Standard English, but as a status code within an Afro-American peasantry employing the variety for performances held totally for a community audience.

THE RUDE AND THE BEHAVED

As discussed in earlier chapters, on St. Vincent there is a good deal of talk about talk. Indeed, it appears that one is constantly being judged by the way in which one talks or acts, judgment being based upon a sense of congruence between expectations and realizations in the carrying out of social life.

There are two basic categories of behavior, the *rude* and the *behaved*; the former involves *playing the fool* or *talking nonsense,* the latter, *talking sensible.* A wide variety of acts and events are categorized and judged in terms of this basic dichotomy. Rudeness is not always judged as inappropriate by any means. Indeed, there are certain ceremonial occasions (like Carnival and wakes) in which it is regarded as appropriate and is encouraged. In everyday behavior, however, rudeness and nonsense are responded to as inappropriate, although expected nonetheless, especially of young men. *Being behave'* is often equated with *talking sweet* (speaking close to Standard English) and rudeness with *talking broad*; thus there is a linguistic dimension to this evaluative procedure. Furthermore, talking sweet has come to be identified not so much with the Euro-American world as with peasant values regarding the importance of continuity, order, and mutual respect. In contrast, *talking bad* is identified with a man's life away from home with his friends. The two varieties are recognized as distinct, then, as part of the native cognizance of the social dichotomy between female and male, the worlds of the household and the crossroads.

This identification of language variety with a social dichotomy does not mean that women always speak sweetly or that men always talk bad. These varieties are associated with the value systems of the two groups and do come into conflict occasionally. But most important for our purposes, the sweet varieties are associated with ceremonies that celebrate household values, while talking broad is stylized for licentious performances.

As part of the training in household values, one of the responsibilities of the head of the household is to assure that each of its younger members develops some competence in learning to eloquently orate. But this cannot always be done by a household member. More characteristically, just as there used to be elegant letter writers to whom one could go for such a service, especially during courtship, there are those who are renowned in the community (often schoolteachers) for their abilities in commanding this eloquence code who give lessons to children sent to them.

There are different speechmaking occasions involving different degrees of difficulty in the attainment of oratorical skills. Naturally, the more elaborate the skill the young person has to exhibit, the greater the chance that he or she will be sent to one of these women- or men-of-words. There are essentially two types of speechmaking occasion in which talking sweet is called for: household ceremonies such as *wedding fêtes,* in which everyone is expected to make a speech or sing a song; and festival ceremonies such as Christmas or Carnival masquerading, the school concert, or tea meeting, in which the more highly trained young people are given a chance to display their eloquence. Of course, the latter occasions call for a speechmaking apprenticeship considerably more involved than the former; and it is on these occasions that the man-of-words is called on to teach.

Paralleling these two levels of speechmaking difficulty, there are two kinds of ceremony, those that are connected with rites of passage and those that arise during calendrical rites. The former are strongly associated with the house and yard, continuity and the maintenance of the family and household system; the latter gravitate in the opposite direction, toward the acting out of licentious and antisocial motives at the crossroads or other places of public commerce.

It is in the household ceremonies that brief speeches occur, ones that nearly everyone in the group is expected to have mastered at some time while growing up. The calendrical festivals are commonly events in which only the most eloquent and inventive performers hold forth, but even here the performances gravitate away from speaking events toward action-oriented ones like dancing, stilt-walking, acrobatics, mock wars, and various performances that bring the audience's focus on the brilliant costuming.

There are intermediate types of activities, however, calendrical events that are either carried out in yards along the road, or in buildings other than the home. These events, which are more public than the licentious festivals but more restricted than the festival, are those in which the great oratorical eloquence traditions flourish. Included here is the Christmas serenading common throughout the English-speaking West Indies, in which songs alternate with praise orations given by the man-of-words, which are included in the performing group especially for that purpose. Here too are the acting groups, the Carnival play mas' troupes or the Christmas mumming groups who play scenes from Shakespeare, *Pilgrim's Progress,* or the St. George and the Turk play (Abrahams, 1964a, 1968, 1968a, 1971). And here also are the tea meeting orators, the fledgling men-of-words who come together to test their eloquent skills in competition with one another and with the rudeness and nonsense of the audience.

Household ceremonies utilize eloquence traditions that equate oratorical and elaborate speechmaking abilities with the continuing order and respectability of the idealized family. By discussing the virtues of family order, responsibility and continuity, this variety of talk comes to be identified with the canons of respect and family maintenance. In asking each person there to make a *contribution* to the sweet proceedings, a declaration is called for in favor of the values appropriate to the household setting as well as the occasion.

By contrast, licentious display occasions employ an emphatically creole, broken manner of expression—talking broad presented dramatically. This, when coupled with the stylized and encouraged rudeness of such performances, indicates that this most creole of Vincentian codes is associated with the antisocial, with the motive of challenge to respectable values.

THE CHAIRMAN'S ROLE

On St. Vincent the organizing idea of the tea meeting is not only to present the most important cultural information (*facts*) about the Gospels or Emancipation in oratorical form, but also to juxtapose the orators against the *rude boys* or *pit boys,* each attempting to confuse the others. Thus, competitive speaking is the impelling motive of the tea meeting. As one chairman, Charles Jack, explains it:

> The pit boys and all that nonsense, that forms part of the enjoyment, the entertainment. Everybody there have their time. You have a time for the chairman, you have a time for the orator, you have a time to say poems and rags and so on. And you have a time to rap, you have a time to get refreshment. You have a time for everything.*

Although Mr. Jack here sets forth the contesting elements in terms of each having its time, the forces constantly contend with one another. Those on the stage, the chairman, choir and orators, must constantly contend for the audience's attention with the rude boys who attempt to seize the limelight and confuse the performers. As Mr. Jack points out, the primary tactics are the pit boys' rapping—banging sticks on the benches and the backs of chairs while chanting, usually for refreshments—and the ragging, rhymes shouted by audience members making fun of an orator's speaking powers, through a curse or a boast. The speaker must learn how to respond appropriately—with a countering rhyme or jest, or simply by proceeding strongly. But the contest motive and the attempt to confuse through the use of rudeness and nonsense in ragging is evident throughout.

> The rag will be coming from the others who want to confuse you. I'll tell you the whole thing—it is that you are going on the platform and when someone starts ragging you, now, if you're not one who has very good memory, you're likely to

---

*This and the following are quotations from interviews held with the principal chairmen-teachers on the island, recorded in August 1968.

forget what you had to say. When you're going on the platform and you begin saying your speech, now you're burst. They could mock you and that is the purpose, the main objective of these rhymes. (Charles Jack)

Both the orators and those *making mock,* then, attempt to confuse the other and it is this contest of confusion that provides the major focus of interest, but the orator must confuse through his command of facts and his ability to keep cool and be sensible, while those ragging operate with the strategy of licensed nonsense and rudeness.

Although the orator has always played an important role in the tea meeting, he has become more central to the ceremony within the last twenty-five or thirty years. Before that time, the major focus of the evening was the chairmen's speeches; they were the reference figures for the orators, the ones who not only trained them but who they aspired to emulate and eventually outspeak. But recently the desirability of learning to speak well has lessened somewhat and thus incentives have had to be provided by the tea meeting entrepreneurs to get the scholars to commit themselves to the ordeal. Thus the chairmen serve as much to bolster the confidence of the scholars as to exhibit their abilities.

> ... those days, the days when I started, the chairman and vice-chairman, secretary had to do a lot of talking, because there was no prize meeting in those days. But since we have a prize meeting we depend [more] on the judges, because you can say we as chairman, vice-chairman and secretary, we can say as much as we like, but the prizes for the children; orators and oratoresses depend upon the judges for the morning [when the prizes are announced]. We have only to congratulate them. Every three persons that speak, boys or girls, the chairman will congratulate such a person . . . and explain to the audience what the children are speaking about. (Clive Richardson)

There has been a shift in the focus of the proceedings, then, in an attempt to keep the young's interest in talking sweet, in speechmaking. This is, of course, one battle in the war to maintain the family system and household values of the past. For this reason, parents continue to encourage their children, if they exhibit speaking talent, to learn the tea meeting techniques and to enter into competition. Parents encourage their children by entering into an agreement with a man of proven oratorical abilities (usually a chairman) to teach speeches to them. They usually pay him roughly the equivalent of a week's wages.

The teachers conceive of this apprenticeship as a school or college for orators or scholars. They teach by meeting with the entire class (generally five to ten students) about a month before the scheduled tea meeting. Usually these sessions are held on Sundays, and the students dress in church clothes, as they will at the meeting. At that point the teachers have written out speeches, lessons, for each, which they read aloud. They also discuss—in terms of the theory of presentational principles—how to stand, speak loudly and clearly, handle the mockery of the audience, make counter jokes, appropriately flatter the judges, and so on. They ask the student orators to read their speeches aloud, acting on the principles discussed. They judge and comment along the way, correcting pronunciation, enunciation, misplaced emphases, and rhythm. In other words, they are charged with the task of teaching not only speeches but also the proper manner of speechmaking, especially in regard to the features that the judges will take into consideration. The criteria of judgment are primarily the manner of delivery, the fluency of speaking, and, perhaps most important, the way in which the scholar keeps himself composed and thus is able to manipulate the audience more effectively.

> The judges give a lot according to how the boy and girl are speaking, how they ascend or descend. He must know how to descend, how to lower your voice, and all that comes in when the judges are judging. [They are concerned] not only in the oration alone but how the boy or the girl go about herself on the platform. (Clive Richardson)

The students are then expected to take the lesson home and commit it to memory within the next two weeks. Again they meet on a Sunday, at which time they perform for the teacher, who makes further comments on their delivery. Usually, at least two and sometimes three sessions of this sort are held, but not always with all of the students present. A student may come to the teacher's house in the evening if he needs special help.

At the end of the schooling, just before the meeting, the teacher generally goes to the student's home to hear the speech and to make comments upon it in front of his parents. "I'll call to their mother or father. They will hear their children's conversation. Any mistakes, I try to correct them" (Ledly Jackson).

This process has recently changed because of the growing literacy of the population. In the past, children were taught their lessons by repetition; in some ways, those days are regarded as more fulfilling for the teachers, because they had a larger part in the training program.

> In some years, if I can remember, I tell you, I carry from here seven—between girls and boys—seven, from here to Kingstown [the capital of St. Vincent, where the meeting was held]. There were seven prizes and carried the whole seven here. And the girl that won the first best prize, I told the judges next morning, "Show her a book and I bet she doesn't know it." And they did and she doesn't know it. They showed it to her and she could never read the alphabet, nothing at all. Those that could not write, you see, I just repeat it over for them and they learn it or I use the strap to you. . . . My children, they must know me victorious that night [of the meeting]. If not, your judges have trouble with me. (Ledly Jackson)

Teachers are thus deeply involved in the outcome of the proceedings, viewing the meeting as a contest of wits, a war of words.

> 'Tis said, "There'll be no peace until the battle is ended and the man who'll be victorious will wear the crown." Supposing we had just one prize. I have my

speakers, and elsewhere you have yours. You would like to see that speaker carry home the prize and what do you think I would like? Well, how can we have peace? (Ledly Jackson)

A teacher gathers a following, especially if his scholars win with any regularity. A good student often comes back year after year to learn new speeches. However, as long as the orator continues to learn the speeches as they are written out, he has no chance of ascending to the place of chairman. It is the speech's underlying structure that must be recognized, and it is the willingness to learn to substitute different content into the structural slots, thus learning to improvise the orations, that enables the young man (or, in at least one case, young woman) to outspeak a chairman and to oust him from his position. As may be imagined, this usurpation rarely occurs, but each chairman has a personal legend (often performed by him in informal gatherings) in which he recounts the occasion on which he ascended to the chairmanship.

The training of the man of words in talking sweet for tea meeting, as with any other involved and improvised verbal form, involves teaching him a repertoire of clichés and commonplaces, or "formulas," as the followers of Parry-Lord's methodology call them (Lord, 1960). At the beginning of the training, these nonmetrical formulaic devices are embodied in the set speech written out by the teacher as a lesson. As the orator progresses, however, he begins to recognize that certain kinds of clichés are appropriate to certain parts of the speech and that he may use substitution if he cares to. It is when he has learned a large number of these and has developed the ability to improvise (perhaps either making up or developing from books some runs of his own) that he begins to think of challenging the chairman.

There are essentially three sections in the oration: the *address,* the *speech* (also called the *topic* or *doctrine* of the body of the speech), and the *joke.* The speech is the central portion and takes the greatest amount of time. The judges are primarily concerned with this section because this is where the demonstration of knowledge, of talking sensibly and factually, arises. In fact, the younger orators are taught only this section and a very brief, one-line joke, for if they do nothing else, they must demonstrate the wisdom of their teachers.

The first section, then, the address, is the optional one, but it is also the one that, when fully developed, develops the skills that allow one to become chairman, for it involves the same kind of elaborate compliments and maca- ronic diction that the chairman must demonstrate. The major focus of the address is the ritual compliment, which may be addressed to the chairmen, the judges, the choir leader (*Mr. Presenter*), or to members of the audience.

> Pleasant evening to these lovely ladies, also to these honorable gentlemen, ad- mitting Mr. Presenter and his choir. Charming ladies. Mr. Chairman, sir, whilst I was sitting in yonder corner, gazing on these *quorum nobis* young ladies with their silver laces and magnificent brooches, they were as bright as the wonderful star that led the wise men from the east into Bethlehem. Charming ladies!! [He then bows.]

This address, which was made by someone we might call an intermediate scholar, is comparatively bare of the eloquent flourishes that characterize the addresses of the accomplished orator.

> Mr. Chairman, judges, ladies and gentlemen, I feel totally ineducate to expiate upon a question so momentously to ourselves. It would be happy and necessary for Africa and the East, for I will be able to express myself before thee. And it is with privilege, hearing my name being called, I stand before you on this rostrum. Chairmen, ladies, and gentlemen, the grandeur of this meeting fills my mind with joy, unremitting felicity and, like Alexander the Great when he having manifest his vicinity at Alexandria and thus explain in the language Athenian, *careto claret primus disjecta membera* of the festivity. But let us please to remember that your Demosthenes *astronema* is here, whose intellectual faculty knows no bounds. Seated in the accidental corner of your rostrum, chairmen, listening to the copious *andoy op dos artac canum nobis,* so it is with concordial *crescentenana felices maniam que dices que quaniam, pacito el picallo gabito quanto.** I have the privilege of arising before this rostrum to give my conversation. As in my lover's lap lying [much laughter], hearing, hearing my name so widely called by your secretary who writes *carenti calemor.* And so it is with great *viventi, due viventi, duos levitii,* that I have arisen to vindicate my call, and to let the vindicators of my evincitation be known. (Ledly Jackson)

The address and the joke, which serve as framing elements for the speech, rely on a combination of erudition and humor; both are presented in as dramatically elaborated a manner as possible (as is made clear by the precise enunciation by the most successful orators at these points). But the hyperbole of the address is commonly directed toward others, while that of the joke takes on a boasting form. One of the continuing features of the speech is the heightening of dramatic effect at the end of a passage by the statement "Tracing on a little further," or the question "Mr. Chairman, must I proceed?" The concluding joke also begins with this question and always turns on some absurd reason why the orator must not continue because of the dire calamities that would ensue:

> No, I will not, for if I continue these beautiful young ladies will fall on me just like the Falls of Niagara. No, if I go on I will break down the stage, leaving none for the common orators. Under these circumstances, I will not continue, but I will take my congratulations, for I am an orator.

> Once my enemy did attempt to run
> But shot and powder has recalled them back to me.
> But if these beasts had dared to run,
> I'll bring them back with machine gun.
> So adieu.

---

*Reasonably accurate orthography is difficult here because the orator begins to alternate between Latin and Spanish allusions.

But, as mentioned, the major portion of the oration is the speech. This is always a direct quotation from a book (or books) chosen because its content is appropriate to the season. This may mean, from the Euro-American perspective, that a passage seems to begin in mid-argument:

> Mr. Chairman, sir, my doctrine I will not inform you of is about Emancipation [Emancipation, thank you.*] Ladies and gentlemen, but while Mr. Clarkson formed a rich reward for his past labors, in the success which crowned his efforts, his triumph animated him for his new exertions. On the month he found himself elevated, he saw the horizon widen, and bright were his hopes for the future. When he said, "But independently of the quantity of physical suffering innumerable abuse to vice in more than a quarter of the globe."
> Ladies and gentlemen. We have reasons to consider, as like you to permit. Mr. Chairman, sir, we have this great probability that Africa is now free from the vicious and the barbarous effect of this traffic may be in a better state to comprehend and receive the sublime truths of the Christian religion. [Fact, Fact†]

The ideal of the sweet-talk man-of-words, whether an orator or a chairman, is to go *higher* than the other speakers; this means not only to ascend the heights of rhetorical inventiveness but to speak long and copiously. Thus the first two of the three sections grow by the addition of compliments and greater portions of memorized text. When this occurs, it becomes necessary to break these sections into smaller units, giving clear enunciation to the beginning of the new unit. This is done generally in the address by having a formulaic series of comparisons with great men, and in the speech by beginning each section with a renewed address or with the addition of the call for the question of whether the speaker will proceed. Here is, as an example, a speech given by an advanced student:

> *Address*
> Mr. Chairman, fellow citizens, ladies and gentlemen, including these ceremonial judges. Admitting Mr. Presenter and choir. Wishing the audience a happy and joyful evening.
> Mr Presenter, sir, while listening to yourself and choir, I think it was Mr. Tennyson's choir singing in the St. Paul's Cathedral. Then sir, to whom must I compare you? I must compare you to the great man George Fredrick Handel, now, the German composer. You are greater. I must now compare you to Admiral Collingwood, Lord Nelson's second in command at Trafalgar. He was born in 1750. He completed his excellence of Cape St. Vincent in 1797. As for you, Mr. Chairman, it is in island spread that you are a biblical and classical presiding officer. Then sir, to whom must I compare you? I must now compare you to that great man John Ephilopótus, who reckon the first King Syria after Alexander the Great. [Thank you.]

---

*An audience interjection.

†This audience interjection is not only an approving continuative, but an indication to the judges that "truth" has been given voice and should be borne in mind in the judging.

Speech
Mr. Chairman, ladies and gentlemen. I dare not close this chapter without repeating what I have said on this occasion. Those who fought for the freedom of their slaves performed their duty heroically, while but their duties still remained for those so early.

Your honor the judge, you know in the economy of God, there is one standard pathway for these races, by beginning at the bottom and gradually climbing to the highest possibilities of his nature. He will send in the years to come, the help, the guidance, the encouragement that the strong convey to the weak.

Ladies and gentlemen, may I proceed? [Proceed.] Mr. Chairman sir, must I continue? [Continue.] My evening doctrine is about emancipation. Ladies and gentlemen, in chapter fifteen, page 179, "Freedom Declared in Antigua in 1834, in Jamaica in 1838." The Negroes continued most orderly, oppressive measure of some planters. The gradual improvement of the freed men. The committee of the Antigua Legislature reported: "We do not, we confess, discover any sufficient reason in the island, why an honorous and strict emancipation should not answer as well in 1834, as in 1838 or 1840." The consequence of this report was such that this emancipation was there proclaimed without the intervention of the mistaken system of apprenticeship.

Chairmen, ladies. Though that system was proposed as a precautionary step it was certainly grounded on many ignorant and imaginary fears of the Negro character which was supposed to the people in Antigua to a bold and most successful experiment.

Joke
Mr. Chairman, sir, must I continue? [Continue.] No, I will not for there is someone else behind whose head's hot, whose heart swelling, just as a rosebud swell and burst out in the month of May listening for the voice of his sweetheart.

As mentioned, the teacher's task goes beyond simply teaching the speeches. Fluency, diction, and, most important, audience command are emphasized. The student orators are taught that they must tread the very fine line between confusing (*amazing*) the audience by using large words and leading them into that special kind of active receptiveness characteristic of Afro-American performances, and confusing them too much and thus losing their interest.

> According to how high is your language, they [the audience] may not understand it. . . . Of course, you'll be talking to a mixed audience, some more educated than you, like the judges, and some less. And in that mixed audience, if you go too high, some couldn't be able to understand you; if you go too low, some will underestimate you. So you have to meet all the sections of your audience. (Charles Jack)

The orator must learn as well how to handle a mistake in his speechmaking:

> If you're talking along, and, for example, you make a mistake, rather than repeating yourself so that those who know will understand that you have made an error, give a joke right there. Or else, turn to the chairman, "Mr. Chairman, must I continue?" and so on. "Your honor, the judges, must I ejaculate?" Well they'll

> answer you and say, "Well, ejaculate" or "Continue," as the case may be. And it
> give you time to pick up. You must be able to do that at intervals. . . . Or you
> might say, "Look, well, I'm going to recite a little poem" and that might work.
> (Charles Jack)

The important feature, stressed again and again in the professorial teachings,
is mental and oral agility:

> The moment decides and you have to be a fast thinker. And when you are in
> control, you must be able to know to think fast, what to do, how to do it, so that
> nobody vexed with you. And you get your call back [assent from the chairmen or
> the judges to proceed]. If they're vexed with you, you know, they'll start to heckle
> you. And when you start getting heckling, well you know the confusion. And
> when they confuse you, you know, that will mean the end of the speaking.
> (Charles Jack)

But the answer for confusion may simply be inaction and silence, for this too
means maintaining one's sense of the cool.

> The boys of Richland Park, they would rhyme the boys at Evesham [two villages
> in the Mesopotamian Valley] . . . when they are ascending the platform. . . . They
> are trying to confuse them. They can sometimes make a joke back or sometimes
> just stand upon the platform for two or three minutes. When the rhyming is
> finished, then they can get to themselves . . . and they can carry on. (Clive
> Richardson)

That confusion and contest rule this occasion is important in order to
understand why this ceremony has developed. This uproarious meeting differs
from similar occasions for eloquence in European and Euro-American cultures
because of the various attempts made to "confuse." The battle of wits is so
organized because the Vincentian would see little value in the demonstration
of the coolness (or lack of confusion) of the orator if it were not tested, contested, surrounded by a heated-up audience. Although the speeches are calculated to obtain the attention of the audience, attention does not mean quiet.
Indeed, if the speaker is not able to obtain the "hot" responses of laughter,
rapping, clapping and continuative words (like "fact, fact" or "proceed"), he
regards his performance as a failure. And well he must, because the alternatives to this guided response are louder noises, generally of a derisive nature.
Thus, learning to talk sweet is calculated not just to show an ability to speak a
code effectively; far more important, it provides an occasion to perform,
edify, entertain, and demonstrate, through the aesthetic of the cool, the
highest values of the group. By this, the group and the performing individuals
achieve a sense of fulfillment—the group because it has come together and
celebrated its overt values; the individual because his abilities have been
utilized and tested in a manner that allows him to achieve status.

SOME IMPLICATIONS

The existence of traditions of this sort does not, of course, contradict the creole language hypothesis; but it does force a reconsideration of the direction traveled recently by those who have been testing this hypothesis on only phonological and morphological grounds. It is clear, however, that even on these levels the data being elicited are not totally representative of the speaking range of anglophonic Afro-Americans. To be sure, the variety of language that young black children in the United States carry into the classroom contains a higher incidence of "archaic" creole features; therefore, if we are to develop teaching tools for helping these children, the analyst must bear these data in mind in determining productive and receptive competence. As David Dalby pointed out in reference to this question:

> Although some educationalists now feel that Afro-American languages and their related European forms should be regarded as "foreign" languages, vis-a-vis each other, it is quite clear to everyone—including their speakers—that they form part of the same linguistic continuum. We are in fact faced with a situation where social and linguistic forces are acting on this continuum in opposite directions. In one direction, we have what might be called "centrifugal factors," drawing the subsidiary foci of black and white idiolects further apart . . . and in the opposing direction we have . . . "centripetal factors," drawing these subsidiary foci more closely together. One result of these opposing factors has been the development of large numbers of . . . idiolects equipped to operate at two or more points along the continuum, according to the social environment in which they are speaking. (Dalby, 1970)

The existence of traditions such as the development of tea meeting orators indicates that there are formal and institutional considerations that attempt to guarantee that there are those in the community who do indeed have a wider range of codes, some closer to Standard English. These varieties are not developed for the purpose of demonstrating upward mobility or an intent to communicate with Euro-Americans. Rather, at least in regard to the tea meeting variety, the code is used almost solely on in-group ceremonial occasions, and it reflects a continuing adherence to traditional African uses and patterns of eloquence. Just how widespread such traditions are and how deeply they affect linguistic performance in other less ceremonial situations are matters that certainly call for study.

CHAPTER NINE

Folklore and Communication on St. Vincent

Folklore obviously communicates. Yet we certainly want to make a distinction between folklore and other kinds of communication. This we commonly do by emphasizing the noncasual aspects of folkloric performances, the ways in which formal and self-conscious performative features of the communicative behavior are so foregrounded that the performer and audience are aware that a specially stylized communication is under way (Ben-Amos, 1970).

In spite of the folklorists' recognition that folklore is a stylization of communicative devices, there has been little interest, evinced by folklorists, in describing the features common to casual communications and folkloric performances within individual communities. This failure of concern occurs almost certainly because the questions addressed in the past by folklorists—questions of provenience, dissemination, generic classification, and description of items of traditional performance—have been directed away from an analysis of the actual performances of these texts. However, recent writings have made theoretical departures toward such descriptive concerns, leading many folklorists (especially in the United States) to develop a performance-centered approach to folkloristics (Paredes and Bauman, 1971; Ben-Amos, 1976). In making these forays, folklorists have been much stimulated by approaches developed in other disciplines concerned with communication: rhetorical theory, sociolinguistics, communication theory, and the ethnography of speaking behaviors. (See especially Hymes, 1971.) But folklorists have traditionally been concerned with the stylistics of their materials, and it is out of this background that they have generated their own perspectives. Exploring the structure of the items of performance and, more recently, the relationship of these items to the situation of their performance, the performance-centered folklorist has been ascertaining the place of creative and stylized communications in the life of specific groups. (See Bauman, 1978, and Toelken, 1979, for reviews of this literature.) It is just one more step in this already established direction to relate everyday communications to the more occasional and artificial ones with which folklorists have concerned themselves in the past.

Casual and noncasual communications might be related in a number of ways. One could demonstrate the relationships between the messages of the two and further relate these to the stated ideals of the community. Or one could fruitfully focus on the formal characteristics of the casual discourse and relate these features to the more stylized characteristics of the performance forms. A third alternative—the one that is pursued in this chapter—is to establish relationships between the structure of the participants' interaction in everyday communication events and more special, planned expressive events.

I shall describe the everyday speaking behaviors in one Afro-American peasant community, Richland Park, St. Vincent. I shall do this by describing some microbehavioral communicative patterns nonverbalized by Vincentians, but these are related to the expressive acts and events that are named and discussed in this community. In other words, the discussion of the speaking patterns of expectation is, as often as possible, given from the voiced perspective of the Vincentian, using his own terms designating social types (those distinguished by their presentational styles) and his named acts and events. The observed patterns are then compared with the more overt stylized communications of ceremonial and play forms—though the greater part of the discussion is given to the casual discourse patterns. Establishing this continuity between the levels of communication is facilitated because the same terms of description and criteria of judgment are used for all levels by Vincentians.

The Vincentian communication pattern is dominated by an overlap of voices and other "presence" indicators; this overlap signals a kind of interlocking between the participants as active members of the performance. Each person in the performance environment is part of—and yet playing apart from—the focal interaction. The result is a richly textured, vibrating interchange, but one that might be regarded as noisy and chaotic by Western norms. Furthermore, most Vincentian interactions, both spontaneous and planned, are open-ended and egalitarian in their patterning; that is, each person in the environment is expected to participate in at least a supportive way, and procedures commonly exist so that the role of local performer is passed from person to person. Yet this is not accomplished through the Western pattern of "I talk, you listen; you talk, I listen," in which markers designate beginning, middle, and end. Rather than looking on communication as calling for the passing on of a message within a clearly defined presentational unit, the Vincentian seeks to emphasize interpersonal relationships established through talk, and information-passing is subordinated to a sense of celebration in coming together for purposes of simply pursuing friendships. This becomes clear as we survey the range of Vincentian speaking roles and communication events.

For the most part, speaking is associated with men, and most of the social types and speech acts and events are regarded as appropriately male activity. This is not to say that women are not expected to talk, but engaging in the kinds of *nonsense* behavior characteristic of public communicative interactions attacks the fabric of female respectability canons in many ways. Furthermore, it is assumed that women primarily speak in their yards and houses and therefore engage in the kind of two-person interactions of *cŏmmess*. Consequently, most of the terms of discussion about talk refer to male types and activities.

Males tend to be typed in terms of how they interact with others in the community. One major feature of designation is how effectively a man handles male-female relationships. Thus, a man may be designated *wild* (one who has a number of women), *macco man* (a cuckold), or *auntie man* (one who is too closely attached to a woman). But, more important for our present purposes, men are classified in terms of how effectively they interact and perform with other men, for male canons of reputation depend upon how well a man establishes and maintains his network of friends. The range of types runs from the *garden man,* who does not successfully maintain his contacts, to the *fool,* who does, but ineffectively through inappropriate performance. Inappropriateness in such a case means anything from misplacing friendship (especially calling someone's name before the friendship is established) to *making boderation* (starting fights). The person who successfully establishes a wide range of friendships because of his ability to perform is a *sporty fellow.* As in other Afro-American communities, status is conferred for speaking ability. The sporty fellow is one so recognized; his presence means there is a constant possibility that casual talk will become more stylized—and more entertaining—performance.

Paralleling the distinctions between these male social types are speech acts that range from the silence of the *selfish* (shy) garden man, who keeps to himself, to the overabundant rude nonsense of the fool, who makes "noise to annoy." It is the sporty fellow who is capable of maintaining a sense of control over the proceedings. Given the constant threat of nonsense performance getting out of hand, it is such *rudeness* that receives the greatest amount of discussion and the largest number of terms designating such speaking activity. But to define Vincentian talk solely in terms of any of these unusual performances would be misleading. Rather, it is more appropriate to recognize that all of these, including the performances of the sporty fellow, are extensions and disruptions of the usual male speaking activity, the crossroads group talking *old talk* or *blagging,* and the kind of casual discourse carried on while *liming*—sitting or standing around in groups.

Artful word use confers on sporty fellows a potential social power that is regarded with admiration and fear, an ambivalence that accompanies all licentious nonsense speech acts and events. The performer of nonsense takes an ambiguous position in the social structure of the community, one not far removed from the fool and the deformed person. The three share an important social characteristic—others are unable to predict the ways in which they will interact, and there is a great possibility that none of them play by the accepted rules of decorum and may therefore embarrass these others. But the major difference between the sporty fellow and the fool is that whereas the former has control over his performance, the latter does not, because of his ignorance, his being *trupidy*.

The gregarious artful talker is therefore less feared and more admired, especially because his becomes an important talent during periods of license. He helps the community confront these recurrent scenes in which the conflicts within or between the systems arise. Thus, even in this traditional type of community in which rudeness is much discussed and discouraged, there are times when controlled rudeness is invoked and highly appreciated.

There is, as with other realms of speech performance, a good deal of discussion about this subject, usually revolving around the ambiguous word *easy*. Easy, when used in regard to an individual, means that he is quiet and for the most part mannerly, though there is a contrary connotation of lack of sociability. Easy may be used in conjunction with the Vincentian terms for shyness, which are selfish and *bashful*. An easy person is not respected for his quietness, because the trait is seen to register an antisocial attitude rather than one of *respect*; however, he is not condemned for *going easy*.

But the often-encountered phrase describing someone—"He ain' easy" —may refer to a number of contrary notions. It may refer to someone's propensities to rudeness, especially stealing, *playing smart*, or its verbal equivalent, having a *fas' mout'* (that is, gossiping, *t'iefing* someone's name). Or it may refer to someone with an ability with words, especially in performing the more elaborate and anticipated genres like Carnival *washovers* (calypsos), *tea meeting* speeches, and Anansi stories at wakes. Essentially, the word *easy* in this set of occasions seems to refer to an ability to lie well. Thus, *ain' easy* may mean either something good or bad. As one informant put it, "If someone says someone ain' easy, we have to say 'Wha' you mean?'"

In the positive sense, when someone ain' easy, he is in the category of sporty fellow. Someone of this type is interested in sport of any sort—not only cricket and football but also Christmas, Carnival, tea meeting, and so on. Being sporty refers generally to loving to *keep company* and to talk. A sporty fellow often defines himself through *flash*: he wears clothes and acts with style, and he considers that in everything he does he is being watched and comports himself accordingly. A sporty fellow is generally admired by the community, but he must know when it is appropriate to be sporty. He therefore runs the risk of being branded a *saga boy* (not a totally negative role) if he sports too much, or a *limey* (or *limer*) *boy* if he uses his flash to *talk with* many women (i.e., have sexual intercourse or make babies with them).

Ain' easy is, then, a valuational term that refers to behavior as performance. It indicates that whether or not one chooses to present oneself in terms of style, one is judged in such terms whenever one's actions are discussed. The difference is that the sporty fellow seems more active in the management of his own image than the shy person.

The importance of being deemed someone who ain' easy can perhaps better be seen in its alternative phrasing, *'e no easy*. This is pronounced much like "noisy," and the pun is fully intended, for this is what the sporty fellow does—he makes noises that entertain his peers, while those in the yard are liable to accuse him of *making noise to annoy*. But the concept of "noise" differs somewhat from the ways we use it in contemporary Standard English. As Karl Reisman has pointed out in reference to speech among a similar group of Antiguan peasants, noise is used in the older and more ambivalent English sense as referring to any constant sounds emanating from an individual (or individuals), whether it signals a pleasant music or a violent quarrel.

> To make "noise" may refer to the assertion of oneself by the sound of one's voice. . . . The phrase also refers to three genres: boasting, cursing and argument. . . . And finally these conventions and genres collectively act to create certain speech events of a striking kind that, following the musical analogy inherent in the word "noise," I want to call contrapuntal—in the sense that . . . each voice has a "tune" and maintains it; and that the voices often sing independently at the same time. (Reisman, 1974, p. 111)

This contrapuntal effect is crucial to an understanding of both conversational and performance interactional styles. First of all, it goes far in explaining speaking characteristics much noted as distinctly Afro-American by Westerners: (1) a constant feeling that blacks argue with one another (or, alternately, take delight in making as much noise as possible), and (2) a mumbling or talking out loud to themselves. In St. Vincent one's voice is regarded as the essence of one's public self. All but the aged person is expected, in a social situation, to lend his voice to a proceeding, whether or not he has the ear of others. This means that one often encounters scenes in which, from the Western point of view, no one seems to be talking to anyone else. In fact, they may not be—they may simply be asserting their sense of presence and their feelings on the occasion.

The act of talking is a social act, but communication of information as part of the discourse is not a necessary component. Indeed, the giving of personal information in a conversational context commonly leads to embarrassment and is usually designed to do so. If someone has information that he either wishes to pass on or to gather, he commonly takes one person off to a non-public place (though not necessarily out of the sight of the others) and engages in an exchange on the subject. The instigator of the interaction generally goes first to the private place and then calls the other over to him, in a direct and abrupt manner without much deference.

This does not mean that no information is passed on in conversations, just no personal and timely local information. Anything else may be introduced and as such may become subject to comment and dispute. But in public discourse, performance and community unity is emphasized. This sense of unity is signaled by the intermingling of voices. The effective talker, the man-of-words, is someone who is capable of making the conglomerate of these individual voices not silent but harmonious. Indeed, he cannot feel successful unless the noise continues and is intensified.

This feeling of the individual presence residing in the voice assumes (as we do not seem to in Euro-America) that a sense of community exists. This sense is the "given" in communicative interactions in St. Vincent (and throughout Afro-America). Using the voice, making noise, is regarded as taking one's place in the group. There is no necessary requirement that when one person speaks all others listen. Only the most charismatic of speakers, and only on set occasions, command such "listening," and then it is not generally silence that is called for but continuative noise (often referred to as "amen-saying" in regard to black styles of talking in the United States).

Further, the system of conversational inclusion demonstrates that the sense of community is the given element of the situation.

> When someone enters a casual group . . . no opening is necessarily made for him; nor is there any pause or other formal signal that he is being included. No one appears to pay any attention. When he feels ready he will simply begin speaking. He may be heard, he may not. . . . If he is not heard the first time he will try again; and yet again (often with the same remark). Eventually he will be heard or give up. . . . But the fact that one is not heard does not mean that one has to stop. One can go right on with perhaps one listener, or perhaps none. (Reisman, 1974, p. 115)

The result is that on occasions in which a strong voice does not assert itself, everyone may seem to be conversing with himself. This pattern cannot be fully understood as long as a conversational unit is envisaged as a face-to-face or huddling type of encounter. But *liming* and *blagging* activities generally are carried on between a group of speakers who are facing in one general direction. There is therefore little physical adaptation called for when another joins the group. Eye contact is not necessarily called for, but if it occurs with anyone passing by, some signal of his presence is made—though this does not also signal a shift in the pattern or content of the conversation. Greetings of this sort are simply another way of recognizing the ever-open perimeters of the group.

The more serious and information-centered the encounter becomes, the closer the participants face each other. The distance between those involved in this "heavier" kind of dialogue is also an indication of how tightly structured the interaction has become. But to see two people very close to each other and face-to-face does not mean that they are either having a secret conference or an argument. It usually means, however, that a verbal contest factor has been introduced into the interaction and that words are therefore flying (or about to).

But even in such a situation, whether serious *vextation* (fighting) or humorous *ragging* is going on, the discussion does not commonly involve a back-and-forth, charge-and-answer pattern of interaction. Rather, each participant (and there may be many more than two) pursues his own argument, ignoring that of his opponent. One may, if one senses that the other has captured the ear of the onlookers, pick up a key word or phrase and embroider it as part of his argument, but that is all. As can be imagined, the sound level rises on such occasions, not just because of the need to outshout the other, but because any noise in the social environment is susceptible to being answered—like a cow's lowing, a radio playing, a baby's crying, a movie's sound, and so forth.

In other words, the appropriate response to noise is noise—sounds that serve as means of asserting the presence of oneself in the group and maintaining one's sense of identity. To participate conversationally, one asserts one's presence rather than engage in anything as formal as an informational exchange. With this approach to speaking focusing on an individual entering into the community-ratifying noise, the structure of conversations (in which each person may be contributing, but with no one else necessarily listening) and speaking or murmuring to oneself are more readily accounted for. The voice is not just to be used for passing on knowledge or for carrying out social amenities. More important, it is the channel for individual feelings and the means of proclaiming the individual presence.

I do not mean to suggest here that the passing of amenities and information does not occur among Vincentians, but rather that the use of the voice is conceived somewhat differently and that therefore verbal interactions do not assume the same shape as what we know as "conversation." Rather, speaking and other verbalizing is a means of dramatizing one's presence and, especially, one's feelings. But the element of the overlapping of the voices and the open-ended character of interpersonal encounters assumes greatest importance here, because similar traits are observable in all Vincentian ceremonies.

As I have indicated, however, there is little expressed distinction made between casual personal encounters and the more ceremonial occasions; rather, the continuities between these realms are emphasized. Perhaps this is because blagging, which goes on especially in the crossroad environment, is not only judged as performance—in terms of the canons of appropriateness —but really is akin to performance when compared to the Western conversational system in the incidence of self-consciously stylized devices and patterned routines. This means, among other things, that hyperbolic effects are frequently encountered in a kind of answering fashion. Just as noise is properly answered by noise in an ever-expanding fashion, so exaggeration is met with a more dramatic exaggeration. The whole interaction is, moreover, commonly begun with that most common of speech acts: the casual, teasing rag, *giving fatigue*. As Reisman reported from Antigua, "this gentle teasing is a steady part of village life. Emotional consolation is hard to come by. If you show you need it you will be teased, until you come back strong" (Reisman, 1971).

This "coming back strong" is, of course, one's demonstration of social self through the use of one's voice. (This is the main reason given why shy people are feared; they cannot be teased.) The appropriate response to ragging is making mock of someone else (usually someone present), sometimes even a stranger, turning the attention-giving device into one of self-dramatization, through a boast or a mild curse. Because any of these devices is liable to be taken up in the antiphonal, responsive manner, any such interaction is apt to become more stylized, turning into an entertainment.

Just as in the more casual blagging, however, there is no attempt to establish any necessary relationship with the content of the participants' discourse. Each person in such an interaction is, after all, dramatizing himself, and the crucial contest feature is one of who can capture the attention and responsive involvement of the others. This is done primarily through the ability to dramatize and hyperbolize most effectively. As in blagging, moreover, repetition is seemingly valued rather than derogated; the greatest test of one's dramatic abilities is staying power rather than invention (Lomax, 1970).

This kind of speaking behavior, because it arises out of the blagging situation, is observed most often among men at the crossroads. Because of this, it is regarded as characteristic of the foolish and rude behavior of men; but this does not mean that women do not engage in interaction very much like it. Teasing does indeed go on in the yard, but because of the stress on yard order and the consequent limitations on noise, the ragging tends to be much milder and more limited in duration. The overlap of voices is also observable, but not leading to the same intensity of dramatic effect as in crossroads situations. Ironically, because the women stay in their yards, their spoken interactions are limited to those who visit; yet as these are commonly between only two conversants, there is a cultural assumption that personal information is being passed on, and women are thus condemned for their propensity to make commess.

This does not mean that women do not engage in such spirited interplay, or that to do so would harm their appearance of respectability. But in line with the restraints of the special dichotomy between yard and road, if a noisy exchange occurs it commonly involves at least one of the participants being out of the yard. Most commonly, this means that a woman passing a yard gives fatigue to one in it; this may develop into a humorous and sometimes lengthy interchange. But more commonly, this setting is used for a *cursing*—an event in which making mock is combined with calling out a name, is directed at one or the other (or both) participant's failure to act respectably, and sensibly. In such a case, the cursing becomes vextation almost immediately, and constitutes *molĕs'*, an actionable offense. The content of the exchange is, like those at the crossroads, a combination of ragging and boasting (the argument is generally about a man). Similar arguments may arise between a man and woman within the confines of a yard, but though this is equally regarded as a social performance, it is classed very differently because so often the argument turns into a physical fight.

Cursing is, however, a speech act that is used in two different senses. One, such as the scene between those in the yard and those in the road, is a special kind of vextation involving a calling out of name and a public demonstration of conflict. It is, in this sense, a synonym for molĕs', though there can be molĕs'es that do not involve the use of the voice and are clearly not curses.

The second sense is simply a name for a self-dramatization in which no one else is involved. There are numerous occasions in which the voice is used, and loudly, to make derogatory remarks (about one's house, for instance, or some other possession) or even about a person (usually not present). These remarks sound, to the outsider, like the beginning of a dispute, but they simply elicit laughter from anyone within hearing range. This cursing is recognized as a kind of self-dramatization or boasting and is not therefore really regarded as derogatory. This is perhaps the most overt way in which the voice is used as a self-dramatizing device, simply because it is the loudest way of talking to oneself.

The cursing that goes on between a woman on the road and one in the yard is not the only situation in which women become involved in such an interchange. There are a number of other occasions in which it is regarded as appropriate for women to congregate outside the yards; they may engage in a wide range of activities of talking nonsense, and in such cases the teasing and boasting in creole broad talk apply. The most notable of these settings are the market (and market women are notoriously adept at making mock) and occasionally outside of a court that is in session. The major difference between the male and female uses of this patterned interaction is that for a woman to become involved, the speaking environment must first be heated up by the instigator who gives rag; men generally seize any such opportunity immediately. As a result, with women the occasion is likely to be more noted by the community and to turn into angry *boderation,* especially because it involves calling a name and an abrogation of the respectability canons of female behavior. In most such cases, of course, the instigator feels that this social upset has already been enacted and that she is simply dramatizing it so that the rest of the community may know of it. But whether this scene is enacted by men or women, it is regarded as a public performance, and enjoyed and judged as such by the onlookers, and by those who later hear about it through the gossip networks.

To recapitulate, then, the components of a casual public interchange are: (1) that anyone may become included in the exchange without any necessary change in its direction of comment or performance focus; (2) that anyone so involved signals his presence by noise, using his voice; (3) that voice overlap is not only permitted but expected; (4) that the interchange has an open-ended quality, in that there is no formal opening or closing of conversation (one reason why others may join freely); and (5) that the interaction tends to focus on, and be coordinated by, the individual who demonstrates his ability to perform effectively. This central role can be taken by more than one in the group, and everyone potentially may play this part—though in practice it is only the most effective talkers in the group who bring about this focus.

The significance of this pattern goes beyond the simple recognition of the system and its distinctiveness. Most ceremonial performance events exhibit characteristics identical or analogous to the patterns of liming or blagging interactions, especially when the ceremonies are connected with a household setting (mainly, life-passage rites). Thus, in a *marriage* or *baptism fête*, a *send-off* and *thanksgiving,* a *wake* or the more spontaneous moonlit night *ring play* occasions, the following traits are observable: (1) an open-ended, protean quality in the interaction, both in terms of spontaneous beginning and fade-out ending and of who interacts with whom; (2) an accompanying emphasis on each person being an active part of the performance, adding his voice, motions, and emotions to the total effect; (3) in many events, a focus on the most persuasive performer, with the others interacting on a call-and-response pattern in which there is no necessary thematic connection between the call and the response; (4) each person in the performance environment is regarded as a potential central performer; (5) the performer (and the performance) is judged with regard to staying power; (6) an open delight in repetition and improvisation out of (or against) the repeated elements; and (7) a constant interplay and overlap of voices, sometimes in noise, sometimes through focused dialogue (or its kinesic equivalent).

In all of the ceremonial performances, noise is a necessary feature. Sounds emanate from one another in the area (except for the aged, who can be exempted if they care to be) and each is expected to become the central performer and is given the opportunity to do so. In other more licentious ceremonies, only those with ability and fortitude are able to seize this role. The former is, of course, regarded as the more behaved and mannerly sort.

Perhaps the easiest way to present these patterns as a whole is through the children's ring play, singing games that are widely played throughout Richland Park on moonlit nights. Here, under the guidance of an older child, the group decides on its game. There are two major types of ring play: in the first, a pair of players face each other; in the second, all players face the center and thus form a ring. In each case, all sing and dance in virtual unison while focusing on a central performer (or a pair) who plays contrapuntally before them. This central role is passed from one child to the next; it is generally determined by the place in which the one in position finds himself or by the choice of the child in the center. The dance and, sometimes, the song emphasize this interactive structure. Generally the child in the center is asked to do special motions while the others move in a more restricted ensemble manner. The song is sometimes in chanter-response form, the chanter usually being the central child. The game and song, being serially organized, is open-ended and therefore can be begun and ended at any time. This same pattern, without the singing and dancing, is characteristic of the other moonlit-night form, riddling. Here, one person seizes center stage by propounding a riddle, then anyone may answer. Often a number of riddles are asked simultaneously. In such a case, the riddles are repeated and the most persistent and vocal riddler eventually reintegrates the focus. The role of riddler is thus available to everyone in the group.

On certain occasions, it is felt that this participation by the entire group must be guaranteed. In such a case, as in weddings and first-night wakes, a *chairman* or *master of ceremonies* is designated to maintain order—it being assumed that both noise and the desire to perform are everpresent.

The further away from a familiar house and yard setting, the more the performance continually focuses on just one central performer or group at a time. For instance, at tea meetings, held in a public hall, there is a much greater rigidity and separation of sensible performers from their audience; the separation is guaranteed by the chairmen and the use of a stage. But in the tea meeting the chairmen also guarantee that anyone who wishes to make a speech will be accorded a place on the program. The more mobile and nonsensical events, such as hangings and Carnival and Christmas groups, depart even further from the household ceremony patterns and have performances in which talented, creative performers are accorded greater license to keep the limelight; the nonperformers' role is restricted to creating responsive noise, setting up an overlap with the performance, often acting as a kind of chorus.

Symbolic Landscapes
and Expressive Events

Richland Park, St. Vincent, is a predominantly peasant community high in the hills leading to Mt. Petit Bonhomme, overlooking the Mesopotamia Valley, and beyond that, the Rathomill Mountains, Fairbaine Pastures, Fountain, Calliaqua Bay and the ocean. The first of the Grenadines, barren Balliseaux and Battaouille, can also be seen on the usual fair-weather days; off their coasts is one of the last of whale-fishing grounds, where whales are hunted in the old way, from the long boats. Kingstown, capital of the island, lies hidden by the Dorsetshire Hills, which come between it and Richland Park. But Kingstown is very much a part of the life of the Richland Park peasant, for there he sends the greater part of his crop in one of the painted bus-trucks (*Lady Madonna, Enterprise, Larwe Go*) that negotiate the winding sixteen miles, going at top speed most of the time, and stopping precipitately to pick up passengers.

In Kingstown, too, are found ships that once a week carry away the *full* if still green bananas to British destinations, bananas produced primarily by those living outside the Richland Park area. Land is hard to buy or lease, but what there is produces the staple tubers: yams, dasheen, eddoes, tanias—sufficient that no one wants, no one starves (though the same cannot be said for all such communities on the island). When the yams sent to market are not bought by the townspeople, they are shipped to Trinidad and Barbados. Some Richland Parkers had the foresight to plant nutmeg trees and thus are able to sell mace and nutmeg for extra cash; the bright red of the drying mace placed along the roads adds more color to an already richly hued environment of flowers and blooming trees and vines. No tropical paradise this, but beautiful in its own rather cool way.

The village radiates from the crossroads, where the school sits along with the two larger *hole-in the wall stores* and rum shops; it is here that the men sit around *liming and blagging* and on occasion drinking *strong* (rum); and here one catches the buses or jitneys that careen into Kingstown or places between.

The houses range along the roads and back up the mountain toward Montreal and its waterfalls and sulphur spring, where many peasants have their fields and where the government has a water catchment and closed reservoir, or along the old road to Greggs (where the superstitious and contentious descendants of the black Caribs are purported to live). Other yards are found on the many footpaths that lead away from the main road up the mountain; less prestigious homes with African-style wattle-and-daub construction appear here and there, mingled with more common clapboard homes.

There is an immediately recognizable sense of community here; for example, when I looked for someone who was not at home, his neighbors could tell me where he was—for all give some notion of where they are going as they pass. And there are strong family bonds; for instance, in conversations others are referred to by their relationship to the speaker or to someone else known in common to the speaker and the listener. Friendships are valued as well, in some ways even more than family relationships; people of the same *sex and size* proudly go as *compé and makmé,* or something like ritual pals. The goodness of life is persistently commented upon; conversation is marked with interjections like "Praise be God," "Nice, nice," and "All right!"

This is, however, no Utopia in anyone's mind. There is much *cômmess* that dramatizes wrongdoings and failures of character; personal doings become public and fights often arise when *business* is discussed. Life is filled with expressions of pleasure and happiness, yet there are also constantly observable tensions and hostility. People here, as everywhere, do not live up to the ideals of the community. But Richland Parkers accept that this is life's way, condemning infractions simply as being all too human. They see that rivalries and sources of dissension are deeply imbedded in life, though they do not approach such moral matters in any systematic philosophical manner. They do have spokesmen for the larger perspective, ones able to see that there are players of certain roles who must always be opposed to players of other roles—the young and the old, men and women, the friendly and the *selfish* (bashful). But these oppositions are not viewed as destructive to the community, even when ideals are departed from dramatically; such contrarieties are part of human nature and therefore, like everything else in life, must be both ameliorated and celebrated.

Although these oppositions are generally discussed by Vincentians in reference to specific personal interactions, they can perhaps best be understood by reference to the basic contrasts made between kinds of social space, the yard and the road or crossroads.

Sidney W. Mintz argues that some version of the living complex described here is widely found throughout this culture area. From his observations in Puerto Rico, Haiti, and Jamaica, he notes that the yard,

> whether of one house or several, is usually surrounded by some land, and set off from the outside by clumps of vegetation, a hedge . . . fencing, or otherwise. . . .

> This yard . . . is frequently viewed . . . as indivisible property. . . . There is special significance to the house and yard, set apart as they are from the outside, and seen as they are, as a unit. This meaning may not always be explicit, but it is readily remarked. Normally visitors approach the yard with care, and do not enter its grounds until their presence is noted and acknowledged by the residents. (Mintz, 1960, pp. 591-592)

Thus the house and yard are deeply identified with the symbolic constraints, concepts, and rules governing the practices of privacy and family. Incursions are therefore regarded not only as inappropriate, but liable to constabulary and judicial intervention, for the police and court systems are much more integral agencies in the day-to-day life of the West Indian than in that of his American counterpart. The word that is used for this kind of actionable offense, *molés*, refers to a physical assault, mayhem offense, public name-calling, or any behavior that emanates from the road and is regarded as violating the privacy of the yard, such as stone-throwing, *cursing* (i.e., loudly calling someone's name), or even urinating on the *hungry* (fencing).

The active life of the road, in other words, is seen as a threat to the maintenance of household order. But the dichotomy goes a great deal further than this. In the West Indian peasant family system, the yard is regarded as the domain of the family, and women who head families are judged in terms of their ability to keep the family in order. Therefore, even in this community, in which there is a high degree of co-residence and family stability, the yard is still strongly identified with the women who maintain its sense of order. By contrast, the road has come to be associated with male activity, primarily because this is the milieu in which men meet to carry on their liming and blagging. It is at the crossroads that the friendship activities that stand at the center of the community's definition of masculinity are carried out. Furthermore, the yard is a circumscribed physical entity symbolic of family continuity and privacy on the one hand, and the ideal of female endurance—the world of order, stability, and decorum—on the other. In contrast, the road symbolizes male gregariousness and mobility—a public world of energy, action, and freedom.

The worlds of the yard and the road are kept apart rather rigidly, not only because of the great regard that West Indians have for family privacy but also because of the dichotomy (and occasional antagonism) within the social system between the approved life-styles and the allocation of resources by women and men. This division between the sexes goes beyond competition over limited resources and division of responsibility to a clash of values and ideals. This is not often noted, because the value system associated with women, the family, and the yard are the overt and conscious values of the entire group, whereas the ideals associated with men and the road life are not often consciously commented upon (though they are equally systematic). Like most sources of recurrent problems, these are commonly dealt with by minimizing the oppositional elements, at least until a confrontation occurs, at which time they are dramatically useful as a resource for a community discussion of how life might best be lived.

Minimization is most easily accomplished by clearly demarcating the physical and social boundaries between the two worlds. There is a casual acceptance by both sexes that the other generally operates in terms of a different code, and its members are judged by different values. Thus the system continues to operate as long as the boundaries are well-defined and maintained. Perhaps more important, the two perspectives establish two world views, each of which finds symbolic expression in the system of ceremony and celebration. It is almost certainly because of these competing elements that the yard-crossroads contrast is relied upon so heavily within Afro-American societies.

ESTABLISHING THE BOUNDARIES

In Richland Park, the physical attributes of the yard provide a family with the basis of status within the community. The yard must be maintained with a firm sense of order, an order both physically and socially determined. The yard is regarded as the domain of the woman who heads the household, even though a large majority of the family units in Richland Park have a resident male who is, in many cases, the father or grandfather of the children.

One way by which a couple first announces to the community that they are involved in what they expect to be a permanent union is working together to purchase *house-land.* As the name indicates, this is ground on which to build a house. This land is then regarded as belonging to the family, rather than to one or another of the pair. After marriage, the male may feel that the land belongs to him and to the children born subsequent to the ceremony, though this feeling is seldom acted upon and the land is seldom broken up except to provide house-land for the children. There is a strong feeling that this land must not be sold to anyone else, especially for producing crops. (See Smith, 1962, and Hill, 1977, for a description of a similar situation on Carriacou.) House-lands are commonly extensive enough to have a *garden* (crop field) attached. These *house-gardens* are contrasted with fields separated from the house-land, which are simply called gardens. When land is purchased and then built upon, it comes to be regarded as family property.

As the locus of family life, the house-lands, with the addition of the house, become the yard, and a number of changes are made in it that articulate the sense of family privacy. House-land must be on the road, and the closer one's land is to a major artery the greater the prestige, due to the easier access to transportation, water, and electricity. But having land on an access route also leaves one's yard open to possible incursions from the street. Consequently, the physical distinctions between road and yard, as well as one yard and another, are firmly drawn by conventional symbolism. The line between the road and the yard is established by the use of *fencing,* which may be any bush, but is most commonly the hibiscus. (Because of this, hibiscus found any place is commonly called *fencing.*) The most crucial area along this line is the place of egress, and this is called the *gate,* though a physical gate is found in only about a quarter of the yards in the community. There are families who love flowers and therefore have a number of flowering bushes. These are most commonly found along the front fencing, or along one of the side boundaries, and only very occasionally by the door of the house. Most of the yard is bare of vegetation, except for an occasional fruit tree. Indeed, the yard is distinguishable from the bush and the garden by the absence of grass and weeds; the land is beaten smooth by much use and kept clean by the children's constant *brooming* (usually using a palm frond). Having a young child in the household is highly valued precisely because he or she can sweep the yard, fetch water, carry messages, and perform other such tasks.

The boundaries between yards are established by bungries, certain trees or bushes that are conventional markers. In other parts of the West Indies, the bungry is commonly a calabash tree, but in Richland Park and parts of St. Vincent it is generally the *dragon* (croton), or, on occasion, a tall papaya. These are always placed at the corner of the property and are also often set out along one entire side of a boundary.

Access to the yard is strongly limited by convention. If someone's yard is not on the road on which the water main lies, there is little problem obtaining permission to walk through another's yard, on a regular basis, to get water. Also it is a simple matter for "family" or for those who have developed a special relationship with someone in the household. Otherwise, visitation is limited. These special relationships are very seldom among peers, for male friendships (which are generally peer friendships) are maintained at the crossroads, and friendship between women is frowned upon after adolescence, because it is seen as a threat to the stability of the household. Hence female socializing in the yard tends to be among women of different generations. The older a woman is, the less she fears that her respectability will be challenged through such visiting.

Naturally, the most important feature of the yard is the house. If there is a co-resident male in the household, he is judged according to the kind of house he has provided for his family, and especially by the kinds of materials used in its construction. A woman usually does not marry a man until he is able to provide a substantial home for her, preferably an *upstairs house.* This is one that has living quarters above a storage area and (most importantly) has a large outdoor stairway, where the bulk of the yard socializing takes place. This need for a substantial house is one of a number of social reasons why marriage takes place so often in middle age.

The criteria for judging the quality of a house and a yard are similar: the more they are sealed off from the world of the road and exhibit a cool and orderly exterior, the more highly they are valued. With the yard this consists of a clearly swept expanse in front of the house, and well-maintained fencing and flowering garden around the *cook shack*; with the house, the capacity for being dramatically sealed. This is why there is such a strongly felt hierarchy of building materials, the best ones being those that give the fullest feeling of completeness and separation.

Thus there are distinctions made between *wattle-and-daub, board,* and *wall* houses. The wattle-and-daub house is regarded as temporary and low-status housing; it is constructed of woven bamboo strips caulked with clay-mud and thus gives the appearance of lack of stability. Constant repair keeps the house sealed against the "cold" night air (and, for some, the *jumbies*). The board house is more socially prestigious, especially if it has been painted. Painting a wall is indeed the most dramatic way of exhibiting the seal of a house, thus a wall house is the most prestigious type. It may be constructed of manufactured pressed brick, stone covered with mortar, or of a molded-sand brick made by the family and dried in the sun. This house type is distinctive because it is sealed with cement and takes a paint readily.

Similarly, a house may be distinguished by its roofing materials. The least prestigious here is the *trash* roof, generally made of gathered and tied lavender grass. More acceptable is galvanized tin, although the grass roof provides more constant cooling in the hot time of day. One hears a dwelling designated on occasion as a *trash house* or a *galvanize house*. The more prestigious houses are usually referred to by the shape of their roof—*pitched* or *gabled.*

Paradoxically, the greater the seal of a house, the more opportunity there is for its breakage, for *flash.* This was done in older houses by adding *fancy work* or *honeycomb* (of the type called gingerbread in the United States and West Indian Chippendale in the Leeward Islands) to the eaves and above the doors and windows—cutout figured woodwork. In more recently built homes, the effect has been adapted to fancy figured bricks. As we shall see in ceremonial performances, this dramatic juxtaposition of oppositions is characteristic of the Vincentian aesthetic.

There are other buildings that may be found in the yard. If one of the offspring of the family cohabits over a long period with someone, another house is erected. It is not considered appropriate (or even socially permissible) for two sets of mates to live under the same roof. As they put it, "Two man-crab can't live in the same hole." Quite often, this second living unit begins as a *cookhouse* or *cookshack,* though the younger couple regard this as not a very acceptable arrangement and plan for a further building if space in the yard permits. This cookshack or cookhouse is commonly made of wattle and daub, but the more permanent materials here too are regarded as more prestigious.

Although there are no conscious rules in the yard's arrangement, there is modal arrangement of buildings that indicates a fine sense of spatial appropri-

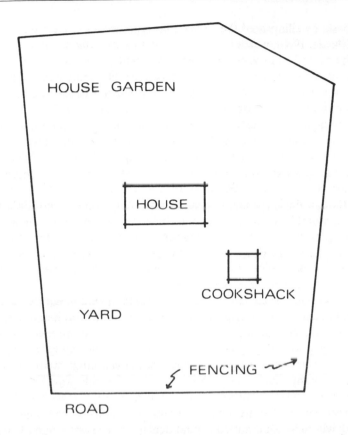

HOUSE GARDEN

HOUSE

COOKSHACK

YARD

FENCING

ROAD

ateness. The house generally faces directly toward the road or path. If there are two houses, they are therefore side by side. The cookshack is commonly slightly in front of, or directly behind and to the right of, the house as it is viewed from the road. The outhouse is in back, also often on the right. There are auxiliary structures on the left of the house, as well, as if to balance the cookshack: a chicken coop, a rabbit hutch or storage shed, or a rack for drying *provisions* (ground vegetables) to be used in the next year's planting. In the yard are also heaped building materials being gathered for future improvements and additions: boards drying beneath the house, a pile of rocks brought from the creekbed, or molded and pressed bricks.

All houses are raised by stilts of some sort, and the space beneath is used as storage of accrued building materials. This is true of the upstairs house as well, though the rooms below are habitable by Western standards. Commonly, not even a kitchen is put in this space. It is considered extremely important that young girls (and, to a lesser extent, boys) are taught to cook, and they are assigned any of the daily cooking chores. The cookshack must be located away from the house for reasons of safety.

The basic dwelling is of the vernacular type commonly called the *creole house* (Glassie, 1968), which is a rectangular structure divided in two by either a curtain or a wall. The room on the right is then called the *sitting room,* and the door leads into it. It commonly has a bed, a table, some cane chairs, and a cabinet in which the prized glassware is kept. If the house is enlarged, the addition is usually built along the front, which sometimes is kept entirely as a sitting room and sometimes divided in two, one side being used for a bedroom. It is not unusual to see three and four additions made, each of which repeats for the most part the construction of the original building. The resultant structure simply looks like two (or three or four) buildings constructed next to each other.

Even though the male family head is most commonly responsible for the construction of the house and the other buildings, it is the Vincentian woman who is responsible for the maintenance of order there. Once the yard is completed, the father of the family has little place there and is expected to spend most of his time in the garden (fields) or at the crossroads, the rum shop, or some other habitual gathering spot.

The paterfamilias is looked to not only to build the home but to continue as the primary provider for the family. He brings into the yard much of the food or income used to sustain the household, but he has an ambiguous relation once there, for he has little authority over the activities and attitudes of the children. Men develop one of a number of conventional relationships with children. In many cases the paterfamilias is especially affectionate to the youngest child, whom he carries about on Sundays or in the evening. However, he may occasionally assume the role of a stern taskmaster, especially with the boys, with whom he is permitted a great deal more authority than the girls. He shares the role of discipliner with his mate and may give *lashes* or *licks,* should that be his inclination. But he has this prerogative (as does any adult) with any child outside the yard if the child seems to be misbehaving, *coming on rude.*

From the point of view of those representing the forces of tradition, order, and continuity within the community, the house and yard complex provides the constant symbolic representation of how fully these values may be attained. The order of the yard is maintained and, celebrated, on the one hand, by fencing out the possible incursions from the road, the crossroads, and the forces from outside—especially *town,* Kingstown. On the other hand, order is also asserted over nature here; this is proclaimed by the various activities carried on within the yard that purify, civilize, transform the natural: in the food preparation and the cooking; in the sweeping of the yard and the planting and maintenance of fencing; and in the amassing of bricks, boards, pebbles, and other building materials. The most profound and the most everyday enunciation of respectability is in the activities going on regularly in which these housing materials are amassed, for these make the symbolic statement that this family is a growing unit, one that is concerned with future

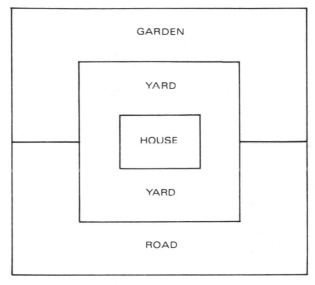

BUSH (PASTURE, MOUNTAIN)

GARDEN

YARD

HOUSE

YARD

ROAD

CROSSROAD, TOWN

generations. All of these themes are made explicit in the speeches that lie at the center of house and yard celebrations.

In contrast to this is the view from those who lime and blag at the crossroads, in which the most significant factor operating is that here action is generated, valued, commented upon. The crossroads is the place of contested and potentially unequalizing exchange; the locus of commerce of all sorts. It is the place in which the cultivated products of nature are shipped to town and the products of distillation and manufacture are received and distributed.

The crossroads comes to symbolize the whole covert set of ideal masculine behaviors, which turns on the expectation of male gregariousness. While the world of women is structured around the order of the house and the yard, the multi-generational, vertical organization of the family, the male world of the road is more horizontally organized around the friendship network system and the kinds of behavior that arise when men get together to demonstrate their masculinity to one another. Women are not encouraged to have close friendships in their home communities because that would take them away from the yard and lead to commess. In other words, the crossroads is not only the place of business transactions, where most of the cash accrued by community members is spent, but also an area in which competitive and often contentious activity is carried out. Thus, the relationships carried out are ones typical of nonfamily members, in which reciprocity of exchange is not taken for granted but must be achieved. This, then, is the area in which friendship is

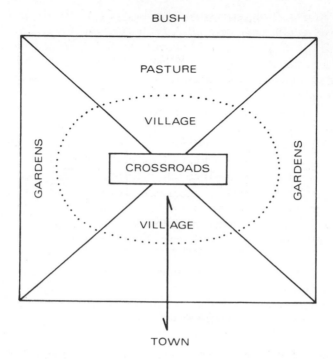

BUSH

PASTURE

VILLAGE

GARDENS

CROSSROADS

GARDENS

VILLAGE

TOWN

achieved through the dramatization of exchanges through strong sharing, playing cards or.dominoes, engaging in playful, contentious talk. *Nonsense* is thus licensed and, therefore, potential *rudeness.* From this perspective, town is an intensification of the crossroads, for here, in the market, one finds the most dramatic playing out of the motives of contentiousness in the bargaining and the badinage of the market people, who are regarded as the sharpest tongued creatures of all.

These contrasted worlds are, moreover, given further definition when the *bush* is taken into account. For the bush symbolizes everything there is to fear, socially speaking. In the bush reside both animals and the spirits who, in former generations, were regarded as a threat. But more important is that the bush stands for potential disorder, from both the agricultural and the social points of view. It is here that the few criminals of the island hide and that the odd ones—strange and sometimes *trupidy* people or drunkards—go to stay for a few days at a time; thus the bush is strongly identified with insanity and unnatural sexual acts. But the existence of this wild world only serves to define more firmly what those in the yard most fear about the crossroads activities.

These perceptions have been affected not only by Mintz's work but also Peter J. Wilson's arguments. In a series of articles and books concerning sociocultural life on the Colombian Anglophonic island of Providencia, Wilson has given us one of our richest and "thickest" descriptions of a Caribbean community (Wilson, 1969, 1971, 1973, 1974). His work, more than any other, has assisted me in formulating the singular character of West Indian life in which life alternatives are used as principles of achieving community solidarity through the competitive dramatization of difference.

The superstructure of his arguments builds upon the distinction between *reputation* and *respectability* that I have heard employed in all of the island communities in which I have worked and, in slightly different formulations, in black communities in the United States. Wilson associates reputation with male, friendship- (or crew-) oriented values, in which life at the rum shop and in other public places is pursued and valued. Reputation-seeking often depends not only upon a deployment of resources with friends rather than family, but is also associated with masculine *flash* (style), big- and loud-talk, and sometimes even drunken unruliness. Respectability represents proper behavior, status-seeking good behavior that demonstrates order, propriety, and various other virtues. Respectability is the overt value system of the community, subscribed to by all when called on to give testimony to what is good and proper. Reputation values are more occasion- and situation-specific, and operate in a more covert manner. Respectability is the bundle of inherited values passively avowed except when challenged; reputation is only gained by being earned and maintained, through expressive and often dramatically coercive means: *cursing, rhyming,* and other kinds of conventional and engaging playful argument. Gossip functions as a way of making these alternative values a matter of discussion. The two value complexes may confront each other in discussions of behavior without causing constant argument, because everyone expects everyone else to depart from the approved ways, to act inappropriately.

The two complexes map to a large extent the symbolic worlds of house and yard, and crossroads. But as the conflicts are registered primarily in the realms of everyday interactions, I shall pursue the reputation-respectability distinction in these domains. In the contrast of these worlds on St. Vincent, what conflicts arise are commonly between old and young, and, even more, between men and women. Relations between the sexes involve an extremely delicate system of role expectations defined in part by one's habitual proximity to the yard. In defining himself in regard to his mate, each man must maintain a balance between dependence and independence. One must not be an *auntie man,* hanging around the yard and checking about the whereabouts of the other. However, the man must not stay so far away that he is liable to be made a *macco man* (repeatedly cuckolded). He is under some pressure from the other men to be a *sporty fellow,* to lime and engage in the usual male activities. If he devotes himself too much to work he is regarded as a *garden man* and thus viewed as somewhat unmasculine, unfriendly, symbolically too close to the bush. A man must also not allow the other sex to be too dominant in the relationship. If he permits this, he is talked about a good deal in unmanly terms. Yet a woman is also involved in *foolishness* if she lets her husband yell at her and beat her too often, for he then threatens the order of the household, and her respectability.

Each parent expects the other to work for the benefit of the family by *gardening* (or by occasionally getting a wage-paying job with the government, such as working for the Banana Board or on a road crew) and by making sure the yard and house are neat and in good repair. A woman commonly has land and income of her own, usually to provide money for the extras for her children, such as school clothing and *treats,* or for the improvement of the house and yard. More often than not, the woman of the family is expected, if possible, to provide the financial assistance to help a son or daughter learn a trade (mason, mechanic, seamstress, secretary) thought to be important for upward social mobility.

One of the central attitudes toward others in the family is that one must not ask for anything. It is assumed that if the father has something, he shares it, and this is true of other members of the family as well. This system works so long as there is a true reciprocity, and no acting upon *lickrish* (selfish, un-cooperative) motives. However, there is a great deal of talk about one member (usually the father) who does not give or share. This may arise because men and women often keep their financial affairs secret from each other; thus imputations of this sort may simply express a fear of a lack of reciprocity. This seems an especially strong motive in those cases in which the father spends a good deal of his time in the rum shop. Both the mother and the other children, in such cases, feel that he is lickrish because he must spend money on himself and his friends there, and on something that is nonsense and that often leads to family fights.

Another by-product of this situation is that the mother may make disparaging remarks to the older children about their father's lickrish ways. Not only does this intensify the antagonism, it also cements an emotional allegiance of child to mother. This is openly discussed by the women, who say they care much more for their children than their mates, because their children's love is more dependable. The result is a mother-child allegiance and reaction pattern, often one of great intensity, which in some families leads to a flow of harsh words between father and older sons. It also results in a great fear of the paternal figure as a source of authority. But there are even stronger counterpressures on male children because of the community expectations of masculine behavior, which force them to the crossroads to lime and blagg. Mother is never forgotten. But peer group pressures and the unconscious expectation that a young man will develop a broad set of friends clears a channel by which an escape from the yard can be made.

In this contest of worlds, a woman is judged almost solely in terms of how well she is able to maintain the order in the lives of those who come into the environment of her yard. She must demonstrate a control at all times, not only over others but also herself. The public discovery of a woman's inability to cook properly, or the dramatic revelation of a long hidden affair, is equally scandalous. These seem as threatening to the respectability or good name of the household.

All yard-centered activity is highly restricted. Children's movement as well as their noise must be confined to the yard. They must be instructed in all of the appropriate household duties, and it must be seen to that these duties are carried out regularly. Proper respect for decorum must be demonstrated within the yard: *boderation* or *vextation* (fighting) is regarded as the ultimate incursion into the decorum of the yard, though of course it happens, and fairly regularly. Circumspection and constancy are highly valued. These virtues are shared with schools and mission churches, and thus the ideal behavior of the yard comes to include *talking sweet* (or proper speech close to oratorical Standard English) and *acting sensible* (exhibiting one's knowledge or discipline). I do not mean to say that this describes actual yard behavior, but only the ideals that household heads attempt to instill in their charges as central to familistic virtues. A mother's respectability is therefore judged primarily in terms of her control over the things, living and otherwise, in her yard—and not really upon her subscribing to any European style of presentation, except in the most public of circumstances, and then in very transformed creolized ways. Young children must therefore remain under the gaze of their mother (and grandmothers), and this means remaining in the yard. There she teaches them proper behavior; she permits them to leave only to fetch water or to do some other errand, or to go to school. If she must tend the garden, she takes them with her and teaches them how to help. She must at all times know of the whereabouts of all children who have not reached early adolescence. She is usually the dispenser of punishment.

Opposed to this highly ordered world of the yard is the freer and more licensed life-style of the crossroads. Here nonsense and rudeness are more tolerated, indeed valued in the rum-shop milieu. A man's reputation as a *sporty fellow* is judged in terms of flash, performance abilities, success with women (including the number of children he has fathered), and the ability to articulate the environment through initiating activity. The stability of the yard is contrasted with the activity valued in the crossroads setting. All of this is solemnized with the drinking of rum, the *nonsense-maker* that rationalizes masculine license.

Because the boundaries between these two worlds are commonly maintained quite successfully, these two sets of ideal characteristics seldom come into open conflict. However, there are two current problems involved with this dual system of behavior. One arises when the father of the family must decide on how he will allocate his resources. His reputation depends upon his willingness to be generous with his friends; but family respectability depends on his devoting his resources primarily to family needs. A precarious balance is therefore established between these two claims upon the man's resources. This is less a problem to the young men who have continued to live in the family yard, because they have less responsibility to share and to cooperate in the family unit. (This has become more pronounced with the development of the job market.) They are instead expected to use this time in their lives to cultivate their friendship network as fully as possible, so that they can call upon it later in life. Thus the young men are encouraged to form close, almost institutionalized friendships as well as to join peer-group crews. When a man becomes a father, coresident, and later a husband he is expected to devote more of his resources to the maintenance of the family.

Thus one of the largest periods of tension within this system is the transitional stage between young manhood and the acceptance of family responsibility. It is usually articulated in terms of the attraction of the rum shop and the attempt to maintain reputation at the expense of respectability. When the decision is made to accept family responsibility fully, a man may seem to be acceding to female values.

Second, men may be judged in terms of reputation, and as reputation is established by the dramatic performance of what are considered rude acts from the perspective of the yard, constant incursions of such nonsense erupt from the road into the orderly world of the yard. This is, of course, especially true when rum consumption is high. It is further intensified by the great mobility of the young men; they travel from village to village to see how many people of both sexes they can add to their friendship networks. However, when a strange group of young men comes into town, social and physical boundaries rigidify, and the young men answer with an intensified rude performance. This very often leads to fighting, and the accusations of *molĕs'* become more common. The rude dimension of the male role depends in part on the stories of incursions he is able to get away with in another community and the tales concerning his ability to protect his home community and its women against such molestations. As the roads have improved and more motor transportation has become available, this has become a greater and greater problem.

The life of each member of the community involves a constant fluctuation between the ordered world of the house and gardens and the activities of the road and town. One may reasonably describe typical Vincentian life careers with reference to the alternative attractions to these worlds.

Throughout their lives women are expected, of course, to be less mobile, to be more firmly committed to life in the yard than the men. And the yard is, for the most part, the entire world a child inhabits. Yet women do have numerous opportunities to escape the yard on occasion or even permanently, while men often maintain their sense of stability by adhering to their yard and garden responsibilities, and by maintaining the values of this world of order and tradition as the only approved overt ideal of the community. The mother of the family attempts to keep the children of the household within the orbit of the yard as long as she can. This she does by making each child part of the working order of the household, teaching each a wide range of skills: food preparation and cooking, washing and ironing, sweeping the yard, fixing hair, hoeing and weeding in the garden, carrying water, running errands, and many other such essentials. The older children are expected to do most of the teaching of the younger ones and to maintain in an active way the order of the yard. Those families with the most children are regarded as fortunate, for the female household head is able to relax more, because she only needs to supervise the activities of her children. When a woman visits another woman's yard, the first subject of conversation is often an enumeration of all the things their children have bought or built for them.

This maternal figure presides over this household with a firm sense of providing a stable place of repose for the rest of her family, no matter how far they may have removed themselves. She guarantees this sense of allegiance by making sure that she has fully trained everyone in her household, including the males, to carry out all of the jobs necessary to keeping a house properly. Through the training period she emphasizes the necessity of learning these things because her charges cannot predict if the person they set up house-keeping with will not betray them in some way. No one, she teaches them, is really to be trusted except their mother.

She regards it as natural for her children as they mature to have sexual liaisons with others, though a mother tries to keep her daughters from such liaisons as long as possible. When one of her children produces offspring, the infant may enter into the family unit and be cared for by its mother (if she decides to remain there); alternatively she may leave the infant to be cared for by her mother while she is employed elsewhere or sets up housekeeping with someone other than the child's father. Thus the young may remain mobile because the older woman provides a stable home base. Young adults are expected to have children by a number of partners, simply because they are young. However, there are people in the community who strongly feel that they only want to have children with one person and regulate their habits accordingly.

The young men are, of course, given much more latitude and are allowed to escape the yard during adolescence, when their crews are forming. In these crews, a lot of boasting concerning sexual experiences takes place. The greatest boast concerns the girls who *make babies* for them. This value is shared both by friends and family, though there is some ambivalence from the latter. Mothers not only countenance but encourage this behavior of their sons, arguing that young girls are fickle anyway and do not know how to treat or keep their sons. The offspring of such a union commonly live with their maternal grandmothers, though paternal grandmothers are usually willing, even anxious, to have the children with them—and this has led to some interesting (usually friendly) rivalry between the two grandmothers.

It is expected, then, that both sexes will be wild in their early adulthood. However, this does not mean that anything goes in the relationships of the young. There is a strong feeling that one should not court—*friend with* or be *gossing with*—more than one person at a time. If a girl is discovered to be having relations with more than one man, she is regarded as being *fas'* (a thief in general parlance, and here meaning not worthy of trust) and will be avoided by most of the young men.

Friending with is encouraged by the older members of the family. There is a tendency for the relationships that produce children to become more regularized, and this is done by having one of the pair move into the home of the other. Should this involve the boy moving to the girl's home, strong friendships often develop between him and the girl's father, for the father is proud in such cases that his daughter has a boyfriend with constancy. These male friendships are commonly maintained if the young man has paid sufficient respect to the father of the house, even if the young man and woman drift apart. The same kind of relationship may develop between the mothers and the young girls should the girl move in with the young man's family. In such situations, the mother feels a great deal of pride toward her grandchild, and should the union not persist, as noted, she often raises the child along with her own. In these youthful alliances, the friendships that develop are seen as more stable than the loves, and even when the split-up of the young ones has been bitter, visits between the mother and the young girl, or the father and the young boy, are not uncommon and are amicable and often jocular. In this system the necessity of accepting responsibility for a family is not usually forced upon the young before they feel they are ready to accept it. Responsibility begins when a separate home is established, and it is finalized—usually ten to twenty years later—in marriage, after the union has proven successful.

It is generally considered out of keeping for young people to get married, for marriage comes when a man can provide a substantial house. For this he must first be able to buy the land (which is not always easily acquired); then he must be able to acquire all kinds of materials, such as lumber and galvanized roofing, out of which he and his friends fashion a house. The most difficult of the carpentry and masonry jobs he may have to pay for as well. Finally, he must have sufficient wherewithal to have a marriage feast. Once he decides to get married, he is assisted in all of these things by his friends and family, but he feels he must have substantial holdings before he can take this step.

Consequently, marriage is commonly an act that says to the community that the man has reached an age of stability and is worthy of some status. He has fully accepted his family and community responsibilities by so marrying. This is commonly done between the ages of thirty-five and fifty; it is generally a celebration of a union that has been in existence for some time and that has produced a number of children.

The young man who seeks respect and who has fewer family responsibilities is charged with putting together a meaningful friendship network. Because he is the most mobile of the community residents, he is expected to roam fairly widely establishing relationships that he can rely on which are separate from the family. This he does by liming with others and by friending with girls in other communities, thereby making friends with her family and neighbors. However, he must be willing to accept the obligations as well as the rewards of friendship. This means that he must give of what he has and ask others for some of what they have.

There is a different sharing procedure between friends from that in the family. Whereas one may not ask for anything within the family, it is regarded as somewhat strange not to ask for something from a friend. But friends also offer things constantly, and a person feels a good deal of pride by being able to maintain a large friendship network by giving gifts, whether asked for or not. To be sure, there are those who are regarded as bad friends because they ask for too much and give too little. These lickrish fellows are often shunned, losing the respect so crucial to establish a positive identity.

Naturally, friendships on this wide-ranging basis are made during the time of greatest mobility, before the establishment of one's own household. This does not mean that this movement is totally unencumbered. Each community expects young men from others to come into it, yet at such times some of the young men there band together and reject the newcomer. They see themselves as protecting their girls, keeping them for themselves. This makes it all the more important for the roaming young men to be able to establish friendships with some in each community, for when there is an attack from the resident boys, there is liable to be *ragging,* then vextation, and, finally, a fight and an allegation of molěs' on the part of both. These encounters often lead to court, and one must have friends from the community who are willing to testify in one's favor.

Such testimony is liable to come not from one's peers in the other community, but from the older people to whom one has not paid proper respect or from the girls who have provided the occasions for the fight. This is because male peers make their crew within a community. They therefore tend to see the honor of the crew deeply embedded in the honor of the community, and this is what they seem to want to uphold when these outsiders come in. But this also means that if one of these outsiders makes a baby with one of their girls and moves in with her family he becomes part of the community and is able to make special friendships there as well as in his home area.

A girl relies on situations of this sort to achieve her reputation, for she also finds a sense of stability in a wide-ranging friendship network. But she is considerably less mobile, only moving when asked to join her boyfriend's family when she makes a baby for him, or, if she is more wild, by moving to Kingstown and getting a job. (It is assumed, if she does this, that she is friending with a number of men at the same time.)

This relative fixity of girls is, of course, dictated by the family arrangement, which insists that the girls stay within the yard except to fetch water, help with the weeding and hoeing, and go to church and school. For the boys to go gossing with them, they must come up to the yard or (more commonly) catch them while going to or from church or school. There are also occasional dances that some are allowed to attend in the company of their peers, as well as dances in other people's yards when some kind of celebration is held.

The crew orientation leads to special male friendships. In these, two or three young men begin to lime and roam together and, sharing these adventurous experiences, may decide on a common economic endeavor (such as renting a field and farming it together, or getting jobs in which they must work jointly). This kind of special palship is encouraged and acted on long after the men begin to set up their own households. Maintenance is possible because of their continued meeting on the street or in the rum shops or on the job, but such friends are given permission to enter each other's yards at will. This is commonly done by a man instructing his mate to feed his friend whenever he comes by, thereby making him like family.

Again, the qualities of this special friendship were most fully exhibited when the decorum of the relationship was broken in a particular instance. Two of my closest male acquaintances had a relationship of this sort when I first lived above Richland Park in 1966. When I went back a few years later they did not seem to be friends anymore. Furthermore, while one of the pair visited me, the other seemed to stay away by design. When I asked members of the community why the two were no longer friends, the condemning response was that the one had abused the friendship of the other by accepting his food and then friending with his woman. As a result, the woman was driven from the home and was forced to set up house with the friend. This did not lead to ostracism by the entire community, but it meant a good deal of talk about the betrayal of friendship, and thus a loss of esteem on the part of the man. The woman in the middle was hardly ever mentioned in the ensuing commess, for her betrayal was regarded as much less egregious than the disruption of friendship.

The members of the community seemed to agree that the problem really was one of how one can bring friendship within the family sphere, because in so many ways the two are antithetical. Family activity calls for the maintenance of order, while friendship, especially among young men, encourages a search for action, and thus the constant possibility of being rude or not fulfilling the economic obligation of belonging to the family. Therefore, while the young man is still living with his family, in most cases, he is not encouraged to bring his friends into the yard. If they do come into it, they must do so with the greatest amount of respect. In some cases, a friend, if he acts in accordance with these strictures, may become a member of the family even to the point of living there, but the relationship then becomes very different between the peers, for they are more like brothers, and the boy added to the household does not generally approach the girls sexually because this would be akin to incest. The mother of the family generally feels that he may be treated as one of her children in regard to his behavior, at least while in her yard. She is, of course, judged as much by his behavior while in the yard as she is for that of any of her own children. She must at all time protect her reputation for running an orderly and behaved household. Rudeness of any sort, especially nonsense, is seen as a reflection of bad upbringing on the part of the mother; however, a certain amount of rudeness while on the streets is regarded as inevitable. Thus, it is only the most egregiously rude—the thief, the vexatious fellow, or the child who has no sense—who directs community contempt on himself and reflects badly on the woman who has raised him. She can control the *melée* (malicious gossip) only by making a kind of repeated public confession, called a cursing, that the boy is unmanageable even in her yard; by this the community ascribes the fault, at least in part, to *bad spirit* in the child and not to bad upbringing.

Another such rationalization for this extreme kind of rude behavior on the part of the boy is that his father has brought out these things in him because the two males are unable to agree on anything. The father is therefore seen (at least by the women in the community) as a provoker who will not adequately share his wisdom, experience, and resources, and who therefore drives the boy away from home and into his bad ways. In other words, though fathers generally take paternal pride in their offspring, children are regarded as the property and responsibility of the mother. She therefore strongly resents anything that the father does to drive the child away. This feeling of responsibility often extends beyond the mother-child relationships to the grand-children, even if they do not live in the grandmother's home.

Given the special orientation to social life, it can be seen that the complementary opposition between the worlds of the yard and the road is only one dimension of the larger opposition between two sets of ideals, reputation and respectability, the one strongly identified with women and the old, the other with men and the young. At the risk of overschematization, the dimensions of opposition might be expressed graphically, as a means of recapitulating some of the major behavioral and conceptual differences:

Yard	*Crossroads*
private world	public world, keeping company
family (generational organization)	friendship networks (crew organization)
order, acting sensible	license, being sporty, talking nonsense
decorum, being behaved	rudeness
stability, passivity	mobility, activity
enclosed, protected	free, adventurous

circumspection	gregariousness, flash, keeping company
quiet, harmony	noise to annoy, vexation, boderation (arguments, usually playful), making mock, giving fatigue (badinage)
feminine values:	masculine values:
respectability maintenance (acceptance principle)	reputation maintenance (heroic attitudes, superphallicism)
truth, honesty, cooperation, loyalty	getting on fas', untrustworthiness, playful trickery, deceit

The ideals of the yard, especially those of cooperation and loyalty, are, of course, regarded as appropriate to any relationship of trust, especially institutionalized friendship. But from the yard perspective, friendships are regarded as frail indeed, as they often prove to be.

The world of respectability finds its fullest expression in celebrations held within the house and yard, the *fêtes* that center on life change: *thanksgivings, send-offs, wedding fêtes, baptismal fêtes.* So, too, the crossroad world has its days of high nonsense: *hangings* (the mock hanging and burning in effigy of social offenders and deviates), and pre-Lenten Carnival, Christmas, and *maroon* (a picnic held around August Monday, Emancipation Day). Just as the household events are, with some exceptions, celebrated with orderly performances, especially with songs and speeches carried out in oratorical Standard English, so the crossroads events involve singing and arguing in deepest creole.

The two worlds are significant because they symbolize different value systems and tend to organize the most important contrast sets of the culture: adult and child; old and young; male and female; public and private. But most important for an understanding of the expressive repertoire of the group, there is a distinction in the kind of talk approved in these different worlds between talking *bad* or *broken* (i.e., in creole) at the crossroads and talking sweet in the house and yard.

With regard to this last distinction, women, as the guardians of respectability, have a kind of investment in speechmaking as the vehicle by which respect is celebrated. This does not mean that women speak in such a code, for no one uses this way of speaking to carry on conversations. Rather, the female head of the household regards it as part of her role to provide instruction for her children in the most important ordering skills of life. Thus, she receives high marks in the eyes of the community if she is able to assist her children in getting a wage-earning trade. So she is also given high respect if she is able to send her children to *colleges,* to learn how to speak successfully on occasions of respect. Thus, to speak well is to honor and respect one's mother and, by extension, the other older females in the family.

As in other parts of Afro-America, in the West Indies the church can best be understood in relation to this value system of respect; and the church service is one of the most dramatic ways in which the control over talking sweet can be demonstrated. In one of the basic ironies common to this culture area, the women of the community in the main—once having established this occasion and place for a demonstration of enduring values through the employment of the oratorical code to speak about respect themes—encourage older men to take the central role in church services and other activities that testify to the importance of continuity and family order.

As with the central place of men in talking sweet occasions, women are ironically regarded as the best performers in talking broad—or at least one species of female, the *market women*. In such Afro-American communities, men and women are both expected to maintain their own gardens, *susus* (saving organizations), memberships in cooperative banks, and to have their own share of family land. Household composition and co-residence of a man and woman is quite stable; yet there is little long-term expectation for this stability, and so there is a great deal of sharing of gardening and house-building tasks within the family, but with a maintenance of separate accounts, as it were. In this system, it is women who are called on to sell the surplus crops. In a sense, then, these peasant agrarians have economic and expressive representatives in town: the sharp-tongued bargainers. Market women are not only major providers of money to the community, they also improvise the argument routines and the routine arguments that are reperformed once they get back home. Most important, they are the female members of the community who are given the greatest amount of latitude within the canons of respectability.

Normally, whenever a disruption occurs in a household, an event is called for in which the transition is given a name. In the main, these events overtly rehearse the norms in respectability, both in words and action. Thus, when someone leaves home for an extended period, a *send-off* is usually given, and when someone returns, or gets better after a sickness, a *thanksgiving* is held. (Henney, 1970, describes these in a church context.) Similarly, weddings and baptisms are major events. All of these call for the establishment and maintenance of order by an established man-of-words, a *chairman* or *master of ceremonies*. He (or she) calls on each person attending (other than the very young and the very old) to give an *offering* of some sort, a *toast*, a *speech*, a *recitation*, or a *sentimental song*. When an argument occurs, it is of a ritual sort and is engineered and led into by the chairman. An example of this is the hilarious argument between members of the bride's family and those of the groom over the cutting of the wedding cake. The groom is called on to cut down with a knife as the bride inserts a fork into the side of the cake in such a way that the knife passes between the tines of the fork. The argument then turns on whether the fork has surrounded and *covered* the knife or the knife has *split* the fork.

Many such occasions are prepared for not only by arranging that a ceremony be performed outside the home (weddings, the first night of wake, and baptisms), but by bringing food (often in the form of live animals) to the home ahead of time and then by cooking together on the day of the ceremony. To eat in the house is unusual; cooking and eating are carried on in the yard. With these ceremonies, however, a readjustment of the symbolic boundaries occurs, and the world of the road is invited into the yard while the friends and family move into the house. Drinking, loud talking, and game playing are carried on by the rest of the village while the household event is carried on indoors. Significantly, after the ceremonial toasts are made, bottles are passed through the windows into the yard, which in a sense encourages nonsense and rude behavior to a point. On such occasions, anyone may come into the yard—at least this is the ideal often given voice.

Another ideal is that everyone in the house must eat and drink together and perform for one another; the central role is passed around the room by the master of ceremonies such as one finds in the *ring plays* performed on moonlit nights. The emphasis in household events is upon people of different generations and sexes coming together as a statement of community togetherness and family continuity.

In direct contrast to such occasions are those carried out on the roads. Here the most important recurring event is carnival, the pre-Lenten celebration that is so raucous, so full of rudeness and nonsense that the boundary between yard and road is intensified. Here the ideal is to carouse, to have *a bacchanal,* to drink, sing and dance, and fight (both by ritual and otherwise), to dress up and to bring the often upside-down and chaos-producing spirit of the natural and supernatural into the community. Thus, some of the common Carnival figures are the devil, donkey, monkey, and bush man. Each such figure has a routine to perpetrate on by-standers, one that calls for exchange (of money or drink) through argument and coercion. Again, for economy's sake I have rendered the contrast between these types of events in the form of parallel lists of traits:

Household Rites	*Road Festivities*
performances in house	performances at crossroads, rum shops, open fields; in yards only when invited
eating; drinking during toasts only within house; bottles passed into yard	drinking of rum emphasized
emphasis on sensible activities in speeches (truth, knowledge, continuity, respect)	emphasis on nonsense in speeches, on lies and other foolishness
texts are logical in organization	texts have numerous *non sequiturs,* puns, other kinds of discontinuities

texts affirm social order and responsibility, focus on individual's acceptance of approved social role	texts satirize social order, hypocrisy of individuals, focus on wrong-doings
performances emphasize the derivation from the past of these social roles; these roles are intensified through stylized actions and formal clothing	social disorder and license emphasized through rude behavior, motley or animalistic costuming; texts oriented toward inducing social confusion and embarrassment
performance coordination; everyone may perform serially when designated by leader	competitive, aggressive performances; much overlap of voices, movements; contantly shifting dramatic focus, as one or another performer or group intrudes
performance speaking variety: talking sweet, good, sensible	performance speaking variety: talking broad, bad, broken

There are a number of occasions that fall between the household and the crossroads events in which one can observe similar encounters between reputation seeking and respect oriented performers, the *tea meeting* being the most dramatic. In principle, as in its history as a Methodist-inspired event, this occasion appears to be a church service simply held in a different environment, usually the lodge hall or some other community place of congregation. Held around Christmas, August Monday, or Easter, the *service* focuses on the oratorical skills of the chairmen and their *scholars.* They come together ostensibly to compete with each other for prize cakes, by speaking out boldly on a seasonal theme. When held at Christmas or Easter, each speech's core is derived from a biblical passage and its gloss.

There are two or more chairmen. One introduces each scholar and attempts to provide the "A, B, C, D's" of continuity and order throughout the event. The chairmen implicitly compete with their scholars and with one another, for each wishes to be known as "the most competent man-of-words." But their main competitors are members of the audience, whom they are charged with controlling. They introduce not only the speeches but also the interspersed anthems performed by the robed choir also seated on the stage. From the perspective of those on stage this is an orderly occasion: they wear their church clothes, fix their eyes on the audience, stiffly stylize any gesture, and otherwise move very little.

Meanwhile, in the other part of the lodge sit and stand the audience—and they are anything but attentive. Its members include *sporty fellows,* who commonly lead in Carnival carousing and other nonsense events, and the market women. They feel that this is their time to show their *style,* their flash. The appearance of a scholar becomes their opportunity for springing up, moving around, making mock, and giving rap in rhymes in the boldest bad talk. It is up to the chairmen and, to a lesser extent, the speakers to maintain their cool and to assert their ability to control through eloquent words. The purveyors of rudeness and nonsense try to make sure that order will not prevail without a struggle.

The major agency of disruption is the group of *pit boys*. They array themselves in the back of the hall, engaging in rapping, beating sticks on the benches in front of them. Commonly the *first chairman* promises the head pit boy one of the prize cakes if he brings his peers under control after they have a chance to have a little display.

Given the way in which the expressive profile of the community divides so neatly, the tea meeting may usefully be regarded as an open confrontation between the words of sense and nonsense, rudeness and behavior, talking sweet and talking bad.

Thus, in a very real sense a number of central features of the symbolic landscape of St. Vincent are brought into the hall used for the tea meeting. But the systematic agon of the event involves not only valorized spaces but a selective drawing upon the vocabulary of the entire range of the island's expressive events. The event is, after all, calendared, but, unlike other seasonal festivities, it is not always held, and, even when it is, it is not regarded in any full sense as part of the seasonal celebration. In part, this is because the event—like a *jump-up* dance, a *concert* or, in earlier times, a *soiree party*—is arranged by a local entrepreneur in order to make money. Not that this motive is absent in Christmas or Carnival, but during these occasions, money-making is secondary. Tea meetings capitalize on seasonal feelings and themes, without actually being built into the sense of seasonal passage.

Moreover, the event in many ways derives its vocabulary and primary ways of preparing and acting from household ceremonies—especially the wedding feast. The sense of formality that dominates the activities on stage is a careful blend of household and church behaviors, as is the way of dressing and singing.

Tea meetings were invented to subvert the all-night *plays* held during and after slavery. But, ironically, the festive spirit of the seasons had a subversive effect on the serious church-based, money-raising evenings; they developed into a type of event in which the entire repertoire of performance techniques is regarded as appropriate. And because the event was held on central ground, as it were, the worlds of order and energy found their way into open competition.

CHAPTER ELEVEN

Storytelling Events:
The Structure of
Nonsense on St. Vincent

The question I address here is quite simple: How do folktales embody and achieve meaning as they are performed within an event? Specifically, I shall describe a body of tales as these tales are employed within a traditional event—the *wake,* or *nine-night,* as celebrated by most Afro-American gardening folk in Richland Park, St. Vincent, and neighboring communities. But as simple as this question is, to reveal the process by which cultural meanings are achieved is always a complex project. For these understandings-in-common draw upon the richly textured weave of group experience as it is imbricated in display forms during such cultural performances.

This chapter is an attempt to place an event, the Vincentian nine-night, within the expressive economy of the community. It does this by looking closely at the content features of the riddles, games, and, especially, tales as they are performed within the event. To be meaningful, these features must be "situated" not only within the structure of the event but also in the ways in which the event articulates the everyday practices and values of the community.

The wake is best understood perhaps in the terms employed by Vincentians themselves in talking about it: "A whole lot people be coming on with nonsense there." *Nonsense,* which is Vincentian for loud, boisterous, rude, argumentative behavior, may seem inappropriate as a way of marking death, but not so in the West Indies. Commonly used to describe the way men behave whenever they get together, but especially at the crossroads rumshop, nonsense takes on another set of meanings in the wake, in which it draws upon the semantic field of *Nansi* as well. Nansi and nonsense are indeed conflated in the terms *Nansi 'tory,* the name given by Vincentians for all wake amusements, whether they are tales concerning the spider trickster, riddles, competitive games, or a fairly broad range of tales including European-style *Märchen.* Also pronounced *nonsen 'tory* and *nas'y 'tory* (i.e., nasty stories), nine-night has come to include not only a way of acting but also a perspective by which the respectable ideals

157

of behavior and decorum have been inverted and commented upon jokingly.

I shall first explore the theoretical underpinnings of event-centered analysis in a study of folktales in general before I explicate the place of the Anansi tales, their telling and their meaning as it emerges through the relationship between Vincentian wakes and the other named expressive events on the island.

EVENT-CENTERED ANALYSIS

Past studies of the folktale have primarily concerned themselves with texts. But recently, in response to the growing ethnographic interests of a number of folklorists, a different sort of study has developed that focuses on storytelling as a cultural activity, and the storyteller as a role in scenes of composition and performance. Such studies, which arise in the general intellectual current of the study of artistic communication, attempt to reveal what the performer brings to the audience so that a performance may be achieved. In these, each performance and thus each narrative is to be regarded as an achievement rather than a rendering.

Taking the text from the realm of the "given" and turning it into a problematic area for discussion enables us to regard both the tale and its telling as aesthetic phenomena. By looking at the performance of tales, one may bring to bear notions of accountability on the part of the performer, a recognition that each performance is a counter in a transaction, and therefore may be judged in terms of its success in "living up to the deal" entered into by performer and audience, in which time and energy are expended in common. But to use accountability in this manner is simply to underscore that an exchange or transaction is taking place, one that is subject to judgment on the basis of certain discoverable notions of reciprocity. As an aesthetic transaction, the telling of the tale is judged in terms of the performer's success in factoring in the physical setting and the audience's size, character, and disposition; the choice made in the repertoire with regard to appropriateness criteria; and the vigor, focus, eloquence, inventiveness, authenticity, and authoritativeness of the rendering. What we are most concerned with turns on the success (or failure) of the performance in heightening apprehension and enjoyment. To actively study such performance traditions entails observation of how the performance skills are developed, how the items performed are learned, practiced, tried out, rehearsed—whatever preparation is appropriate to the type of performance (Bauman, 1978; Toelken, 1979). Moreover, notions of accountability include appropriateness of style and repertoire—that is, what the criteria are brought to bear with regard to what may be talked about, in what manner and at what language level of formality or informality, openness or fixity.

All performances draw upon a learned repertoire of conventional devices, but some have larger units to be learned and replayed exactly as learned. This presents a real descriptive problem in discussing folktales, for there is always a question of how much a tale is learned and must be performed exactly as heard, how much must be presented in a more spontaneous style of stitching together. Here we are concerned with elements of style and context that enable us not only to look at the creative process of various performances but also to distinguish one type of performance from others in the expressive economy of a community, as well as to relate the expressive dimensions of everyday experience and the more intensely focused and stylized performance. Such a point of view, then, enables us to see the connection made by Vincentians between nonsense activities at the rum shop as they occur everyday and at a low level of intensity, and more formal nonsense as it arises during *Carnival, hangings* (effigy burnings with comic songs and plays), and nine-nights.

While this argument in favor of relating the ordinary to the extraordinary in terms of manners arises directly out of sociological phenomenology—especially the work of Erving Goffman on the one hand, the Hymesian ethnography of communication on the other—it really reflects the common intellectual tradition in which all American ethnography seems to flourish: the tradition of the pragmatists, of William James and John Dewey and George Herbert Mead.

In line with the apparent openness of the movement across North America, a philosophy concerned with the frontiers of the mind emerged, along with pluralism and openness of a more psychological sort. This project invoked a peculiarly American notion of "frontier," in which the term refers not to fixed boundaries between states but to "natural," "wild," unpopulated regions in which the not-yet-apprehended and the as-yet-unordered provides the term with its center of meaning. In pursuing such matters, "experience" became the key concept for notions of life as being constructed of constantly emerging phenomena.

The Deweyan distinction between "experience" and "*an* experience" epitomizes this approach by distinguishing between the flow of quotidian activities in which meanings and feelings are taken for granted, and the sense of the episodic that emerges from time to time, often from the least choate dimension of our existence. A happening emerges that has a sense of intense wholeness to it, implying that it is somehow to be interpreted apart from that flow. To a great extent the difference has to do with how focused the engagement is, whether that focus emerges because of preparation or through an external disruption of sufficient magnitude to bring it about. One way or the other, we expect an experience to be reportable, sufficiently interesting to talk about it later, and to make it a story.

There is a wide range of experience that is susceptible to achieving this intensity of focus, especially those that become "occasions" and "events." The latter, especially, has resonances of meaning indicating that when the flow of activities becomes *an* event, the activity is more bounded and more framed than *an* experience. Event in such a case, means a focused interaction that has been anticipated and prepared for. We recognize an event not only because of the intensity of involvement in common carried by the participants into the encounter but by their special rule-regulated behaviors, their manner of coordinating and regularizing the activity. Included here are all of those events that involve celebration: the festivals, ceremonies, and rituals that call for specially stylized and occasion-specific behaviors and performances.

There is a major ontological shift to be made between everyday experience and these prepared-for events, because our manner of deriving meaning from the engagement is so different. In the flow of everyday activities, our exchanges are judged in such terms as liveliness, spontaneity, informativeness, and responsiveness, or openness to the flow of the talk; any nonspontaneous acts tend to be bracketed and regarded as temporary and not the norm. We place frames—or at least quotation marks—around such an episode, regarding it as a little performance introduced into an everyday exchange. We judge interactions marked as performance- (or some other kind of play-) events in terms of the degree of control of those involved. Rather than look for intensity we anticipate redundancy and other self-consciously stylized acts.

My objective in outlining this approach to behavior is to establish storytelling as a type of performance that lives best in the special occasion I have been calling *an* event. Sometimes, of course, the event itself is the telling of tales. But often tales arise in the midst of other, more large-scale events and may be usefully studied with regard to their placement within that context.

Strangely enough, we have few situated studies of either tales or tale-telling events in spite of the call sent forth by Robert Georges ten years ago. Even more disappointing is the lack of studies of tales and other forms of performance in ethnographic accounts of the expressive culture of any community, for anthropologists have collected texts for at least a century as expressions of culture, but they have largely failed to relate stories or storytelling to recurrent activities. (Perhaps this poverty exists only in ethnographies in English.)

In spite of the recent interest in events as cultural performances, I have been able to uncover very few analyses of storytelling events. Only the recent books on storytelling among certain West and South African groups by Finnegan, Scheub, Ben-Amos, Cosentino, and LaPin have presented us with texts, situating them within the life of the community. And most of these studies have focused more on the process of composition and performance than on relating the tales and their telling to the expressive resources of the culture and to the recurrent occasions on which they are told. Even Linda Dégh's remarkable monograph on the Szeklers of Hungary and Rumania treats these occasions in passing, and she only tantalizes us with brief references to the larger events in which storytelling arises.

Only two very recent books have begun to carry out the ethnographic ideal with regard to story-making, storytelling and interpreting. Henry Glassie's analysis of Irish narrators, narration, and narrative scenes, occasions, and events in *Passing the Time in Ballymenone* is an exhaustive and rhapsodic work that will cause us to reexamine folktale methodology. If we read it in combination with his *All Silver and No Brass*—an excursus into mumming and mummers in the same community—we can begin to get a feeling for the range of expressive events, forms, and repertoire of devices in one small group of peasants.

Even closer to my present design is Alessandro Falassi's remarkable *Folklore by the Fireside,* an ethnographic and folkloristic account of the Tuscan *veglia.* Here, by focusing on the range of expressive forms that arises in one kind of family and community event (usually taking place in the kitchen), storytelling is related to riddling, social dancing, and singing, among other practices. Moreover, the tales are given in a context of how they are usually performed, the idiosyncrasies of specific narrators, the ways in which the kitchen space is articulated, who is locally identified with specific stories and why.

This is not to argue that there have been too few analytic studies of cultural events by folklorists or ethnographers. Rather it has been difficult to relate such focused occasions to other dimensions of the culture receiving ethnographic notice. Even the "classics" describing rituals, festivals, or play occasions have rendered specific named events in depth without tying them to the expressive system. More characteristic are those such as Gregory Bateson, Clifford Geertz and Victor W. Turner, who give us multilayered discriptions of the event within the system of world order and value. Van Gennep and Malinowski, Radcliffe-Brown and Raymond Firth give us objective descriptions of the yearly in-gatherings in a kind of calendar of affairs. There are two major exceptions: Gary Gossen's *Chamulas in the Land of the Sun,* which is an in-depth analysis of world order through expressive codes if not thickly described events; and Fredrik Barth's *Ritual and Knowledge among the Baktaman of New Guinea,* which focuses on the initiatory rites but places them (briefly) in the context of the range of expressive forms, scenes, and events.

An activity can be made to seem significant simply by calling it an event. But the events analyzed by folklorists are those already set apart by the folk, associated by them with occasion-specific ways of behaving and performing. These traditional events establish themselves outside the flow of the everyday because they are named, anticipated, and involve intensive preparations and conventions of play and performance.

RESPECT NORMS AND REPUTATION-SEEKING PRACTICES

Examining the meaning system articulated in the Vincentian wake as an event is difficult because it is an inversive encounter. Only by spelling out the norms and the common practices that are turned upside down can it be understood. Moreover, such inversive social and cultural play, as one form of nonsense, is regarded as normal behavior in public places under everyday conditions. To understand how these stories and their telling are interpreted as both normative and inversive, I shall describe the Vincentian expressive economy as it relates to the range of social events.

As elsewhere in Afro-America, on St. Vincent there is an observable tension in daily life between domains of order and continuity on the one hand, and those of action and the pursuit of friendly encounters on the other. This is most easily understood as an opposition between the complex of the house and yard and that of the road, the crossroads, and the town with its gathering place, the market. Throughout the agrarian segment of Afro-America, family life takes place as much in the yard as in the house. The house and yard are the appropriate places to display acts of order, continuity, and, most importantly, respectability. Although this is the most private of domains, the place of "nobody's business but my own," whenever private happenings become public (because of sickness, birth, death, travel), the household world and its values are put under strain, and the response often takes the form of a traditional ceremonial display. These traditional events that occur in the house and yard have a strong sense of having been prepared for. They are sequenced and focused displays. This cannot be said of either the everyday activities at the crossroads or of the festive events that are carried on in such public places, encounters that seem to erupt into nonsense performances.

Each pattern of conduct is associated with different places, with differences in age and sex, and with alternative codes of stylized speaking and acting as I explored in the last chapter. The ordering and maintaining of life in Richland Park is associated with *respect*. This is constantly contrasted with behavior that is regarded, from the respect-seeking perspective, as being chaotic, or, to use those most common Vincentian terms, *nonsense-making, coming on rude*. Problems seldom arise between these two worlds, for they exist in different places and the areas where they abut are clearly delineated.

Except when explicitly celebrated in detail, respectability is dramatized on an everyday basis through the observable order-making activities carried on within the yard—activities that go beyond cooking and sweeping to the making of building materials. Most dramatically, in the yard cultural things are constantly fashioned out of natural products. We see this, of course, in gardening and cooking, but also in the sawing of boards, the breaking of rocks, the molding of bricks—and all of those other activities that go into house-building as well as order-maintaining. Thus, the yard gives off the message that this is a growing family in good order and worthy of being regarded with respect.

When a *fête* is called for in the house or yard, a breakdown of social and physical boundaries occurs. This happens in response to threats to one or another member of the family, through sickness, leave-taking and return, birth and marriage. All of these call for a fête: a *thanksgiving*, a *send-off*, a *wedding*, and a *baptism*.

Although these are house-based ceremonies, everything that goes on within both the house and the yard is an interruption of everyday life there. For instance, food, which is commonly cooked and eaten in the yard, is served within the house to the seated guests. The world of the road is invited into the yard while the friends and family move into the house. Drinking, loud talking, game playing, and other dramatic examples of nonsense and rudeness are brought into the area that commonly is the seat of order—the yard. After a speech or song celebrating respect values is made, a toast may be drunk, and bottles are passed through the windows. Noise from the yard constantly threatens to interrupt the proceedings, especially when fights break out. By licensing the drinking of rum on such occasions (albeit in combination with food), a kind of brinksmanship is being practiced, for rum is regarded as the *nonsense-maker,* thus introducing the constant possibility of rudeness in the proceedings.

The alternative crossroads world brings action, especially that of contest exchanges, into play. The crossroads is the public space in which competitive commerce is carried on. The most representative place in the crossroads world of St. Vincent is the market in Kingstown, for here one gets as far away from the norms of house and family as possible, and here one expects to engage in contests to see who is able to do the outsmarting, the exploiting.

Crossroads events highlight the symbolic dimensions of everyday actions by building upon the dramatic possibilities of even bargaining coercively, or at least through the use of vigorous acts and dramatic talk. Moreover, these occasions are public and celebrate nonsense-making in all its forms, from indulging in all activities to the point of excess, to cross-dressing and engaging in other topsy-turvy behaviors, to making fun in every dimension, especially through songs of derision. The most important of these crossroads events on St. Vincent is Carnival, but other such activities are: the mock-trial called hanging; the *maroon* (picnic on Emancipation Day); Christmas *serenading, tea meeting,* and *soiree party and dance,* now called *concert.* All underscore the excitement of action through performances that bring coercive begging from the bystanders, attempts by those in costume to frighten as well as delight, the constant passing of bottles, and contest encounters of many sorts.

But unlike the household events, those held in more public places seem to develop their primary impetus by their positioning vis-à-vis the yard or respectable behavior. For instance, the Christmas serenading explicitly distinguishes between the licentious carousing while the serenaders are on the road, and the *sweet* orations, playing, and singing done at the *gate,* the entrance point to the yard. In the latter, formal modes of address are used, and leave to enter the yard is made before the formal speech is given.

Hangings, too, are deeply implicated in household norms, for they enact scenes that occurred in a specific yard, which deeply challenges respect norms. Specifically, the misdoings generally arise from a man's inability to control his *nature* in this setting. Hangings, then, involve dramatized *cómmess,* but carried out in such a public and joking way that social wounds are actually salved through community laughter and celebration (Rubinstein, 1974).

In an even more pragmatic manner, in tea meetings (and the closely related concerts) respect practices actively confront the powers of license. In the form of an oratorical contest, the two conflict on a neutral ground, a lodge hall or some other enclosed public space. Here the space is divided in two: the stage, where the respect-side is represented with dressing up and orations are delivered talking sweet; and the seats below, where the audience attempts, through *making mock,* to shout down the speakers and to entertain one another in the process.

THE WAKE: ORGANIZED RUDENESS

Nine-night is an anomaly, but one that accrues power precisely because of the ways in which it differs from other expressive events. For in these wakes, the entire crossroads world seems invited not only into the yard but also into the house itself, thus readjusting the boundaries by which the value- and performance-orientation of the community usually is put into place. In this environment of license stories are told, stories that celebrate life through the dramatization of inversive motives. Just such a distinction was pointed out to me by one of the great chairmen of the island, Charles Jack. Commenting on the difference between making speeches and storytelling, he noted:

> When you say a speech, you couldn't talk nonsense. That's a *speech.* The one who studies [thinks about, practices] 'Nansi 'tory, it's nonsense story, and there're little or no truth in a nonsense story, right? The one who studies *oration,* he's studying facts. . . . The Nansi storyteller . . . he talks broad, of course, that's the best part of it. He doesn't care how he talks, because Nansi can't talk good.

Talking nonsense and acting *rude* is what, indeed, the character of Compé Nansi does, and it is this kind of talking and acting that describes the event as well as the motives embodied in the stories. The 'Nansi storyteller *talks broad,* and this is explicitly related to Compé Nansi's inability to speak correctly. Nansi not only speaks as the other animals do, in conversational creole, but his speech is even more *bruck-up,* for he lisps and stutters.

Furthermore, nonsense is associated with outrageous actions, as are both Nansi himself and the stories to which he gives his name. To have actions of any sort happening within the house normally challenges the respectability of the woman who is head of the household. This would especially apply to any competitive activities or, to use the Vincentian terms, getting on *vextatious* or *contrady.* But this is precisely the kind of action encouraged in wake. Or as Charles Jack pointed out:

Talking Nansi story without action in it doesn't mean much. It's the action that amuses, so you must see him making action and so on. Sing a little note, dance. . . .

Here he is describing not only the way in which Buh 'Nansi acts within the stories, but the manner in which the stories and other expressive genres within the domain of Nansi 'tory are performed. These other activities are contrady in structure: riddling contests and forfeit games. Moreover, they involve rude activities carried out rudely, by young men seizing power, at least for the moment of play.

Rudeness in the everyday is feared because it leads to embarrassment for those who are socially manipulated by the activity. A rude person upsets all expectations of how an interaction goes (or should go). He not only causes embarrassment but does so while having the embarrassed one feel as if the social encounter is one-sided and out of control. What is often referred to as *disbehaving* is therefore an illegitimate device of social confusion, for it leads to a feeling that there has been a breakdown of the social order. This point is emphasized in discussions of rudeness from the point of view of the respect-seeking element of the community. These discussions most commonly focus on young people (especially young men) forgetting their "place" in the order of things—*playin' man before 'e time.*

Seizing the central place in an encounter involving a mixture of generations leads to an allegation of *boasting*—which here refers to any activity that a person can use to focus attention on himself. It is regarded as appropriate for men to boast, but not before they are considered men by the community. *Calling name* is one way of boasting, for it reveals that you regard the one so named as being equal, being your *sex and size.* But calling the name of someone older than yourself is always chancy. The young *rude boys,* then, are often accused as *being out of place* or *not company.* A standard way of pointing out such disbehaving is to level a proverb at the offending one, usually focusing on the noisy dimension of the disorder: "The more you talk to pig, the more they tell you 'hunh hunh'"—that is, the more you try to talk with someone about his or her rudeness, the ruder he or she becomes.

It is precisely this set of motives that are drawn upon in riddling, forfeit games, and 'Nansi stories. But what in everyday life is regarded as disruptive, in play form creates fun and the community of laughter. One person seizes the position of leadership, then uses it both to engineer and to describe confusion, that is, games, riddling, and storytelling are all noisy, contentious, spirited forms of licensed boasting and disbehaving. But they are all concerned with describing chaotic social conditions as well as embodying the motive of disbehaving in the performance. For just as the stories are often about confusion and even social dissolution, so the games are concerned with forms that describe tested relationships of power, even while they test them in real life. The content of the games and the riddles, in others, is paralleled by the way they are enacted. The point is perhaps most easily seen in the way the lashing games are played. In these, one person grabs a towel or large handkerchief and begins to gain control over the proceedings either by leading the singing of one of the songs that accompanies a game or by announcing what will be played. At some point he has to give over control to other young men—which he does by giving lashes to those who make mistakes in the game.

A common game used in these situations is Barkodey. This game subverts one of the most important acts of friendship: taking care of the hair of another. Here the leader sings one line and all others answer "Barkodey" as the chorus:

> Barkodey, me buddy.
> *Barkodey*
> Them send me to shave you,
> *Barkodey*
> With me ten pound razor,
> *Barkodey*
> And if you laugh me go cut you,
> *Barkodey*
> Me buddy, bark, oh, bark,
> *Barkodey*
> [*ad lib, etc.*]

The leader has a comb, which he holds, like a razor, in his hand, passing it under the noses of those seated. He tries to get them to smile by the manner of using the comb, by taking the attacked person by surprise, or by making some kind of rude comment or strange noise. If the player does laugh, he is hit with great gusto with the towel around the head and shoulders by the leader, who then moves on to someone else.

Another such game, this one parodying the courtship process, is Contrady Partner. A leader chooses pairs couples on the basis of the strangeness of the sexual combination embodied in the supposed partnership. He jests that the two picked will soon marry. He then goes to one of the partners and begins to make disparaging remarks about the other in as intense a style and as broad a way of talking as possible. He argues that the other should "leave she" or make remarks on how *fas'* (thieving, untrustworthy) one of the partners is or other similarly disorienting remarks. (The same all too obviously parodies devices of social control like cõmmess.) If the person to whom these remarks are directed laughs, she or he is rewarded with the same lashes.

In these games, then, there is contrived confusion through a calculated rudeness that brings to bear social motives actively into an unreal game contest. The players are constantly aware that play borders on the real in readily perceptible ways, for the leader is manipulating feelings and sentiments that real people have for one another.

Riddles, too, contrive a confusion, both in their texts and their telling. A great majority of the riddles deal with imposing contrasts, ones that in everyday life often refer to power relationships. But in the riddling context, this element appears playfully subverted if not inverted. In the main, these are what folklorists call "true riddles" ones that describe an object or action through a list of traits, but ones that either do not fill in the picture sufficiently to guess the referent or have such an innate (apparent) contradiction of terms within the description that the solution is difficult or impossible to arrive at.

Like the games, the riddling draws on social relationships of the most troubling sort—between father and child, white and black, man and animal, life and death. Here the conventions of the relationships are given; but the mystery at the heart of the relationship, rather than a subversion of it through trickery, is the central feature of the riddles.

For instance, as many as one third of the texts emerging in an evening of riddling refer to the attributes, abilities, and powers of "my father" or, alternatively, "an old man," underscoring the generational basis of the conflict. We are asked to guess what their source is. But repeatedly strength and ability are revealed as not inhering to the father at all but merely being attached to him by convention:

> My father has twelve sons, and he put them off to go on a journey. And they all going but they cannot touch each other 't all—January, February, March, April, May, June, July, August, September, October, November, December . . . 'c falls to the days, man, otherwise the hours.

Here it is the conventions of time-marking—rather than the father—that have the power:

> An old man built his house
> Can' get in or out.
> And only a man outside can get him out.
> —Oh, chigger; chigger and needle.

> My father have thirty-two white sheep . . .
> There came a red bull and overlook* them
> all.—Teeth and tongue.

The power of *overlooking* is, of course, one of social and sexual control—an attribute of "my father" found in many riddle questions, only to be undercut somewhat in the answer.

> My father have a cock and every time it crow,
> it crow fire.—A gun.

> My father build a house with one post
> and many sill.—Umbrella.

Similarly, the white man or whitie plays a powerful—if often bumbling—role in a number of these mock mini-dramas.

---

*oversee

Whitie-whitie send whitie-whitie over whitie-whitie. Whitie-whitie see half of whitie-whitie' garden.—A white man sent a white man drive a white man' sheep, a white man have, out a white man' garden.

Whitie, blackie inside whitie; whitie 'pon top blackie and white come out.—Your crack a matches, put it on top the tobacco in the pipe and smoke comes out.

Reddie-reddie* gi' whitie-whitie; blackie-blackie gi' whitie-whitie; brownie-brownie gi' whitie-whitie.—Cows and milk.

My flesh is white, my children are black, my skin is green and bumpy.—Soursop.

Perhaps the most striking riddles, given the occasion, are those that articulate the opposition of life and death. Again, the powerful one, death, is comprised through equation as well as opposition with life, the two being juxtaposed in a jocular fashion. Repeatedly, the contradiction that is the source of confusion turns on the dead somehow sustaining the living:

As I was going down the road, I saw the dead carrying the living.—Boat and man.
A man take a dead man to maintain† a living man 'body.—Carry a dead worm‡ to catch a living fish.

Clearly, then, a kind of vibrancy is established through the self-consciously clever confusion of categories and the witty inversion of the power relations.

THE STORYTELLING

In riddling, then, we see a structural process operating on the level of systematic meaning and sentiment that is closely related to the joking seizure of power, for the moment, by performers. The process of structural inversion operates within the spaces of the house and yard temporarily taken over by the forces of nonsense, and in the kinds of performance called forth and the content of the performed texts. The explosive fun-making energy and vitality of the crossroads ways of talking and acting becomes a cultural resource for the family and community in the encounter with death.

All of these same patterns of performance and thematic inversions of manners and sentiments are most fully explored in the storytelling sessions of the nine-night. Just as the riddling and lashing games involve a bold seizure of the spotlight by a sporty fellow, so, too, stories are commonly begun by someone successfully contending for the attention of the group. This is often done by choosing a story to perform that has a song embedded in it. Vincentians

---

*Red and brown here refer to different shades of Afro-American coloration, not to American Indians.
†Obtain.
‡Or crawfish.

distinguish between *wet* and *dry* stories, the former being considered better because they have songs. Before a performance, someone is likely to spring up and begin a song. If the others begin to sing along, the same song will be repeated for a fairly extended period (thirty seconds to a couple of minutes). This may also cause people to get up and begin to dance together; if this occurs the singing goes on even longer. Commonly, then, the one who began the song leaps up and proclaims "Crick-crack!", to which the others respond "Rockland come!". He or she may have to say "crick-crack" a number of times before the response occurs—if it occurs at all, for there is no rule that says once a story or its song is begun it must be finished. Moreover, the story may proceed and be stopped again and again for the singing and the dancing. Here the storyteller tries to move things along by yelling out "Crick-crack!"

The stories told in this welter of confusion are commonly concerned with describing the trickery of Nansi or some other such minatory character who manages to shake up the social and natural order of things through his doings. The following is an example of such a story:

> Well once upon a time, Massa King had a daughter. And the daughter that he had was so beautiful that he have she into a showcase. And he had a large stone was out into his yard. And when he had this large stone there, he said anybody that come and dance this stone into smoke shall receive his daughter, and the palace likewise too. And everybody went and dance on this stone, they cannot get no smoke.
>
> Well, little Anansi heard about this beautiful girl and he was well-dress. He went to the chief town and did buy a piece a clot' and he carry to the tailor. And when he went to the tailor, he make it inside with pure inside pocket right way down [motioning to the ground]. And he get to a building where they boil sweeten, he full every pocket with ashes. And he went down to Massa King.
>
> And he said when he going, "Good morning, Massa King." Tell him, "Good morning, Compé Anansi." He says, "Well I heard you had a work to perform here sir. And I come to see if I could try to perform anyt'ing for you." He said, "Oh, yes Compé Anansi, this is the girl and there is the stone in the yard who want and dance into smoke, and you shall receive my daughter." And Compé Anansi has went. He say, "Massa King, well, let me go and try and see if I can do anything with the stone." He said, "Oh sure, Compé Anansi." And Compé Anansi has went to the stone. And when he is going to the stone, his shoe is speaking to him going now. And when he went on the stone start. (I want everybody to sing this tune with me.) He went up and the stone. He start:
>
> Ying-ee-ding-ee-ding,
> The girl-a for me.
> Ying-ee-ding-ee-ding,
> The girl-a for me.
> Ying-ee-ding-ee-ding,
> The girl-a for me.
> Ying-ee-ding-ee-ding,
> The girl-a for me.

And Massa King has 'top him. He says, "Wait Compé Anansi. What you said?" He said, "I just humming a little tune, sir." He says, "Hum that tune again and let me hear."

Ying-ee-ding-ee-ding,
The girl-a for me.
Ying-ee-ding-ee-ding,
The girl-a for me.

And he curse him. He said, "Yes, Compé Anansi, I would glad if you should gain that girl." And Compé Anansi went up to he say, "Well, Massa King, I am going to begin now." He say, "Oh yes, Compé Anansi, you can go ahead." And he start now, he going to make his motion now. Went up, he said [slapping sides]:

Ying-ee-ding-ee-ding,
The girl-a for me.
Ying-ee-ding-ee-ding,
The girl-a for me.
Ying-ee-ding-ee-ding,
The girl-a for me.
Ying-ee-ding-ee-ding,
The girl-a for me.

[Every fourth line he slaps all the way to the ground.]

And there was the ashes, caused fly so great until Massa King could not have see Compé Anansi where he is. And he has to stop him, for dance, smoke the stone into smoke. And the wire bend and the story end.

Like trickster figures everywhere, Nansi is clever with words and with transforming (and bewitching) performances in general. Although he is small and childlike, he manages to trick those larger and supposedly wiser. And like other tricksters, his appetites are only matched by his immense power to confuse and mislead others. In keeping with his role as lord of nonsense, he manages to commit every act of rudeness conceivable and, beyond this, violate all canons of behavior and friendship relationships.

Thus, it seems especially significant that those who identify themselves with Anansi by telling his stories resemble Spider in their social position within the community. The Vincentian taletellers I worked with were ones who, because of their peculiar character or in-between social situation, lived alone (with one exception, a young man of twenty-five who still lived with his mother). Moreover, many of them were regarded as *selfish* (i.e., bashful) by others, a subject that was discussed because of the change that seemed to come over them when they began to perform. Indeed, two of them in Richland Park stuttered, except when leading a story.

This in-between status is significant if only because it mirrors the anomalous character of Spider, who is neither a creature of the bush, nor the field, nor the house and yard, but one who lives between all of these realms. He is wild yet not wild, in the house but not of the house. He is an outrageous contaminator.

We can understand his status in these stories better by using these anomalous rule- and boundary-breaking characteristics. With Vincentians, we can laugh at his antics—ruining families and friendships, wholesale killing, eating all of the available food (even while his children go hungry), stealing all of the women—although we are shocked and even repulsed by them.

Almost half of the stories that go under Compé Nansi's name are concerned with Massa King and his attempts to protect the fortune of his beautiful daughter—and not just from Nansi but the other animals. In the other type of story most commonly encountered the protagonist is commonly the Old Witch Boy—also called the Jiggerfoot Boy because of his club foot, or the Chiggerfoot Boy because of having troubling mites in his foot—who is the son of Massa King, and therefore the younger brother of the beautiful daughter. A great many stories are told in which the daughter's hand is won by one who is able to pass the king's test and who takes her away to the bush. There he reveals himself as an animal or devil creature who keeps his wife in bondage. But her little brother sneaks into the bush, discovers what has happened, and manages to free her by revealing the sources of his power, usually, a transforming set of words, or (as here) a song. Oedipal motives as well as deep sibling rivalry are the primary themes, and in line with this, the ending often involves a castratory killing of the man-animal. Crucial to an understanding of what is going on here, the Old Witch Boy is, though of the royal family, associated with filth, contamination, and social unworthiness. Although he wins this contest, we see no signs of his social acceptance in any of the stories about him, and some explicitly reject such a possibility.

> Scalambay, scalambay,
> Scoops, scops, scalambay.
> See me lover coming dey,
> Scoops, scops, scalambay.
> [*Ad lib, etc.*]

Once upon a time, it was a very good time, Massa King he have one only daughter and all the young fellows were all time going to marry to she. Say, "No, Daddy, this fellow here, I don't like he." And the last one that 'e choose was a boarhog.

Well, one day the young fellow come in and when he came in from work, 'e have a little Old Witch Boy dey, dey back in the home. 'E say, "Daddy, Daddy, you know that fellow that marry to my sister is a boarhog." "What? Shut your mouth and get underneath the bed."

Well, it happen so now, married, the father came up on the mountain, and show 'im a big piece of land for work there. Well he going off, he going by the land to mind the tania* them. Going so, he noticing everything. Watch the time a piece. Father show him a house where he could go and take off he clothes and everyt'ing. Say, "O.K."

---

* An edible tubor in the taro family.

So this day now, well he going up to work now. Going up very early in the morning, and when he go up now, he going in the side of the watch-house, and he take off 'e clothes, he put on 'e dirty clothes. But when when he go now to take off the dirty clothes, instead that he putting on a . . . he don't know he a boarhog. And you know the boarhog love the tania piece. He say [making a rooting motion with his head]:
  Scalambay, scalambay,
  Scoops, scops, scalambay.
  Scalambay, scalambay,
  Scoops, scops, scalambay.
  [*Repeat four times*]

Well, he judge the time is twelve o'clock. He jump inside the room, he take off the boarhog suit, and he put on the ordinary suit he come in with. Eat 'o food. This young fellow go home, tell his daddy, say, "Daddy, dis fellow who marry to my sister up dey, he's a boarhog." He say, "It is true." He said, "Boy, shut your mouth." His sister said, "Get underneath the bed, you little scamp you."
  Next day, going up again, hear:
  Scalambay, scalambay,
  Scoops, scops, scalambay.
  See me lover coming dey,
  Scoops, scops, scalambay.
  [*Repeat three times*]

All right, he go down the next day, 'e tell he daddy [that his tania field is being eaten and who is doing it], and daddy, father load the gun. He say, "Daddy, everytime I up there, 'e eat them down." And the father load up the gun and he come up. Boarhog up dey fus' [before him]. Then he say la tania field [the tanias emerge out of the ground because of this magic song]:
  Scalambay, scalambay,
  Scoops, scops, scalambay.
  See me lover coming dey,
  Scoops, scops, scalambay.
  [*Repeat four times*]
  Said, "Boy, me going and see a me tania piece." Wait see the boarhog going on so. And he lower the gun and he going out:
  Scalambay, scalambay,
  Scoops, scops, scalambay.
  See me lover coming dey,
  Scoops, scops, scalambay.
  [*Repeat nine times*]
And Massa King leggo bow! And he take Mr. Boarhog. And they carry Mr. Boarhog. When they go and clean Mr. Boarhog, they have to bring home Mr. Boarhog go an' have he quartered. And I been on the spot and I take one of the grains [testicles]. It serve me [as meat] nearly a week. Crick Crack. Sweet-O. (Percy Silva)

The oedipal character of the struggle becomes displaced from the father to the brother; but, significantly, both Massa King and the Jiggerfoot Boy are regarded as having the power of witchcraft rather than any political power. There are no witches in the community, and no one regards witchcraft as a problem there; *obeah,* which involves curing techniques and potions, is not considered witchcraft. However, Massa King and his son are often described in the same terms as the *obeahman,* who is regarded as a bush creature, an older person who has elected to live outside of the village and therefore has no friends in the usual sense.

The oedipal face-off is never far from the surface in such stories, some of which pit an old man against a young one for the favors of a young girl who happens to pass by. Even more open in its examination of this is the story depicting a battle between an old bull and his secret son. The old bull kills all male calves as they are born. But one of his cows sneaks off into the bush to have her calf and raises him there. When he is old enough to toss a huge boulder and mow down a forest with his horns, his mother allows him to go to meet his father. They have a butting contest in which the father loses one leg after another and finally his head. Then he goes off with one of the cows, with all the others singing and dancing in his honor:

Now this story about a bull-cattle. This bull-cattle was a black one. You know black cattle can't stand much sun, the heat of the sun. And that bull-cattle—every cow that bull-cattle go and have the range with. If they have any bull-calf, he kill 'im.

So there was one, one of the cows, and that cow decide to go into the bush and bring forth that baby, which she suggest would be a bull. And so said, so done. The calf grow and grow, he reach to a certain age, and he say, "But mommy, where is my daddy; I want to see my daddy." The mother say unto him, "Boy, if you go and see your daddy, he will kill you, because every bull-calf that born, the father kill them, and he's the only bull alive." A look as Superintendent, he's young that Superintendent. Lot o' colors, pretty-looking fellow, man, so that fellow, man, he would stand any heat of sun, when his father only black. And the mother was speckled in color.

Well it so happened that the mother said, "For you to go and see your father, you will have to go to that big stone out there, and when you reach it, you will just have to go and when you t'row it over your back, can go an' see you fadduh." Superintendent run off with speed, man. Soon as he reach, run 'round and pitch it over 'e back. Well 'e pitch it over 'e back, mother say, "Yes you have done it but you have los' t'ree month' strenk and you have to stop t'ree months before you can pick up you strenk again and can go an' see you fadduh. Because soon as you lif' that, part of you strenk gone."

Well he spen' another t'ree months. 'E carry um to a tree this time, 'e say, "You can go to dat tree, but befo' you go to de tree remember you have to go an jus' dig it out an' t'row it over you back without leavin' any of the san' on you back when you finish." Superintendent run, but soon as he reach, he na even go with a force more than 'e have to jus' throw over the back. Shake off san'. So pretty and skin so smooth that none the san' leave on' e back.

Well arright, he decide now, 'e say, "Mommy, I want to go an' see daddy." mother said, "No, boy, if you go, your father will kill you." 'E say, "No, I want to go." Say, "Arright, you can go, but remember, y' have to spen' six more months before you can go, becau' you los' as much strenk for six months."

Arright, Superintendent, now he eager, if he even have to run away, he going. An' Superintendent he run away until he reached to where he fin' strickly grass. No other thing but grass. An' 'e began to feed. Feed there for four months., An' the other two, go back to his mother. When he reached back to his mother, say, "Mommy, I want to go an' see daddy." Mother say, "Yes, I believe you can go an' see your daddy. But if you dead, remember, I dead too, and you wouldn't see me anymore, I wouldn't see you, because he would hate us."

So Superintendent he took he mother all outside with him now. When he reach to a certain place that he can call out, the mother say, "Is over yonder your fadduh livin'." an he want to fin' out if he strong enough to go an' meet he fadduh. Sung with the voice sang out like this:

A-me Superintendent-eh,
A-me Superintendent-eh;
No more man grand champion ground,
No more Bully Manger.

From the time Bully Manger heard that, he look around. When he look around now, an' he saw one was missin', missin' from the couch [herd] he said, "My god, Old Nanny have gone, an' look 'e bringin' back now a son." Because the mother of Superintendent, name of that one was "Old Nanny." So when he look around now, he get mad and he song, sing out, he sing:

A-me Bully Manger-eh,
A-me Bully Manger-eh;
No more man grand champion ground,
No more Superintendent.

You know the fadduh was singing out those words.

So he step until he reach right up to 'e fadduh. Bu' 'e didn't go right into the premises, like a barrier. Stopped to de edge. An' he stop to de edge. Fadduh call to him, say, "What you want now?" When 'e look, 'e muddah to de side, an' if you see this, if didn't see this little fellow man. An' there was one young heifer in the crowd. That one name "Fireling." So when from the time he see the little fellow out there, man he begin to run all around now, becau' he believe 'eself that this young chap will kill the fadduh. An' e love this chap even more than the fadduh. Jus' by hearing the voice 'e loved eh more 'an de fadduh. So Superintendent march up. When he march up now, soon as 'e reach up an' 'e see Fireling he run, run boy. He feel nice, too. An' when everytime he do so [kicks up his heels] turn 'e heels right up. An' he decide that he was going to kill the fadduh. The fadduh say, "Now remember how you want to get too rude here." Son said, "By fighting. An' if I kill you I reign an' if you kill me you reign." Fadduh said, "All right, but when you would like to fight?" Old Nanny say, "Tell 'im twelve o'clock in the day when the sun dey." So well, he say so. Young Superintendent say, "I will fight you. But remember it would not be later or earlier than twelve o'clock in the day when the sun is in the middle sky." You know that black cattle can't stand much sun. Well arright, he look aroun' he can see a shade that he can get to, go an, fight under the shade. Have to fight in the open air. An 'e decide, 'e say, "Arright, if you say so an' you come to try, I would meet you." De next day was for the fight.

So all the cows now, the only two bulls in the crowd was Superintendent and his old fadduh. So he decide now that he have to kill the fadduh in order to reign. He went to 'e fadduh, soon as he reach 'e fadduh, He sing out:

A-me Superintendent-eh,
A-me Superintendent-eh;
No more man grand champion ground,
No more Bully Manger.

Bull, he didn't rush to his fadduh; fadduh now he goin' to rush to him. Soon as the fadduh saw him coming up close, 'e fadduh rush to 'im an' 'e sing out:

A-me Bully Manger-eh,
A-me Bully Manger-eh;
No more man grand champion ground,
No more Superintendent.

An' he pick up Superintendent and he t'row him up in the air, an' Superintendent, he didn't even spend two minutes, he dropped back on his four legs. Superintendent say, "All right, my turn." Say, "Yes, your turn." But still remember he's annoyed because it seem like he didn't do anything to him, neither leg nor nothin' was broken. Superintendent went to him now, an' he sing out:

A-me Superintendent-eh,
A-me Superintendent-eh;
No more man grand champion ground,
No more Bully Manger.

An' 'e pick up 'e fadduh Bully Manger an' he shoot him up in the air, an' meanwhile he up in the air, he and Fireling and they began to dance and sing:

Fire girl,
Fireling,
Fire tonight,
Fireling.

Fire girl,
Fireling,
Fire tonight,
Fireling.

Fire tonight,
Fireling.
Fire tonight,
Fireling. [etc.]

Crick!

When old Bully Manger drop back, he drop back with three legs; one was missing. From the time Fireling saw that, that is when he want man, to run all aroun' new. An' if you see how Superintendent mother feel joyful now, becau' 'e son going win. Well arright, Bully Manger went to Superintendent, sing out again:

A-me Bully Manger-eh ['e vexed now, you know],
A-me Bully Manger-eh;
No more man grand champion ground,
No more Superintendent.

Pick up Superintendent up in the air, Superintendent only drop back and laugh.
Arright, when 'e finish laughin', Superintendent sing out:

A-me Superintendent-eh,
A-me Superintendent-eh;
No more man grand champion ground,
No more Bully Manger.

Pick up Bully Manger, shoot 'im up in the air. Meantime he up there, he began to sing:

Fire girl,
Fireling.
Fire girl,
Fireling.

Fire tonight,
Fireling.
Fire girl,
Fireling. [*etc.*]

Crick!

When old Bully Manger drop back, remember, he drop back with two legs this time. Well arright, Superintendent, he feel joyful. Old Bully Manger went to him again:

A-me Bully Manger-eh,
A-me Bully Manger-eh;
No more man grand champion ground,
No more Superintendent.

Pick up Superintendent, up in the air. When 'e drop back solid again. Even more shine up, becau' a little drop a rain drop in 'e back, so he's col, nah? [Much laughter and comment occurs here, both about Superintendent and the veracity of the storyteller.] Soon as he drop back, Superintendent went to 'im again an' sing out:

A-me Superintendent-eh,
A-me Superintendent-eh;
No more man grand champion ground,
No more Bully Manger.

Pick up Bully Manger up in the air again, an' while he's up there he began to sing:

Fire girl,
Fireling.
Fire tonight,
Fireling.

Fire girl,
Fireling.
Fire tonight,
Fireling. [etc.]

Crick!

When old Bully Manger drop back, this time he drop back on the one, all the other cows now began now to run, run, becau' they know, even though he try to rush at them, he cannot walk on the one leg. Well arright, he went to Superintendent, again, an' he sang the same song, Sen' 'im up in the air an' 'e drop back this time look up even shinier than before. Because you know, more an' more, soon as they look at him, they saw he feel nice and jumping around, come like he swell now an' look more flashy, more shine. He went to the fadduh again, an' he sing out:

A-me Superintendent-eh,
A-me Superintendent-eh;
No more man grand champion ground,
No more Bully Manger.

He pick up the fadduh again, up in the air, an 'e grab that Fireling there this beautiful damsel and 'e began to sing:

Fire girl,
Fireling.
Fire tonight,
Fireling.

Fire girl,
Fireling.
Fire tonight,
Fireling. [*etc.*]

Crick!

When Bully Manger drop back 'e drop without any head. An' all that they could see all over his body partly was slime. And that is the reason today one of the chief reason why sometime when a cattle have a calf and go to that calf and a on the cattle, sometime you don't find 'e birt' [afterbirth] at all; sometime eat it. And Superintendent reign up to today. You would notice that if you have a black cattle, always look worse than those speck colors most of them. Cun' stand too hot sun, that is the black one. So that come like me, Superintendent. (Lester Frank)

We can see, through using the Vincentian concept of nonsense, the characteristics and the expressive vocabulary drawn upon the inversive activity contained within the event of nine-night. In the wake we witness a primary breakdown of both physical and psycho-social boundaries; with the admitting of road behaviors into the house, numerous other adjustments occur, not least of which is the license given to marginal ones to perform in an outwardly rude fashion, to the enjoyment of all. Moreover, the motives brought to bear underscore the vital role of contests of wits and words—including tales centering on and named for the trickster. Significantly, not only are power relationships inverted in these stories, but all of the other social orders and boundaries implied in Vincentian ideals and sentiments are broken. Thus, we see inversions—and a resultant sense of freeing up—exhibited on the levels of: the system of everyday behavior in the way in which different social spaces are articulated, along with the different ideals and sentiments that came to be associated with those spaces; and in the relationship between these behavioral ideals and the patterns by which the performances are carried out; and the structure of approved relationships and sentiments as they are reported upon within the texts of the stories themselves.

To enter into the universe of meanings by which these stories take on life, it would be necessary to explicate the significant actions, role expectations and role relationships within the Vincentian household—a task that is obviously impossible in this chapter. Characteristically, in limited resource peasantries, one finds a good deal of repressed (and not so repressed) hostilities between parents, and between children and parents; they arise because of competition over scarce resources. This scarcity is, of course, exacerbated in large families such as one finds on St. Vincent, because the child commonly is weaned away from maternal nurture and care at a fairly early age. Moreover, displays of child care and order are regarded as a central feature of respectability. Chastisement of infants is the one family act that is carried out in such a way that others can hear, observe, and laugh at the child when it cries. This *giving lashes* or *licks* may be done by anyone in charge, and it is one activity that adults of either sex enter into seemingly with little provocation.

In line with this, adults speak a great deal among one another about how unruly and untrustworthy children have become. Indeed, one of the standard ways in which one may align oneself with respectability norms is to extemporize a speech on this subject. Thus is the antagonism between the generations both voiced and acted upon as a piece of everyday display behavior. Such set speeches are paralleled with others on how little women can trust men, and vice versa.

It is often *Mommy,* the keeper of order and respect, commonly the oldest woman of the household, who makes these speeches about the unreliability of others—male or female, adult or child. At first, the vision of relational possibilities seems bleak until one begins to recognize the underlying message of these speeches, no matter who makes them, and that is that there is only one person in life you really can trust—Mommy.

This is exceptionally important, of course, in the establishment and maintenance of respect values. But more than this, in a scarce resources economy, it is important for children to leave home to go to work at wage labor, and to send home money so that Mommy and the other family members still there are able to get by. This remittance economy flourishes on St. Vincent. But it means that there are always ways in which the young can dream of escaping from the repressive aspects of a peasantry in which rights and responsibilities are passed on to the young rather slowly (at least from their perspective). By working at a job rather than in the family *garden,* the young can open up life for themselves—and, in this remittance economy—their families. If they are able to find a job elsewhere, they emigrate; indeed, the system encourages it. And if they happen to have children when they are away, there is a good place to send them to be raised properly.

In this system, however, the most troublesome spot is among the young men who still live at home but do wage labor or are in the market for such work. They are structural in-betweeners, unable to really assert themselves except at the crossroads, where they *lime and blag*. That is, of course, where nonsense behaviors are the norm, and where the *sporty fellows* dream up how they will *play* in the various *sports*—from cricket and football to Carnival and Christmas. It is these rude boys who associate themselves with the *sly mongoose,* who sneaks into "the mistress kitchen, stealing out her fattest chicken," the Monkey, and Nansi and the Old Witch Boy.

To be sure, the games, riddles, and tales that go under the name of Nansi 'tory are performed by others. But, as mentioned, these others are often ones who have found themselves stuck in a marginal social position. In some dimensions, these stories must be seen as reflections on the tellers and their cohorts. They are texts about living voraciously and energetically at the margins. But the message that they deliver is not an especially optimistic one, for both friendship and family are seldom achieved, except in the case of the remarkable young bull—protected by his mother—who is able to do in his rapacious father.

Nine-night is, then, in many ways a time of in-betweenness held by and for in-betweeners. This is indeed precisely what Nansi and nonsense mean, both in the event itself and in the acts recounted in the stories. This vibrant if eccentric behavior must also be understood in terms of its contrast, not only with everyday manners and the other display events, but also how it focuses, through exclusion, on the other in-betweeners of the community, the very old.

From the perspective of the Vincentian speech economy, growing up involves learning the value of speech, and speaking appropriately—if not always correctly, for that is reserved for ceremonial house-based occasions. As I noted, in those occasions, nearly everyone is expected to enter into the event by singing or talking sweet when their time comes to *share*. But the older members of the community are not expected to enter in; they sit on benches along the walls while the performances or games go on in the center of the room. They have earned the right to be silent. But far from being honored in the community, the very old are feared, because they are only half of this world.

They are placed somewhat in the same class as *jumbies,* except they are on one side of the line between life and death, the jumbies on the other side. Jumbies are vexing spirits, who, for some reason, were not put into their appropriate resting place in the proper manner. Thus, they continue to wander through the place of the living, causing apprehension to everyone. They are subject to discussion in terms analogous to *commess,* because their continuing presence brings up questions of their character and activities while alive.

Today most Vincentian peasants disavow any belief in jumbies—but nearly everyone has stories on the subject, which are told with smiles and giggles. Jumbies are not regarded as malevolent spirits so much as troubled ones who cause upset of some sort. Thus, Richland Parkers continue to draw chalk figures (not unlike the Haitian *vevee,* but without the elaborate iconic significance) in front of their doors and make sure their houses are closed tight at night to dissuade jumbies from disbehaving.

The first night of wake is given over to singing and anthems over the body of the dead one. To be sure, there is drinking, and merriment is provided by conventional arguments between chairmen over what hymns should be sung, and why. There is a feeling, however, that nonsense should not be encouraged until the interment, which commonly takes place the next morning.

Even for those of this old-time persuasion, there is not a high level of concern that the burial service must be done correctly or that the body be buried in the right place. However, when asked why jumbies persist, most say because they were not put to rest properly. And to these people, feeling this way, nine-night is a part of the right way to put the dead to rest. Furthermore, for sometime afterward, one is likely to see the first drops of any liquid being drunk thrown on the ground, whether for the *daddies* (as the ancestors are called) or for a specific dead person. This is especially important to do at the crossroads or where people congregate in public.

One must keep the dead ones silent and inactive, then; to those on this side of the line, the old ones, quietness and disinvolvement is also anticipated. The older one gets, moreover, the more one is likely to live alone, and apart from the major gathering places; food is brought in by the younger members of the family. Women therefore attempt to maintain their place in the community as long as possible by keeping young children in their yard. Thus, there are often arguments between women of different generations as to who most deserves to keep this child or that, usually one who is the outcome of a liaison between a couple too young to have a household of their own. Children often become scared of the older members of their household, because they tend to get snappish in their demands. Also the young are often discussed in terms of how rude they have become.

The attitude toward power figures exhibited in the riddles and stories must be interpreted, in some part, in the light of this complex attitude. Fear of the old seldom takes precedence over notions of respect as displayed and celebrated in the household-based events. But there is a cultural bind here that pulls both ways whenever an old one is present. This is especially felt in wakes, of course, for one of the topics of animated discussion is the things the dead one did in his or her lifetime, and the old ones often give amusing testimony here. But in the performance of nonsense in wake, they do not enter in except to laugh and applaud.

Moreover, the subject of the interpenetration of life and death emerges in a startlingly open fashion in nine-night texts. In addition to the riddles previously noted, the following was the opening discussion of a riddle session in one wake recorded:

Between the living and the dead there is seven tongue in one head.
Come on, come on, don't stop now.
Come on then, go tell them fas'.
There was a head.
What kind of head?
Little cattle head.
Yeah.
And the seven blackbird go inside that head.
Not so man. Speak your riddle good, your answer good.
He there now. Was a ol' cattle go in the mountain.
And then the head remain and a bird go and he lay six egg in the head.
And after the six egg hatch, six bird, six young bird 'ey come out.
And the mother' tongue.
There is seven tongue in one head between the living and the dead.

And again, a riddle emerged, turning on someone being between the two states:

> Going down the road within [between] the living and the dead; the living can't talk and the dead could talk. — Green peas and dried peas.

Somewhat later in the same session, moreover, a riddling description of the interment process emerged:

> I have a boat. The boat work with six oars. I carry the boat to shore, to town. The six oars come back and the boat can't come back.

The answer makes direct reference to the occasion:

> "The old man die?" "Yeah." "Six bearers didn't carry him?" "Yeah." "Well, they leave the corpse, the six bearers leave the corpse and the six bearers come back."

The tales tell of Nansi or, in his name, approach the same subjects in a number of interesting ways. Nansi himself is, for instance, portrayed as one who is able, through trickery, to go back and forth between life and death. In one much told story, for instance, Nansi and his wife convince their friends Compé Hawk, Compé Bullcattle, and Sheep that Nansi is dead. As each comes near, Nansi kills him. However, Compé Ground Dove witnesses the whole thing and is able to wait around until Nansi reveals himself in a ridiculous way — by fainting.

> Well this is Compé Anansi again. He have his wife, and real hungry time dey in. Well now, he said, "Me wife, saltfish dey fo [is appropriate for my] food dey but saltfish no dey [there is not any there]. But anyhow I could play like I dead, [you] go out and sing, go out and bawl dead, say, "Me husband dead." He say, "Me wife, you t'ink you can do dat?" Say, "Yes, me husband, I can do it." 'E say, "Me husband, if I no do it, God dead." 'E say, "I will do it."
>
> Well she come out now, "Ohh." She tie up jaw, tie up 'e jaw, you know, ev'y God t'ing, and 'e set 'em dey, you know. 'E say, "Ohhm God. Me husband dead,

oy, and me one whe' got a burial t'ing what'." Well, my friend, 'e come back, boy. She come out now, she band she waist* say:

Poor me 'Nansi dead-o,
Oh ting-wa.
Poor me 'Nansi dead-o,
Oh ting-wa.
And me one go got de burial,
Oh ting-wa.
Lemme ban' me wais' fo' cry-o,
Oh ting-wa.
Lemme band me wais' for cry-o,
Oh ting-wa.

Compé Hawk pass. Compé Hawk say [bawling noise], "You see Compé Hawk do dat? You see. Bother so, 'e goin'," Betime he goin' [carrying on wailing], Compé Anansi stretch off like 'e dead. 'E shut 'e eye tight. 'E say, "Well, Compé. You have choose the better path" [in a high voice imitating a hawk's call]. He say Compé choose the better path. So anyhow, "Thy will be done." Betime 'e turn his back, Compé hear "Whoop!" and Compé bawl. 'E say, "Me wife, me wife?" [screaming]. His wife come in. "You kill 'im." He said, "Yes." He said, "Me wife, me never been know you so brave. But anyhow, we go make living."

Anyhow, he come boy. 'E say, "Me wife, part one dey, two dey.† 'E go out again, she start. "Ohh God! Me husband dead, oy: And me one got de burial, ting-wa!" Well, she start:

Poor me 'Nansi dead-o,
Ting-wa.
Poor me 'Nansi dead-o,
Oh ting-wa.
And me one got de burial,
Oh ting-wa.
Lemme band me wais' fo' cry-o,
Oh ting-wa.
And me one got de burial,
Oh ting-wa.

Crick boy!‡ Well, my friend, 'e go dey now, Compé Bullcattle pass. "Unnh. Wha' do you so?" 'E say, "Me husband dead." 'E say, "You talking fart." 'E going in, so see 'im. When 'e go in, go see 'im. 'E say, "Well, man," 'e say, "Now Compé Anansi do 'e time, 'e choose the better path." Well after Compé going, 'e turn 'e back, come out. 'E say "Maaah." 'E drop a ground again boop.

'E say, "Me wife, go back again." Come out wid de same bawling again. 'E start:

Poor me 'Nansi dead-o,
Oh ting-wa.
Poor me 'Nansi dead-o,

---

*The proper mark of respect for the dead by a widow, putting a sash (usually white) around her waist; it is often called a *jumbie band.*
† If you go out again, another will come along.
‡ A way of stopping the group singing.

Oh ting-wa.
And me one got de burial,
Oh ting-wa.
Lemme band me wais' for cry-o,
Oh ting-wa.

Crick! Compé Sheep pass, 'e go in again, de poor lamb sheep say, "Maaah." Sheep dead. Fowl pass, 'e same t'ing, 'e kill 'im. All animal in dis world pass, kill 'um de same t'ing.

Compé Ground Dove dey up on a tree watchin' 'im now, watchin' the doings a he now. Compé Ground Dove reach out, 'e start, "Ooh God, Compé. I need help here. Compé Anansi dead, dead, dead," 'E say, "Dead, dead, dead?" 'E said, "Yes." 'E said, "Dead, dead, dead?" 'E said, "Yes." 'E say "Dead? And you ha' de place shut up so? Dead could dey in a place like this yah? Open up, open up, open up." 'E say open up all the window and them. 'E say, "Open up the blind." 'E open up the blind. 'E go up on the ledge. 'E say, "Compé, you dead?" 'E say, "Yes." 'E say, "But anyhow, if I want to believe Compé he have to break a fart." Compé Anansi let go boop. 'E say, "Yes, yes, yes. You can hear a dead man fart. When a man dead he done wi dis world." 'E say, "Fart again." Well, my friend. And Compé Ground Dove go back down. And that's why you see 'e have fools in this world today. Some wiser than some, till today. And that is the end a de story. (Sephus Jobe, Greggs Village)

This kind of story, which details the dissolution of friendship and community, though characteristic of West Indian narratives (Dundes, Haring) is not so commonly found in the Vincentian repertoire as another. This pattern creates dramatic interest by introducing an older man as power figure, usually Massa King, who is set upon protecting his beautiful daughter by making her inaccessible. At this point, as in the story about Nansi making the stone smoke, a suitor or suitors emerge, the old man proposes a test that the protagonist passes through trickery or hidden powers. In the case of the father, the structural pattern is doubled, as we saw in the Massa King and the boar hog story, for now the King's son, the Old Witch Boy, comes into the action. He follows his sister and her husband to their new home, which is in the midst of the bush. As befits those who live in the bush, the husband proves to be a shape-shifting superphallic animal, as we saw in the story of the boarhog. The Old Witch Boy matches power, then, with his new brother-in-law and shows him up for what he is, an animal. So this pattern, too, ends with a dissolving move, in which the ultimate messages delivered have to do with the unreliability of nonfamily bonds. (For Jamaican parallels, see Beckwith, 1924 which reports a number of stories about the Old Witch Boy.) Most important, the battle is waged by in-betweeners: a protean human-animal and a club-footed outcast boy endowed with magical powers. The result is a demystification of power.

The pattern is neither complex nor difficult of access, especially if this story is compared with the earlier one regarding the old Bully Manger and the young Superintendent. Controlling power resides in inherited position, skin color, or bush animality. The only ways to counter such power, from the perspective of the small, outrageous Anansi or the outcast and solemn Jigger-foot Boy, is through either magic or trickery. But the transformations they bring about deliver a message that is clearly opposed to those carried by traditional texts in most household ceremonies: endurance, respect, and a valuing of the clean and the orderly. But Nansi 'tory in all its forms operates within the atmosphere of license, one in which it is precisely the chaotic in-betweeners who have their way for the moment. It should provide no surprise in such a case that their protagonists betray a similar social condition and that they are encouraged to prevail in the face of death.

The matter becomes a bit more clear in the following tale featuring a *jumbieman* protagonist. The despised but clever Old Witch Boy again saves his sister from the power of one who would marry her and take her away to a place other than a human habitation. Usually, this means following her and her new husband to the bush, as in the boarhog story. In this tale, it is the burying ground. The Jiggerfoot Boy reveals the husband's disguise commonly by singing a key song dance that brings out the bestial nature; here, he hands his sister a cross to protect her as she is led into her new home, the grave. The story, as it is told here, is localized. The marriage takes place in Richland Park; the jumbieman comes from the burial ground in Kingstown. His trip involves coming up through the Rathomill hills to Arnos Vale, then across another group of hills to Mespo (the Mesopotamian Valley, at the foot of Mt. Petit Bonhomme), then on up the mountain to the village.

Just as Anansi speaks with a lisp, the animal husbands, as they go back to their home, resume their animality through voice modification. So too with Mr. Jumbieman, who here speaks as if he had a cleft palate.*

> Once upon a time, Master King have a daughter, and everybody come for this daughter, the daughter refuse them. 'E could be minister, lawyer, doctor, any-one—do love no one.
>
> And this day, Mr. Jumbieman hear about this and Jumbieman dress up in a nice, beautiful black suit. . . . And when Mr. Jumbieman come up, the girl upstairs in the house and say "Mommy, mommy, *that's* the man I want."
>
> When Mr. Jumbieman a want meet up one, a meet this girl and have a con-versation, the girl ain' know about love and t'ing. Well, Mr. Jumbieman break up right there, introduced to the mother, introduced to the father, introduced to the girl.

---

*This makes transcription of the recorded text difficult, of course, a problem exacerbated by the laughter occurring whenever such voice modification occurs. Moreover, the narrator portrays the jumbie as being very excitable. Finally, the storyteller was not regarded very highly, so he was interrupted constantly. It was clear that he did not know the story well. In other renderings, the story is closer to its African antecedents, with body parts rather than horses and wheels being borrowed at each burying ground. This African story is best known from Amos Tutuola's literary handling of it in *The Palm Wine Drinkard.*

Well, 'e mek time and so, when marry her and so. Pay respect and do that.

Well, 'e have a Little Ol' Witch Boy dey, Chiggerfoot Boy wi' tobo [i.e., trouble—infection, puss, with gnats flying around] there in the corner, and sit down there. 'E say when Mr. Jumbieman gone, 'e say, "Mommy, you dey that man sister going married to is a jumbie." 'E say, "Go on now, Chiggerfoot Boy, you mu' catch 'em both 'e tails." [They are making fun of the boy because of his foot.] 'E say, "Go on now boy, Chiggerfoot Boy, dig out a ground both his tails."

Mr. Jumbieman going to [is resolved to] marry today. He bring up 'e cart. Well when he reach, he bring a carriage [to carry his wife and her goods with him in appropriate style]. He take a cartwheel and a horse from Kingstown, that's Kingstown burying ground. When he meet by [go to] Arnos Vale, he take a cartwheel and a horse. When he meet by Belmont, he take a cartwheel and a horse. When he meet by . . . he go round Dumbarton, he take a cartwheel and a horse. He come back by Roman church, he take a cartwheel and a horse. When he meet by Anglican church, he take a cartwheel and a horse. When he reach by burying ground by chapel out they [pointing to Richland Park cemetery] he take a cart and horse.

Well he came right up, he said he want to keep his horse and cart out there. When 'e take 'e last vow, 'e go out there. Right, they go home and they marry [are married] and t'ing. When they finish, Mount a' burying ground, they going back now. Goin', the carriage pack up everything, and going back home now. The Old Witch Boy start following them.

Well, all right, when they reach at first burying ground out there, they leave one of the wheel and one of the horse, going down. When 'e reach Mespo, 'e leave one. When 'e go round, 'e leave one, one, one.

When 'e read—Belmont, 'e wife say "What's one horse a have no wheel? [Mumbles speaks as if he has a cleft palate.]

Well, all right, when they go down . . . 'is brother, the tobofoot brother is still following. Anyt'ing at all 'e go, anywhere 'e go, 'is brother still following she.

Well, when 'e meet no by town, that is the las' burial ground. All the cartwheel and the horses disappear. Only [the] three of them [people] standing up, but only two seeing face-to-face, and one seeing two. [The husband and wife cannot see the Old Witch Boy because he has made himself invisible.] The Old Witch Boy the one they won't see there. An when the jumbieman go down, 'e say, "Me live here. Now, me father live jus' so [pointing] me mother live there, me brother live there, me sister live there, me grandfather live there, and me, wife, me living dey jus' so." In the middle of the ground he lived there. All around 'e family and them.

All right. 'E say "Me wife. When a see me go down, you mustn't step in there face up [do not look back]. You must put there two [feet].

'Kay. When 'e go down, his wife land, down his only first one, then twist so, there were de hole. 'E goin' to put this one wooden stake. Right. Where 'e go she hand 'nother one, so 'e brother say, "Lord, me sister, me sister, no put down so, put down so."

The jumbieman in the hole now "Jeshus Shishe. I can' ge' hol' me wife,

"Me sister, me sister. No put down so, put down so" [do not get into the save that way]. Jeshush Shiske! [more ranting and raving]. (That a jumbieman, you know 'e coming to put just a cross in there, ya know?) [The Witch Boy hands her a cross.] 'E say, "Jeshus Chirishe me wife you no put that so, put that so."

"Me sister, me sister hold on dey. Me sister me sister, hold on dey." [The jumbieman is now ranting and raving.]

Well, all right, then in 'e hole he can't come up. They hol' em until first cockcrow. When first cockcrow, 'e raise 'e sister up. So Mr. Jumbieman going down there and the wife up there.

Well the boy brought 'e sister just go back just so. And she pained [free?]. And her brother going take she up, take she home and so on. Rough she up and so, the girl get better. And the girl cleaned the brother, take out all the tobo from 'e feet and so on. Right then story end and, the wire bend. (Cherry Hazell)

This story suggests that all mysterious power may be metonymically related to death and the living dead. Perhaps the objective of nine-night, then, in invoking the languages of nonsense, is to properly consign the dead to their appropriate place, by revealing death as nothing more than fear embodied. But then we must see the event as an ongoing paradox: a demystifying act of practices that nevertheless maintains the basic mystery of life and death. By establishing the opposition as a contrariety—that is, in a form in which there is no real dramatic resolution—we are not presented with a happily-ever-after type of ending. Rather, in a more typical African and Afro-American pattern, life is seen to be most fully celebrated through the contrarietous presentation of oppositions. Thus, the same story is infinitely repeatable, for it has no ending; rather, it is of the to-be-continued sort. This, in combination with the joyous overlap and interlock of voices and movements characteristic of public aesthetic activity throughout the black world, is the deepest manner in which celebration may be carried out in these parts of the world. This is, as I described in chapter nine, a pattern of performance that ties together everyday liming and blagging with the larger celebratory events. The pattern is, when imported into the house and yard, put in the service of continuity and community celebration.

Moreover, we must not forget that Nansi 'tory—the riddles, lashing games, and tales—are played for laughs. In this case, laughter masks the mystery that it marks and seems to give a name to. But this should be what the structural and symbolic analyst expects when working with the processes of cultural inversion.

Bibliography

Entries with asterisks are reprinted here, some in slightly different form.

Abrahams, Roger D. 1962. Playing the dozens. *Journal of American Folklore*, 75, 209-20.

_____. 1964. *Deep down in the jungle: Negro narrative folklore from the streets of Philadelphia*. Hatboro, Pa.: Folklore Associates.

_____. 1964a. The cowboy in the British West Indies. In Mody Boatright, Wilson M. Hudson, & Allen Maxwell (Eds)., *A good tale and a bonnie tune*. Dallas: Southern Methodist University Press, Publications of the Texas Folklore Society, 32, 168-175.

_____. 1967. The shaping of folklore traditions in the British West Indies. *Journal of Inter-American Studies*, 9, 456-480.

*_____. 1968. Public drama and common values in two Caribbean islands. *Trans-Action*, 5, 62-71. Reprinted as Patterns of performance in the British West Indies in *Afro-American anthropology: Contemporary perspectives*. New York: The Free Press, 1970, 163-180.

_____. 1968a. "Pull out your purse and pay": A St. George mumming from the British West Indies. *Folklore*, 79, 176-201.

_____. 1968b. *"Speech mas"* on Tobago. In Wilson M. Hudson (Ed.), *Tire shrinker to dragster*. Austin: Encino Press.

*_____. 1970. A performance-centered approach to gossip. *Man*, 5, 290-301.

_____. 1970a. *Deep down in the jungle* (Rev. ed.). Chicago: Aldine.

*_____. Traditions of Eloquence in the West Indies. *Journal of Inter-American Studies and World Affairs*, 12, 505-527.

_____. 1971. British West Indian drama and the "Life cycle" problem. *Folklore*, 82, 241-265.

_____. 1972. Talking my talk: Black English and social segmentation in black communities. *Florida F/L Reporter*, 10, 29-38.

*_____. 1972a. The training of the man-of-words in talking sweet. *Language in Society*, 1, 15-29.

*_____. 1972b. Christmas and carnival on St. Vincent. *Western Folklore*, 31, 275-289.

————. 1976. *Talking black.* Rowley, Mass.: Newbury House.

————. 1977. The West Indian tea meeting: An essay in creolization. In Ann M. Pescatello (Ed.), *Old roots in the new world.* Westport, Conn.: Greenwood Press, 173-209.

*————. 1979. Reputation vs. respectability: A review of Peter J. Wilson's concept. *Revista/Review Interamericana,* 9, 448-453.

*————. 1981. Symbolic landscapes on St. Vincent. *Canadian Journal of Anthropology/Revue Canadienne d'Anthropologie,* 2(1), 45-53.

————. Forthcoming. (Ed.) *Folktales of the black world: Subsaharan Africa.* New York: Pantheon Books.

*————, & Bauman, Richard. 1971. Sense and nonsense on St. Vincent: Speech behavior decorum in a Caribbean community. *American Anthropologist,* 73(3), 262-272.

————, & Szwed, John. Forthcoming. *After Africa.* New Haven: Yale University Press.

Adams, Richard N. 1962. The formal analysis of behavioral segments: A progress report (Paper presented at the Sixty-first Annual Meeting of the American Anthropological Association, Chicago, 16 November 1962.)

Albert, Ethel M. 1964. "Rhetoric," "logic," and "poetics" in Burundi: Culture patterning of speech behavior. *American Anthropologist* 66 (Pt. 6), 35-54.

Babcock, Barbara A. 1978. *The reversible world.* Ithaca: Cornell University Press.

Barth, Fredrik. 1975. *Ritual and knowledge among the Baktaman of New Guinea.* Oslo and New Haven: Universitetsforlaget and Yale University Press.

Bascom, William R. 1941. Acculturation among the Gullah Negroes. *American Anthropologist,* 43, 43-50.

————. 1952. The focus of Cuban Santería. *Southwestern Journal of Anthropology,* 6, 64-68.

————. 1972. *Shango in the new world.* Austin: African and Afro-American Research Institute Occasional Publication, University of Texas.

Bateson, Gregory. 1958. *Naven.* Stanford: Stanford University Press.

Baudet, Henri. 1965. *Paradise on earth: Some thoughts on European images of non-European man.* New Haven: Yale University Press.

Bauman, Richard. 1978. *Verbal art as performance.* Rowley, Mass.: Newbury House.

————, & Sherzer, Joel (Eds.) 1974. *Explorations in the ethnography of communication.* Cambridge: At the University Press.

Beck, Jane C. 1979. *To the windward of the land: The occult world of Alexander Charles.* Bloomington: Indiana University Press.

Beckford, William. 1790. *A descriptive account of the island of Jamaica.* (2 vols.) London.

Beckwith, Martha Warren. 1924. *Jamaican Anansi stories.* New York: G. E. Stechert.

————. 1929. *Black roadways.* Chapel Hill: University of North Carolina Press.

Bell, Hesketh. 1889. *Obeah: Witchcraft in the West Indies.* London.

Ben-Amos, Dan. 1970. Towards a componential model of folklore analysis. In Dan Ben-Amos (Ed.), *Proceedings of the VIII International Congress of Anthropological and Ethnological Sciences of 1968.* Tokyo, 309-310.

————. 1976. Introduction and Analytic categories and ethnic genres. In *Folklore genres.* Austin: University of Texas Press, ix-xiv, 215-242.

Bohannon, Laura. 1966. Shakespeare in the bush. *Natural History*, 28-33.

Bowen, Eleanor Smith [pseud.]. 1968. *Return to laughter*. Garden City, N.Y.: Doubleday and Co.

Brockhurst, Rev. H.V.P. 1883. *The colony of British Guiana and its labouring population*. London.

Brown, H. Rap. 1969. *Die nigger die*. New York: Dial Press.

Cabrera, Lydia. 1968. *El Monte* (2nd ed.). Miami: Rema Press.

Calame-Griaule, Genevieve. 1965. *Ethnologie et langage: La parole chez les dogon*. Paris: Gallimard.

Carr, Andrew T. 1956. Pierrot Grenade. *Carribean Quarterly*, 4, 281-314.

Cash, W. J. 1941. *The mind of the south*. New York: Vintage Random.

Chinua, Achebe. 1964. Foreword. In W. H. Whitely (Ed.), *A selection of African prose*. Oxford: Clarendon Press, iix.

Colby, B. N. 1966. Ethnographic semantics: A preliminary survey. *Current Anthropology*, 7, 3 32.

Collymore, Frank C. 1965. *Notes for a glossary of words and phrases of Barbadian dialect* (3rd ed., Rev. and enlarged). Bridgetown, Conn.: Advocate Co.

Conklin, Harold C. 1968. Lexicographical treatment of folk taxonomies. In Joshua A. Fishman (Ed.), *Readings in the sociology of language*. The Hague: Mouton.

Crowley, Daniel J. 1953. American credit institutions of the Yoruba type. *Man* (n.s.) 53, 80.

_____. 1956. The midnight robbers. *Caribbean Quarterly*, 4, 271-272.

_____. 1959. Towards a definition of calypso. *Ethnomusicology*, 3, 2, 3.

Dalby, David. 1979. Reflections on the historical development of Afro-American languages: A discussion of Mervyn C. Alleyne's paper, "The linguistic continuity of Africa in the Caribbean," 1970. Unpublished manuscript from the symposium "Continuities and discontinuities in Afro-American societies and cultures." Mona, Jamaica, 2-5 April, Wenner-Gren Foundation.

Day, Charles William. 1852. *Five years' residence in the West Indies*. London, 1:23, 2.61.

DeCamp, David. 1968. Mock bidding in Jamaica. In Wilson J. Hudson (Ed.), *Tire shrinker to dragster*. Austin: Encino Press.

_____. 1971. Toward a generative analysis of a post-creole speech. In *Pidginization and creolization of languages*. Cambridge: At the University Press.

Dégh, Linda. 1969. *Folktales and society*. Bloomington: Indiana University Press.

De La Beche, H. T. 1825. *Notes on the present conditions of the Negroes in Jamaica*. London.

_____. 1827. *Letter from the West Indies*. London.

Dillard, J. L. 1972. *Black English*. New York: Random House.

Douglas, Mary, *Purity and danger*. New York: Praeger.

Dundes, Alan. 1971. The Making and breaking of friendship as a structural frame in the African folktales. In Pierre Miranda and Elli Köngas-Miranda (Eds.), *Structural analysis in oral tradition*. Philadelphia: University of Pennsylvania Press.

Edmonson, M. S. 1966. Play: Games, gossip, and humor. In Manning Nash (Ed.), *Handbook of Middle America Indians*. Austin: University of Texas Press.

Edwards, Bryan. 1793. *The History, civil and commercial, of the British colonies in the West Indies*. Dublin.

Edwards, Jay. 1978. *The Afro-American trickster tale: A structural analysis.* Bloomington: Monographs of the Folklore Institute, Indiana University.

Elder, Jacob. 1966. Kalinda: Song of the battling troubadours of Trinidad. *Journal of the Folklore Institute,* 3, 192-203.

Falassi, Alessandro. 1980. *Folklore by the fireside.* Austin: University of Texas Press.

Faris, James C. 1966. The dynamics of verbal exchange: A Newfoundland example. *Anthropologica* (n.s.) 8, 235-248.

————. 1968. Validation in ethnographical description: The lexicon of "Occasions" in Cat Harbour. *Man* (n.s.) 3, 112-124.

Ferguson, C. 1959. Diglossia. *Word,* 15, 325-340.

Finnegan, Ruth. 1967. *Limba stories and story-telling.* New York: Oxford University Press.

Firth, R. 1940. *The work of the gods of Tikopia.* London: London School of Economics.

————. 1961. *History and traditions of Tikopia.* (Memoirs of the Polynesian Society 33.) Wellington, New Zealand: Polynesian Society.

Fishman, Joshua A. (Ed.) 1968. *Readings in the sociology of language.* The Hague: Mouton.

Frake, Charles O. 1964. A structural description of Subanun religious behavior. In Ward Goodenough (Ed.), *Explorations in cultural anthropology.* New York: McGraw-Hill.

————. 1964a. How to ask for a drink in Subanun. In John J. Gumperz and Dell Hymes (Eds.), *American Anthropologist,* 66 (6, Pt. 2), 127-132.

Frucht, Richard. 1966. *Community and context in a colonial society: Social and economic change.* Ann Arbor: University Microfilms No. 66-13, 640.

Geertz, Clifford. 1973. *The interpretation of cultures.* New York: Basic Books.

Genovese, Eugene. 1974. *Roll, Jordan, roll: The world the slaves made.* New York: Pantheon Books.

Georges, Robert A. 1969. Toward an understanding of storytelling events. *Journal of American Folklore,* 82, 313-328.

Glassie, Henry. 1968. *Patterns in the material folk-culture of the eastern United States.* Philadelphia: University of Pennsylvania Press.

————. 1976. *All silver and no brass.* Bloomington: Indiana University Press.

————. 1982. *Passing the time in Ballymenone.* Philadelphia: University of Pennsylvania Press.

Gluckman, Max. 1963. *Order and rebellion in tribal Africa.* New York: The Free Press.

————. 1963a. Gossip and scandal. *Current Anthropology,* 4, 307-316.

————. 1968. Psychological, sociological, and anthropological explanations of witchcraft and gossip. *Man* (n.s.) 3, 20-34.

Goffman, E. 1968. *Interaction ritual.* Garden City, N.Y.: Doubleday and Co.

Goodenough, Ward H. 1957. Cultural anthropology and linguistics. In Paul L. Garvin (Ed.), *Report of the seventh annual roundtable meeting of linguistics and language study.* Washington, D.C.: Georgetown University Press, 167-173.

————. 1963. *Cooperation in change.* New York: Russell Sage Foundation.

————. 1964a. Explorations in cultural anthropology: Essays in honor of George Peter Murdock. New York: McGraw-Hill.

Gossen, Gary. 1974. *Chamulas in the world of the sun: Time and space in a Mayan oral tradition.* Cambridge, Mass.: Harvard University Press.

Gumperz, John J., & Hymes, Dell (Eds.). 1964. *The Ethnography of Communication. American Anthropologist,* 66 (6, Pt. 2).

Hammel, E. A. (Ed.). 1965. *Formal Semantic Analysis. American Anthropologist,* 67 (5, Pt. 2).

Handler, Jerome C., & Frisbie, Charlotte J. 1972. Aspects of slave life in Barbados: Music and its cultural context. *Carribean Quarterly,* 2(4), 5-46.

Hannerz, Ulf. 1967. Gossip networks and culture in a black American ghetto. *Ethnos,* 32, 35-60.

_____. 1969. *Soulside.* New York: Columbia University Press.

Haring, Lee. 1972. A characteristic African folktale pattern. In Richard M. Dorson (Ed.), *African folklore.* Garden City, N.Y.: Doubleday and Co.

Henney, Jeannette H. 1970. *Spirit possession: Belief in a religious group in St. Vincent.* Ann Arbor: University Microfilms No. 69-11, 648.

Herskovits, Melville J. 1941. *Myth of the negro past.* New York: Alfred A. Knopf.

_____. 1941a. *The interdisciplinary aspects of negro studies.* Washington, D.C.: American Council of Learned Societies Bulletin No. 32.

_____. 1943. Some next steps in the study of Negro folklore. *Journal of American Folklore,* 56, 1-7.

_____. 1955. *Cultural anthropology.* New York: Alfred A. Knopf.

_____. 1955a. "The Social organization of the Candomble." *Annais do XXXI congresso internacional de Americanistas,* 1954, Sao Paulo, 505-532

_____, & Herskovits, Frances S. 1947. *Trinidad village.* New York: Alfred A. Knopf. See also Simpson, George Eaton, & Hammond, Peter B.

Hill, Donald R. 1977. *The impact of migration in the metropolitan and folk society of Carriacou, Grenada.* New York: American Museum of Natural History (Anthropological Papers, 54, Pt. 2).

Hill, Errol T. 1972. *The Trinidad carnival: Mandate for a national theater.* Austin: University of Texas Press.

Hunt, Leigh. 1873. *Wishing cup papers.* London.

Hymes, Dell. (Ed.). 1964. *Language in culture and society.* New York: Harper & Row.

_____. 1964a. A perspective for linguistic anthropology. In Sol Tex (Ed.), *Horizons of anthropology.* Chicago: Aldine, 92-107.

_____. 1967. Models of the interaction of language and social setting. *Journal of Social Issues,* 23(2), 8-28.

_____. 1968. The ethnography of speaking. In Fishman 1968:99-138.

_____. 1971. The contribution of folklore to sociolinguistic research. *Journal of American Folklore,* 84, 3-15.

Jones, Eldred D. 1971. *The Elizabethan image of Africa.* Charlottesville: University Press of Virginia.

Joos, Martin. 1967. *The five clocks.* New York: Harcourt, Brace & World.

Keesing, Roger M. 1966. Comments on Colby. *Current Anthropology,* 7, 23.

Kirke, Henry. 1898. *Twenty-five years in British Guiana, 1872-1897.* London: BG edition, 1948.

Landes, Ruth. 1971. Review of Afro-American anthropology. In Norman E. Whitten, Jr., & John F. Szwed (Eds.), *American Anthropologist,* 73, 1306-1310.

Lanigan, Mrs. 1844. *Antigua and the Antiguans.* (2 vols.) London.

LaPin, Dierdre. Story, medium and masque: The idea of art of Yoruba storytelling. Unpublished doctoral dissertation. University of Wisconsin.

Latrobe, Benjamin Henry. 1951. *Impressions respecting New Orleans.* New York: Columbia University Press.

Lauria, Anthony, Jr. "Respeto," "relajo," and interpersonal relations in Puerto Rico. *Anthropological Quarterly,* 7, 53-67.

Laws, Malcom. 1957. *American balladry from British broadsides.* Philadelphia: American Folklore Society.

Leach, E. R. 1954. *Political systems of Highland Burma.* London: Bell.

————. 1961. *Rethinking anthropology.* London: Athlone Press.

Lewis, M. G. 1836. *Journal of a West Indian proprietor.* London.

Ligon, Richard. 1673. *A true and exact history of the island of Barbadoes* (2nd ed.). London.

Lomax, Alan. 1968. *Folk song style and culture.* American Association for the Advancement of Science, Washington, D.C., Publication no. 88.

————. 1970. The homogeneity of African-Afro-American music style. In N. E. Whitten & J. F. Szwed (Eds.), *Afro-American anthropology: contemporary perspectives.* New York: The Free Press, 181.

Lord, A. M. 1960. *The singer of tales.* Cambridge, Mass.: Harvard University Press.

Luffman, John. 1788. *A brief account of the island of Antigua.* London.

Lynch, Louis. 1964. *The Barbados book.* London: André Deutsch.

Malinowski, Bronislaw. 1935. *Coral gardens and their magic,* Vol. 2. *The language of magic and gardening.* London. Republished 1965. Bloomington: Indiana University Press.

Marks, Morton. 1972. Performance rules and ritual structure in Afro-American music. Unpublished doctoral dissertation, University of California at Berkeley.

————, & Szwed, John F. 1971. Afro-American cultures on parade. Paper read at the American Anthropological Association's Annual Meeting, New York City, 1971.

Marsden, Peter. 1788. *An account of the island of Jamaica.* Newcastle.

Mayer, Philip. 1951. The joking of pals in Gusii age-sets. *African Studies,* 10, 31-32.

Merrill, Gordon C. 1958. *The historical geography of St. Kitts and Nevis.* Mexico City: Instituto Pan-American de geografia e historia.

Metzger, Duane, & Williams, Gerald. 1963. A formal ethnographic analysis of Tenejapa Ladino weddings. *American Anthropologist,* 63, 1076-1101.

Mintz, Sidney. 1960. The house and the yard among three Caribbean peasantries. *VIe congrès international des Sciences anthropologiques et ethnologiques* (Vol. 2), 590-596.

————. 1970. Foreword. In Norman E. Whitten, Jr., & John F. Szwed (Eds.), *Afro-American anthropology: Contemporary perspectives.* New York: The Free Press.

————. 1975. *Caribbean transformations.* Chicago: Aldine.

Moreton, J. B. 1793. *West Indian customs and manners.* London.

Norbeck, Edward. 1963. African rituals of conflict. *American Anthropologist,* 65, 1254-1279.

Paine, R. 1967. What is gossip about? An alternative hypothesis. *Man* (n.s.) 2, 278-285.

Paredes, Américo, & Bauman, Richard (Eds.). 1971. *Towards new perspectives in folklore.* Austin: University of Texas Press.

Pares, Richard. 1950. *A West India fortune.* London: Longmans, Green. Reprinted 1968, Hamden, Conn.: Archon.

Peacock, James. 1968. *Rites of modernization.* Chicago: University of Chicago Press.

Perdue, Robert E., Jr. 1968. African baskets in South Carolina. *Economic Botany,* 22, 289-292.

Pierpoint, Robert. 1916. Negro, or coloured, bandsmen in the army. *Notes and queries,* 2, 303-304.

Powdermaker, Hortense. 1968. *After freedom: A cultural study in the deep south.* Boston: Atheneum.

Price, Richard. 1970. Saramaka woodcarving: The development of an Afro-American art. *Man* (n.s.) 5, 363-378.

Puckett, Newbelle Niles. 1968. *Folk beliefs of the southern negroes.* Patterson Smith. (Originally published, 1926).

Radin, Paul. 1969. Foreword. In Clifton H. Johnson (Ed.), *God struck me dead.* Philadelphia: Pilgrim Press.

Rampini, Charles. 1873. *Letters from Jamaica.* Edinburgh.

Reid, Ira De A. 1927. Mrs. Bailey pays the rent. In Charles S. Johnson (Ed.), *Ebony and topaz.* New York: National Urban League.

Reisman, Karl. 1970. Cultural and linguistic ambiguity in a West Indian village. In Norman E. Whitten & John F. Szwed (Eds.), *Afro-American anthropology: Contemporary perspectives.* New York: The Free Press, 129-144.

_____. 1974. Contrapuntal conversations in a Antiguan village. In Richard Bauman & Joel Sherzer (Eds.), *Explorations in the ethnography of communication.* Cambridge: At the University Press, 110-124.

_____. 1974a. Noise and Order. In *Language in its social setting.* Washington, D.C.: Anthropological Society of Washington, 56-73.

Rigby, Peter. 1968. Joking relationships, kin categories, and clanship among the Gogo. *Africa,* 38, 150-165.

Rubinstein, H. 1974. Incest, social control, and biculturation in an Eastern Caribbean Village. In University of Manitoba Anthropology papers, number 9, Winnipeg: Department of Anthropology, University of Manitoba.

Sahlins, Marshall. 1976. *Culture and practical reason.* Chicago: University of Chicago Press.

Scheub, Harold. 1975. *The Xhosa Ntsomi.* New York: Oxford University Press.

Scott, Michael. 1833. *Tom Cringle's log.* Edinburgh.

Simmonds, W. Austin. 1959. *"Pan": The story of the steelband.* Printed as a booklet by West Indian Airways.

Simmons, Donald. 1962. Possible West African sources for the American Negro dozens. *Journal of American Folklore,* 75, 339-340.

Simpson, George E., & Hammond, Peter B. 1960. Discussion. In Vera Rubin (Ed.), *Carribean studies: A symposium.* Seattle: University of Washington Press, 46-53.

Sloane, Sir Hans. 1707. *A voyage to the Islands, Madera, Barbados, Nieves, St. Christophers, and Jamaica.* London.

Smith, M. G. 1962. *Kinship and community on Carriacou.* New Haven: Yale University Press.

Stewart, James. 1823. *A view of the past and present state of the island of Jamaica.* London.

Stewart, William A. 1967. Sociolinguistic factors in the history of American Negro dialects. *Florida F/L Reporter,* 5(2), 11-29.

————. 1968. Continuity and change in American Negro dialects. *Florida F/L Reporter,* 6(1), 3-14.

Stuckey, Sterling. 1969. Relationships between Africans and Afro-Americans. *Africa Today,* 16(2), 4-9.

Sturtevant, William. 1964. Studies in ethnoscience. *American Anthropologist* 66(3, Pt. 2), 99-131.

Szwed, J. 1966. Gossip, drinking, and social control: Consensus and communication in a Newfoundland parish. *Ethnology,* 5, 434-41.

————. 1969. Musical adaptation among American Negroes. *Journal of American Folklore,* 82, 117-118.

Thompson, Robert Farris. 1966. Dance and culture. *African Forum,* 2, 98.

————. 1969. African influence on the art of the United States. In Armstead L. Robinson, et al. (Eds.), *Black studies in the university: A symposium.* New Haven: Yale University Press, 122-170.

Toelken, Barre. 1979. *The dynamics of folklore.* Boston: Houghton Mifflin.

Turner, Victor W. 1969. *The ritual process.* Chicago: Aldine.

————. 1974. *Dramas, fields, metaphors.* Ithaca: Cornell University Press.

Vidich, A. J., & Bensman, J. 1968. *Small town in mass society* (Rev. ed.). Princeton: Princeton University Press.

Watson, John F. 1857. *Annals of Philadelphia and Pennsylvania, in the olden times.* Philadelphia.

Webster, Staten W. 1966. *The disadvantaged learner.* San Francisco: Chandler.

Wentworth, Trelawny. 1834. *A West Indian sketch book.* (2 vols.) London.

Whinnom, Keith. 1965. The origin of European-based creoles and pidgins. *Orbis,* 511-526.

Williams, Raymond. 1973. *The country and the city.* New York: Oxford University Press.

Wilson, Peter J. 1969. Reputation vs. respectability: A suggestion of Caribbean ethnography. *Man* (n.s.) 4, 70-84.

————. 1971. Caribbean crews: Peer groups and male society. *Caribbean Studies,* 10, 18-34.

————. 1973. *The social anthropology of English-speaking Negro societies in the Caribbean.* New Haven: Yale University Press.

————. 1974. *Oscar: An inquiry into the nature of sanity.* New York: Random House.

Wood, Peter H. 1975. "It was a Negro taught them": A new look at African labor in early South Carolina. In Roger D. Abrahams & John F. Szwed (Eds.), *Discovering Afro-America.* Leiden: E. J. Brill.

Zahan, Dominique. 1963. *La dialectique du verbe chez les Bambara.* The Hague: Mouton.

Index

JOHNS HOPKINS STUDIES IN ATLANTIC HISTORY AND CULTURE
RICHARD PRICE AND FRANKLIN W. KNIGHT, GENERAL EDITORS

The Guiana Maroons: A Historical and Bibliographical Introduction
Richard Price

The Formation of a Colonial Society: Belize, from Conquest to Crown Colony
O. Nigel Bolland

Languages of the West Indies
Douglas Taylor

Peasant Politics: Struggle in a Dominican Village
Kenneth Evan Sharpe

The African Religions of Brazil: Toward a Sociology of the Interpenetration of Civilizations
Roger Bastide; Translated by Helen Sebba

Africa and the Caribbean: The Legacies of a Link
Margaret E. Crahan and Franklin W. Knight

Behold the Promised Land: A History of Afro-American Settler Society in Nineteeth-Century Liberia
Tom W. Shick

"Alas, Alas, Kongo": A Social History of Indentured African Immigration into Jamaica, 1841-1865
Monica Schuler

"We Come to Object": The Peasants of Morelos and the National State
Arturo Warman; Translated by Stephen K. Ault

A History of the Guyanese Working People, 1881-1905
Walter Rodney

The Dominican People, 1850-1900: Notes for a Historical Sociology
H. Hoetink; Translated by Stephen K. Ault

Self and Society in the Poetry of Nicolás Guillén
Lorna V. Williams

Settlements, Trade, and Polities in the Seventeenth-Century Gold Coast
Ray A. Kea

Atlantic Empires: The Network of Trade and Revolution, 1713-1826
Peggy K. Liss

Main Currents in Carribean Thought: The Evolution of Caribbean Society in Its Ideological Aspects, 1492-1900
Gordon K. Lewis

The Man-of-Words in the West Indies: Performance and the Emergence of Creole Culture
Roger D. Abrahams

About the Author

Roger D. Abrahams is Alexander H. Kenan Professor of
the Humanities at Scripps and Pitzer Colleges in
Claremont, California. He has served as president of the
American Folklore Society and is author or editor of
more than a dozen books, including *Talking Black;
Between the Living and the Dead: Riddles Which Tell
Stories; Afro-American Folk Culture—An Annotated
Bibliography* (edited with John Szwed); and *Counting
Out Rhymes: A Dictionary* (edited with Lois Rankin).

The Johns Hopkins University Press

THE MAN-OF-WORDS IN THE WEST INDIES

*This book was composed in Times Roman Text and
Baskerville display by David Lorton, from a design by
Susan P. Fillion. It was printed on 50-lb. Glatfelter Off-
set and bound in Holliston Sturdetan by Port City Press,
Inc.*